THE APHORISMS OF ŚIVA

SUNY Series in Tantric Studies
Paul E. Muller-Ortega, editor

THE APHORISMS OF ŚIVA

The *ŚivaSūtra* with Bhāskara's Commentary, the *Vārttika*

Translated with Exposition and Notes by
Mark S. G. Dyczkowski

STATE UNIVERSITY OF NEW YORK PRESS

I gratefully acknowledge the financial assistance given to me by the Indian National Trust for Art and Cultural Heritage (INTACH).

Grateful acknowledgment is also given for the use of photographs from Bharat Kala Bhavan, Banaras Hindu University, Varanasi, India.

Published by
State University of New York Press, Albany

Printed in the United States of America

For information, address State University of New York
Press, State University Plaza, Albany, NY 12246

Production by Marilyn P. Semerad
Marketing by Theresa A. Swierzowski

Library of Congress Cataloging-in-Publication Data

Vasugupta.
[Śivasūtra. English]
The Aphorisms of Śiva : the ŚivaSūtra with Bhāskara's
commentary, the Vārttika / translated with exposition and notes by
Mark S. G. Dyczkowski.
p. cm. — (SUNY series in tantric studies)
Includes bibliographic references and index.
ISBN 0-7914-1263-6. — ISBN 0-7914-1264-4 (pbk.)
1. Kashmir Śaivism—Doctrines. 2. Vasugupta. Śivasūtra.
3. Bhāskarabhaṭṭa, 10th/11th cent. Śivasūtravārttika.
I. Dyczkowski, Mark S. G. II. Bhāskarabhaṭṭa, 10th/11th cent.
Śivasūtravārttika. English. 1992. III. Title. IV. Series.
BL1281.1592.V38A27413 1992
294.5'95—dc20

91-36927
CIP

10 9 8 7 6 5 4 3 2 1

CONTENTS

This book is dedicated as a tribute to my family
and as an offering to the Supreme Being
Who makes all things possible.

FOREWORD

It is indeed a pleasure to introduce this book as part of the ongoing program of publication by SUNY Press in the Tantric Studies Series. With this translation and exposition of the *Śivasūtra* and two of its commentaries, Mark Dyczkowski makes a serious and weighty contribution to the study of the Shaiva traditions of Kashmir. The importance and usefulness of this book—which includes a first rendering of Bhāskara's *Vārrtika* on the *Śivasūtra*—may be stressed on several grounds. First of all, because the *Śivasūtra* stands textually at the fountainhead of the nondual Shaivism of Kashmir, the present translation of the *Aphorisms of Śiva* expands our understanding of the early phases of this tradition. Moreover, while previous translations of this text have primarily focussed on the influential commentary by Kṣemarāja (known as the *Vimarśinī*) Dyczkowski has chosen to translate along with the aphorisms the important comment by Bhāskara as well as another, anonymous commentary on this foundational text. These commentaries—here rendered for the first time in English—open a wider commentarial panorama within which to read and interpret the aphorisms. Finally, Dyczkowski has added his own lucid and patient exposition of each *sūtra*, with the added benefit of continuously comparing Bhaskara's commentary to Kṣemarāja's position. In this way Dyczkowski brings forth the many levels of meaning contained in this fundamental text and weaves them together into a rich interpretive tapestry for the delectation of the reader.

In the various commentaries on the *Śivasūtra*, one encounters several versions of what might be called a textual myth of origin. A deceptively simple story narrates the events by which the aphorisms are revealed in a dream to sage Vasugupta either by Śiva directly or by a Siddha, a perfected being. In some versions, this dream-state revelation is then confirmed when Vasugupta receives additional instructions to proceed to a rock on the Mahādeva mountain which at his touch turns to reveal the aphorisms inscribed on it. This myth fragment—which purports to tell us about the historical source of the text—serves as a useful entry point into the symbolic framework of the text, the cluster of fundamental meanings within which the text takes shape.

For most of us, to dream is to partake of the evanescent, to float nightly in images of unreality, shards of memory, bizarre and frightening episodes that may yield without warning to beautiful and alluring scenes. But the luminous dreams of a Siddha, a perfected being, escape this chaotic fragmentation and function as transparent filters for the apprehensions of truth. Having recognized the living truth of the freedom-imbued declaration, *Śivo'ham*—I am Śiva—the Siddha lives in a state of attunement, a powerful, sacrificial translucence through which the great light can shine. While the ordinary, contracted being exhibits only a resistive opacity, the Siddha yields to the truth even in dreams.

Vasugupta is said to have dreamt the aphorisms. Sage Vasugupta, who was himself appropriately termed a Siddha, was one who had ecstatically, and in some irrevocable fashion, recognized the fundamental and uncontracted egoity, the uncontainable consciousness that is called Śiva. Thus, when the Siddha Vasugupta dreamed, it was reality rather than illusion which was projected on the inner screen of his awareness. Of such a revelatory character were the dreams of Vasugupta, to whom and through whom the paradoxical reality of Śiva is said to have revealed itself.

There is more to this metaphor of the dream. The ordinary dreamer withdraws from the outer world coiled into the oblivion of sleep. In the dream, the dreamer is completely self-enclosed and thus capable of creating whole, if temporary, worlds of experience. But when the Siddha withdraws from the ordinary waking world of the senses, then the wholeness of absolute consciousness is set free to move within itself. Its movement unfolds a systematic revelation of its own inherent structure, its inbuilt patterns of coherence. So Vasugupta the sage dreams and a sequence of transcendent truths comes to light. That which is Śiva, the absolute light of consciousness, reveals itself to him in these aphorisms.

The dreamer's posture of self-enclosure precisely parallels the self-reflexive stance of the absolute consciousness. This stance is revealed in the first of the aphorisms, an axiomatic and apparently tautological dictum which is curiously reminiscent of the Upanishadic saying *ĀTMĀ EVA BRAHMA*. The first *sūtra*—*CAITANYAMĀTMĀ*: Consciousness is the Self—displays the original and multidimensional self-encompassing of that which is essentially unencompassable. In the process of translating the *sūtras*, we insert the verb form "is." However, without in any way impugning the accuracy of this translation, we might for a moment entertain the notion that in this aphorism the verbal form "is" forms part of our own Western grammatical and philosophical intrusion on the Sanskrit text. In the Sanskrit, the aphorism is quite direct and bald. It states: Consciousness—Self. The *sūtra* is telling us: Consciousness faces into the Self, into Consciousness itself.

In this first revelation, Śiva reveals his own inherent stance. The unimpeded consciousness that is Śiva is perpetually in a state of self-enclosure, or self-reference known as *vimarśa*. This is the stance of the great cosmic dreamer who is Śiva. Even when this stance of self-enclosure apparently opens out to give way to the manifold universes of transmigratory experience, to the creation of the worlds of form and content, Śiva is never forced to abandon his self-reflexive and self-enclosed posture. Indeed, Shaivism teaches that what we perceive as our ordinary life experience emerges from, is energized and sustained by, the *vimarśa-śakti*. Thus Vasugupta dreams and in his dream the nature of the various states of consciousness is taught to him along with the truth of the fundamental, underlying reality that is behind these ever-changing states of consciousness. The Siddha thus functions as a lively intermediary, a living spring through which the primordial and unspoken perception that the ultimate consciousness has of itself is able to emerge into language.

Such is the revelation of Lord Śiva. It emerges as the sequence of transcendent and revealed truth that Śiva unfolds within himself as he expounds this new revelation. Out of the honeyed richness of the inner experience of Vasugupta, there flowed the ecstatic teachings of Śiva. The aphorisms are thus not merely a dry philosophical elaboration, but are rather a conceptual adoration of the supreme, a slowly revolving vision of the absolute.

Vasugupta's dream: the oneiric and lithic revelation of the foundational text of a new lineage. While previous āgamic revealed texts will remain very important in the formulation of this tradition, the *Aphorisms of Śiva* will come to serve as the immediate textual basis for the early tradition of the Shaivism of Kashmir. To confirm their oneiric revelation in a more substantial medium than the delicate tissues of a dream, Śiva directs Vasugupta to the Mahādeva mountain and to the Śiva rock where he finds—miraculously engraved in stone—the lithic counterpart of the dream, the compelling and irrevocable teachings of Śiva, carved into the rock. Thus these inner and essentially private revelations are given substance by the stony exhibit on the mountain and a new and creative manifestation of truth emerges.

The reader is invited to investigate these teachings and to explore their subtlety and relevance. Thanks to the patient labors of Mark Dyczkowski, Vasugupta's dream continues to illuminate our lives.

Paul E. Muller-Ortega
Michigan State University
Mahāśivarātri, March 2, 1992

THE ŚIVA SŪTRAS

The First Light Called THE DESCRIPTION OF THE NATURE OF THE LIGHT OF UNIVERSAL CONSCIOUSNESS

1. Consciousness is the Self.
2. Knowledge is bondage.
3. The group of sources constitutes the body of obscuring energies.
4. The ground of knowledge is *Mātṛkā*.
5. Bhairava is upsurge.
6. When the Wheel of Energies fuses together, the universe is withdrawn.
7. The consciousness which is the expanse of the Fourth State (abides constantly in) the various (states) of waking, dreaming and deep sleep.
8. Knowledge (born of sensory perception) is the waking state.
9. Dreaming consists of thought constructs.
10. Deep sleep is Māyā, the lack of discernment.
11. The enjoyer of the three states is the Lord of the Heroes.
12. The planes of union are wonder.
13. The virgin is the will, the supreme power.

14. The perceptible is (His) body.
15. By fixing the mind in the Heart (the yogi) has a vision of the perceivable and of dreams.
16. Or (the yogi can realise Śiva) by contemplating the Pure Principle.
17. Energy established in its own abode.
18. Right discernment is the knowledge of the Self.
19. The bliss of the Light is the joy of contemplation.
20. The body comes into being when the energies unite.
21. The union of the elements, the separation of the elements and the union of the universe.
22. (The yogi) attains mastery of the Wheel by the arising of Pure Knowledge.
23. (The yogi) experiences the vitality of Mantra by contemplating the Great Lake.

The Second Light Called THE ARISING OF INNATE KNOWLEDGE

1. The mind is Mantra.
2. Effort is that which attains the goal.
3. The secret of Mantra is the Being of the Body of Knowledge.
4. The expansion of the mind in the womb (of consciousness) is the slumber of (all) particular forms of ignorance.
5. When the knowledge innately inherent in one's own nature arises, (that is) Śiva's state—(the gesture of) the one who wanders in the Sky of Consciousness.
6. The Master is the means.
7. The awakening of the Wheel of *Mātṛkā*.

8. The body is the oblation.
9. (This yogi's) food is knowledge.
10. The withdrawal of knowledge heralds the vision of dreams that arises from it.

The Third Light Called
THE VIBRATION OF THE POWERS

1. The mind is the Self.
2. (Empirical) knowledge is bondage.
3. Māyā is the lack of discernment of the principles beginning with *Kalā*.
4. The forces are withdrawn in the body.
5. The withdrawal of the vital channels, the conquest of the elements, freedom from the elements and the separation of the elements.
6. (The yogi attains) perfection through the obscuring veil of delusion.
7. (But) by conquering delusion and by (his) infinite expanse (the yogi) achieves Innate Knowledge.
8. Waking is the second ray (of consciousness).
9. The Self is the actor.
10. The stage is the inner Self.
11. The spectators are the senses.
12. The pure state is achieved by the power of the (illumined) intellect.
13. (Once this has been achieved) freedom is achieved.
14. As it is here, so is it elsewhere.
15. The nature (of consciousness) is emission and so that which is not external abides as such.
16. Constant attention to the seed.

17. (Confortably) seated (the yogi) sinks effortlessly into the lake (of consciousness).
18. (Śiva) fashions the world by means of His mother.
19. Once (limited) knowledge is destroyed, rebirth is destroyed.
20. Māheśvarī and the other mothers of the soul in bondage reside in the gutterals and the other classes of consonants.
21. The Fourth should be sprinkled like oil into the three.
22. Merged (in his own nature, the yogi) must penetrate (the phonemes) with his mind.
23. The emergence of the lower (plane) occurs in the centre.
24. When the breath moves uniformly one has an equal vision of all things.
25. That which was destroyed arises once more in the course of the unifying awareness of one's own perception of the individual units of experience.
26. He becomes like Śiva.
27. The activity of the body is the vow.
28. Common talk is (his) recitation of Mantra.
29. Self-knowledge is the boon.
30. Knowledge and the cause reside in the cosmic nature and the source (of the universe).
31. The universe is the aggregate of his powers.
32. (Such is also the case with) persistence and absorption.
33. Even when these are operant, (the subject) is not lost because (he is) the perceiving subjectivity.
34. (The yogi's) feeling of pleasure and pain is external.
35. The one who is free of that is a liberated soul.
36. A compact mass of delusion, the soul is subject to *karma*.

37. When diversity has been eliminated (the yogi's) action is to give rise to another creation.

38. The power of the senses (is proved) by one's own experience.

39. That which is preceded by the three states vitalizes them.

40. The same stability of mind (should permeate) the body, senses and external world.

41. Due to (one's) craving, that which is transported moves outside.

42. Then (when the yogi) is established in pure awareness (his craving) is destroyed and so the individual soul ceases to exist.

43. (The soul) clad in the cloak of elements is not free but, like the Lord, becomes supreme once more.

44. The link with the vital breath is natural.

45. (The movement of the vital breath is stilled) by concentrating on the centre within the nose. Of what use (then) are the left and right channels or *Suṣumnā*?

46. May (the soul) merge (in the Lord) once again.

INTRODUCTION

The *Aphorisms of Śiva* (*Śivasūtra*) have been translated a number of times into several languages along with Kṣemarāja's commentary.[1] Up to now, however, no English translation of Bhāskara's commentary on the *Aphorisms* has been published nor has an analysis been made of the many differences between them. The present work is intended to fill that gap.

The Aphorisms of Śiva and the Stanzas on Vibration

In my *Doctrine of Vibration*[2] I have already discussed the history of the *Aphorisms of Śiva* and how they were revealed to the Master Vasugupta in the middle of the ninth century in Kashmir. More information will be supplied in my forthcoming *Stanzas on Vibration* to which the reader is referred. Suffice it to say here that the *Aphorisms*, despite their brevity and cryptic form, are very important in the history of Kashmiri Śaivism as they represent the first of a series of works composed in Kashmir by monistic Kashmiri Śaivites from the middle of the ninth to the thirteenth century that together constitute the greater part of the corpus of Kashmiri Śaiva literature. Inspired by the Śaiva Tantras and the earlier dualistic Śaiva philosophy of the *Śaivasiddhānta*, they are a monument to the brilliance of the Kashmiri teachers of those days. Especially great among them was Abhinavagupta who lived from approximately the middle of the eleventh century into the first quarter of the twelfth. The importance of this great polymath's contribution to the monistic philosophy of Kashmiri Śaivism, the Pratyabhijñā, the exegesis of the Tantras prevalent in the Kashmir of his day and Indian poetics and aesthetics, cannot be exaggerated. His greatest disciple was

Kṣemarāja who wrote a number of important works, among the first of which were his commentaries on the *Aphorisms of Śiva* and the *Stanzas on Vibration* (*Spandakarikā*) to which they were closely related.

Utpaladeva, the author of the *Stanzas on Recognition,* the *Īśvarapratyabhijñākārikā,* was, along with his teacher Somānanda, the founder of the monistic Śaiva philosophy of Kashmir, the Pratyabhijñā, that drew its name from his work. He was Abhinavagupta's grand-teacher and a major source of inspiration for him. Bhāskara, who wrote one of the commentaries translated for this volume, was either his contemporary or lived soon after him, as we know from the fact that he paraphrases one of the verses in the *Stanzas on Recognition* in his commentary on the *Aphorisms.*[3] He was known to Abhinavagupta who quotes him in his works[4] and so must have lived sometime in the middle of the eleventh century. We know nothing else about him except that he was the son of one Divākarabhaṭṭa and was, therefore, like the other Kashmiri Śaiva authors, a Brahmin by caste, as *bhaṭṭa* was a title bestowed to learned Brahmins in Kashmir at that time.

In his introductory remarks to his commentary, Bhāskara links his spiritual lineage directly to Vasugupta and his direct disciple Kallaṭabhaṭṭa. Kṣemarāja nowhere does so in his commentaries but simply acknowledges Abhinavagupta as his teacher. He was, moreover, critical of Kallaṭa's interpretation of the *Stanzas on Vibration* thus clearly indicating that he had chosen a different line of interpretation not only of the *Stanzas* but also of the *Aphorisms* which were consistently characterised by later Kashmiri Śaivites as related more or less directly to them.[5] Indeed, both Kṣemarāja and Bhāskara refer to them throughout their commentaries.[6]

Bhāskara and Kṣemarāja: Two Visions, One Truth

This is not the place to go extensively into an exposition of the metaphysics and theology that these works presuppose. I have already done this in my previous work, the *Doctrine of Vibration,* and will add further remarks in my forthcoming translation of the *Stanzas on Vibration* and their commentaries to which the reader is referred. The exposition I have added to each aphorism should supply the reader with the necessary theoretical background as he proceeds through the work. One or two preliminary remarks are, however, necessary here.

Kashmiri Śaivism is a form of monism which teaches that there is only one reality identified with one universal consciousness adored as Śiva, the one God. It is also an idealism in so far as it teaches that things exist as objects in the external world because they are perceived to exist. In other words, 'to be is to be perceived' (*esse est percipii*). Both these views are also held by other schools of Indian thought. The most famous exponent of the former is Advaita Vedānta and of the latter the idealist school of Buddhism know as the Yogācāra.

The most distinctive feature of Kashmiri Śaivism is not, therefore, its monistic idealism but the doctrine that this one reality is a universal egoity. It is a pure 'I' consciousness that we can, and do, experience by simply being aware that 'I am'. This egoity is contrasted with the petty ego which is based on a false notion of oneself as the body or a particular temporal personality, which we strive to support and protect by the exertion of our trivial pride and selfishness and that is, therefore, the cause of man's many troubles both with himself and in relation to his fellow man. The authentic ego, this pure sense of 'I am', on the contrary, does not cling to self and personal ambitions. It has no fear of being less than anyone or of anything else. It makes room for others and does not deny their place and value in the economy of life. It is not a victim nor does it victimize. It is not foolish, selfish, proud, full of desire, ambitious or fearful but the very opposite of all these things. Moreover, it is infinite, eternal, all-powerful and omniscient. It is, in other words, not only free of everything which limits us and cuts us off from one another and God, Who is Himself this pure 'I am', but actively creates, sustains and withdraws all things in and through its perception of them and itself.

This important teaching was first expounded by Utpaladeva[7] and was so quickly assimilated by later Kashmiri Śaivites and others who accepted their teachings that few have noticed the fact that this was his own distinctive contribution. This is largely because within a few decades of its formulation Abhinavagupta had already applied it systematically throughout his extensive interpretation of the Tantra, notably in his *Light of the Tantras*, the *Tantrāloka*, but also throughout his works, including those on aesthetics and poetics. We should not be surprised, therefore, to notice that this important concept is missing in both *Stanzas* and *Aphorisms*. Scholars have failed to miss this absence largely because they have viewed these works through the interpretation of them offered by Kṣemarāja who, as one would expect, followed in his Master's footsteps by systematically encoding this concept into them at every possible turn. This is one major difference between his commentary on the *Aphorisms* and the one translated here by Bhāskara. The latter, despite the fact he knew of Utpaladeva's work, seems totally oblivious of this important idea.

Another point of divergence between Bhāskara's commentary and Kṣemarāja's is the absence in the former of the teachings of another important school of Kashmiri Śaivism, namely, Krama. Unlike the Pratyabhijñā, which is a purely philosophical-cum-theological school of thought that, therefore, rightly belongs to the history of Indian philosophy rather than religion, the Krama system is a distillate of a purely Tantric tradition or, to be more precise, several closely related traditions. By this I mean that it finds its original formulation in the Tantras and was transmitted for several generations by teachers who were initiated into these specific Tantras and were initiating their disciples into them, and handing down interpretations of their meaning to them. They also wrote independent works of their own. The earliest of these works were short tracts that portrayed themselves as Tantras in their own right that were 'brought into the world' by their exponents. One of the earliest figures in this development that marked the initial emergence out of the anonymity of the Tantras was Jñānanetra. Also known as Śivānanda, he probably lived sometime in the middle of the ninth century. He was, therefore, if our dating is correct, a close contemporary of Vasugupta. Śivānanda felt himself to be simply a vehicle of a higher revelation through which the Tantras were brought into the world. Similarly, according to tradition, Vasugupta did not write the *Aphorisms* himself but was merely the recipient of a revelation the authorship of which is ultimately attributed to Śiva, as are the Tantras. One could say that Vasugupta, like Śivānanda, marks a point of transition from scripture to the learned treatise technically called *śāstra*.

The treatises of the Krama school developed independently and a number of them have come down to us. Mostly relatively short tracts, they deal with the sophisticated symbolism of a number of 'Wheels' (*cakra*) or aggregates of energies that are responsible for the manifestation of the spheres of existence. These are understood in idealistic terms as spheres of the manifestation of the one energy of consciousness that ranges from that of pure awareness through the mental and sensory right down to the physical level. All these energies and their deployment through, and as, the flux of time and space are part of an infinite, unconditioned flux of energy known as the Great Sequence (*Mahākrama*) from which this school draws its name. The energies are worshipped in a sequence (*Krama*) as aspects and forms of the Supreme Deity which is the Goddess, rather than the God. She is variously named in the different allied Krama traditions but all Her forms are essentially characterizations of the Goddess Kālī, the Goddess of Time (*kāla*). Such ideas are not at all alien to Bhāskara who also understands manifest reality in terms of flux which is a 'non-flux' of energy, but his characterizations of it fall in line with general representations that agree with an archetype common to a number of notions found in the earlier Tantras, particularly, but not exclusively, the more monistically oriented ones.

Just as common notions link Kṣemarāja's specifically Krama orientated interpretations with the less sectarian ones in Bhāskara's commentary, similarly the former's presentation of universal 'I' consciousness is linked with the latter's more loosely defined presentation of the Self and one's 'own nature' (*svasvabhāva*) which he takes over from the earlier teachers in his lineage, particularly Kallaṭabhaṭṭa. The 'abiding in one's own nature' central to the teachings of the *Stanzas on Vibration* as the goal and ultimate ground of all conditioned existence, perception and the ego is here given a brilliant new dimension. Bhāskara presents us with a mysticism of Light. The Divine, our true nature, our 'own Being', is Light. Its realisation is therefore a powerful vision of Light, expanding and unfolding as all things. To realise this is to acquire 'Pure Knowledge', to miss it is to be subject to the impure knowledge of thought constructs that, far from revealing reality, hide it. The attentive reader will notice Bhāskara's continous reference to this Light throughout his commentary. This approach distinguishes him from Kṣemarāja who does not ignore this important mystical experience but prefers not to treat it as his guiding theme in the way Bhāskara does.

About This Translation

The printed edition of Bhāskara's commentary is accompanied by another commentary the origin of which is not noted by the editor of the text. Apparently, this commentary was found in the manuscripts used for this edition and was added by the editor as an aid to understanding Bhāskara's interpretation of the *Aphorisms.* I have choosen to translate this commentary as well, as it does in fact serve its purpose in this respect. Moreover, it often serves as a bridge between Bhāskara's and Kṣemarāja's interpretations drawing as it does from both, although tending to stick to the former rather than the latter. This is true even though the anonymous commentator takes the notion of the absolute ego, to which we have referred above, as axiomatic much the same way that Kṣemarāja does. The commentary on each aphorism is thus in three layers. First comes Bhāskara's commentary, the translation of which has been printed here in bold characters. This is followed by the second anonymous commentary in normal type after which I add my own exposition where, among other things, I compare Bhāskara's commentary with Kṣemarāja's.

In making my translation I have avoided including Sanskrit terms wherever possible in the running text. But, in deference to the fact that the terminology in these works is highly distinctive and each term carries a wealth of meaning that no single word, or even phrase, in English could capture entirely, I have supplied the original term in parentheses. The reader who is not interested can simply ignore them. Like all languages, Sanskrit has its own peculiar forms of syntax and turns of phrase that translated literally do not make good reading in English. Moreover, not infrequently, one can express in a few words of Sanskrit what would require a long sentence in English. Inevitably, therefore, any translator must make additions and alterations to the literal meaning of the Sanskrit in order to present it in reasonably good English. These additions may, at times, become interpretations, which is also virtually inevitable. My own way out of this dilemma is to place these additions in parentheses. The reader should not allow himself to be distracted by these parentheses but read the text in continuity as if they were not there. Those who are interested can see what I have done to make the original sound right in English and those who are not need not bother.

Concluding Remarks

Finally, the reader who has a personal spiritual commitment to Kashmiri Śaivism may well ask himself what the presentation of such elevated experiences and Yogic practises has to do with him. As most of us are far from the developed spirituality that lends access to these mystical experiences, the question is certainly quite valid.

From the Kashmiri Śaiva point of view, the seeker after truth who sincerely seeks spiritual growth is first and foremost a yogi. He is, in other words, a person who practises Yoga in one or more of its many forms, and it is a very special form of Yoga that the *Aphorisms* teach. Yoga means union. This union is taught here in many ways, all of which essentially amount to the realisation of our true inherent nature which is infinitely greater than our thoughts could ever conceive. Ultimately, the ancient Kashmiri Masters teach we will realise that we are, and have always been, as we always will be, perfect, free, eternal, blissful and infinitely spiritually conscious. We are, in short, ourselves the ultimate goal of all spiritual endevour, the very same God Śaivites call Śiva or Bhairava Who has helped us throughout whether we know it or not. This realisation does not make us more proud or selfish but less so because as Abhinavagupta beautifully puts it :

> People, occupied as they are with their own affairs, normally do nothing for others. The activity of those in whom every stain of phenomenal existence has been destroyed and are identified with Bhairava, full of Him, is intended only for the benefit of the world.[8]

Although it seems to most of us that we are very far from this, the supreme realisation, yet we are as close as one could ever be. This is all the more true of the many and wonderful states that lead up to it and so they relate to all of us however underdeveloped we may seem to be. In other words, we are as close or as far away as we want be at any time. Some teachers prefer to leave these matters for later when their disciples are more developed for fear that they may be misguided or seek something that is less than ultimate, but others, like the ancient Masters of Kashmir, felt that it was right to reveal these secrets, trusting in that inner purity that nothing can sully. Their revelation is not an invitation to simply take pleasure in their often strange and wonderful descriptions, far from it. As the attentive reader will notice, the yogi is constantly admonished to be attentive, to press on beyond his present state. That is the great secret of growth: whatever level of development we have reached, we must keep on growing.

Now Begins the First Light Called

THE DESCRIPTION OF THE LIGHT OF UNIVERSAL CONSCIOUSNESS

May (all) prostrate before the Lord, the bestower of boons Who is the beloved of the daughter of the Snowy Mountains that bears as a crestjewel the budding moon and sustains, destroys and creates (all things).

* * *

The immediate outer meaning of this verse is quite clear (and is as follows). May (all) penetrate into their own true nature (*svātman*) which bestows the boon of the highest level of self-realisation (*svātmalābha*).This is the Lord (*deva*) Who performs the five divine operations of creation, (persistence, withdrawal, obscuration and grace). He is intent on pouring everything out of Himself and other games and He is the brilliance (which illumines all things) (*dyotana*)[1] and all the rest.The hidden digit of the moon (*amākalā*)[2] which gives life to the universe is His crestjewel and finest ornament while He is the beloved of (the Goddess) Who is His power of freedom that unfolds from the supremely pure abode of Absolute Stability (*anuttaradhruvapada*).

(The verse also) implicitely refers to the three sections of the *Aphorisms of Śiva* in the following way :

a) The first quarter of the verse, [namely, (He) Who is the beloved of the daughter of the Snowy Mountains] refers especially to (Śiva), the possessor of power, and so stands for the section called "The Nature of Universal Consciousness."

b) The second quarter of the verse [namely, '(He) Who bears as a crestjewel the budding moon'] refers especially to Śakti and so stands for the second section called "The Arising of Innate Knowledge."

c) The remaining part of the verse deals with that which enacts the cosmic drama and so stands for the last part (of the *Aphorisms* called) "The Vibration of the Powers."

* * *

Obeisance to Śiva Whose body is unique, perfectly full consciousness, unobscured by the radiance (*sphurattā*) of His own eternally manifest (*nityodita*) light (*ābhāsa*).

* * *

The contracted, individual Self (*āṇavatman*) is made manifest by the radiance of Śiva's obscured form (*avṛtākṛti*) which flows incessantly out of His own eternally manifest light. At one with Him, it consists of (the many forms), such as the colour blue, that appear, each distinctly manifest, (to constitute the phenomenal world). In reality, even in this state, (Śiva's) perfectly full, compact being and consciousness is not obscured. The third section (of the *Aphorisms*) elaborates on this point in the context of practise.

The particular work we are reflecting on contains the teachings transmitted through the line of Masters which amount to this, namely, that one's own true nature is Śiva. As is written further on: "the Śiva-nature inherent in the Self of all (living beings) is not destroyed (*akhaṇḍita*)."[3] But how can (a soul) subject to transmigration possess this Śiva-nature? (In reply we) say that (although our Śiva-nature) is seemingly obscured due to the power of delusion (*vimohanī-śakti*), in reality it is unobscured because it shines perpetually. If it were (really) covered over, all daily life would come to an end. As (Bhāskara) will go on to say: "That (Śiva-nature) is enveloped by the manifestations, etc., of consciousness (*jñāna*) consisting of subjectivity, objectivity and the rest."[4]

What then removes this (obscuration)? (We say that) nothing but the Lord's grace (can do this). Accordingly (it is said): "O Goddess, it is by the power of grace (*śaktipāta*) that one is led to a true Master."

When (one has) this grace, one's own true nature, as described above, becomes clearly apparent. In this way all things are possible for one who is such. As (Bhāskara) will say later: "One's own true nature (*svasvarūpa*) is Śiva directly apparent (*sakṣāt*)"[5]

* * *

(The line of transmission of the Aphorisms and of their teachings)

Originally, the *Aphorisms of Śiva* of the Master Vasugupta appeared on the hallowed Mahādeva mountain at the divine command of a Siddha. Subsequently, he transmitted (them) along with (their) secret to the venerable Brahmin (*sūri*) Kallaṭa who (wrote) the *Aphorisms on Vibration* (*Spandasūtra*) as a commentary on (the first) three of its four sections and *The Wishgranting Gem of the Purport of Reality* (*Tattvārthacintāmaṇi*) on the last. He transmitted the secret in this way to his maternal cousin, the venerable Pradyumnabhaṭṭa who, in his turn, gave it to his son Prajñārjuna who told it in the same way to his disciple Mahādevabhaṭṭa who gave it to his son, the venerable Śrīkaṇṭhabhaṭṭa. (Now), I, Bhāskara, the son of Divākara, having received it from (Śrīkaṇṭhabhaṭṭa) reverently write this commentary (*vārtika*) on the *Aphorisms* at the insistance of my disciples. I will now explain these *Aphorisms* (for them, for they are) young and, having strayed from the (true) tradition (*āgama*), their minds are confused by erroneous notions.

Indeed, the Śiva-nature inherent in the Self of all (living beings) is not destroyed (*akhaṇḍita*) (but) it is constantly enveloped by the manifestations, etc., of consciousness consisting of subjectivity, objectivity and the rest.

* * *

One's own true nature itself is Śiva Who is consciousness (*cidātman*). It does not differ from Him as others believe it does. This Śiva-nature is proved to exist by the experience everyone has of their own existence (*svānubhavasiddha*).It is the abode of the sovereign power of the Self which is perfect, transcendent and the cause of (all) phenomena (*kārya*). It is the place wherein all things repose.The freedom to generate emotion (*bhāva*) and other such (creative) functions is the sign of its presence, which only the aesthete can realise, in the individual centres of consciousness (*cidaṇu*) (which presence) inspires its recognition at every moment in the course of daily life. The individual soul fails to realise (his true nature) because it seems to be obscured by the objectivized consciousness (*idantājñāna*) engendered by the conditioned (*māyīya*) subjectivity he freely chooses to will into existence. Therefore, Lord Śiva, desiring to enlighten those who are the objects of His grace so that they may realise this, brought the *Aphorisms* (into this world).

* * *

Śiva, overcome with compassion, spoke these aphorisms (one after the other) in an ordered sequence of revelation to remove this enveloping obscuration and make known His own nature.

One's own true nature is Śiva directly apparent (*sakṣāt*). The universe which is the body of consciousness[6] and the Wheel of Energies (*kalācakra*) is generated by His expansion (*unmeṣa*) and contraction (*nimeṣa*). (All things) arise and fall away in consonance with the extension and withdrawal of (His) power.[7]

There are many conflicting views concerning His true nature (*svarūpa*) and (so) Śiva composed the (following) aphorism to refute them.

* * *

The *Aphorisms* are arranged in an ordered sequence for the benefit of those fit to receive them. The reason for this is that they lead progressively to the highest state of realisation in stages as one climbs stepwise to successively higher levels. Thus, those blessed with the most intense grace (*tīvratara-śaktipāta*) (are enlightened) by the knowledge of Śiva (directly) (*śāmbhavajñāna*), those blessed with a middling degree of grace (*tīvramadhya*), by a knowledge of (Śiva's) power (*śākta-vijñāna*) and those whose grace is weak (*manda*) by a knowledge of the individual soul (*āṇavajñāna*).

The universe, which is nothing but pure consciousness, the Wheel of the Energies of consciousness, will and the rest as well as its attendent causes, namely, the five (pure) principles beginning with Śiva and the expansion of the powers *Khecarī* (*Gocarī, Dikcarī* and *Bhūcarī*),[8] are (all) generated and persist in consonance with (Śiva's) expansion and contraction, which correspond to the extension and withdrawal of (His) power.

Philosophers belonging to various schools disagree with one another because of the differing order of impurity to which they are subject. Thus the materialists (*laukika*) think that the Self is the body endowed with consciousness; the logicians (*naiyayika*) that it is the intellect endowed with the qualities of knowledge etc.; the Mīmāṃsakas (believe it to be) the subtle body (*puryaṣṭaka*) and the Buddhists, a flux of perceptions; certain Vedāntins and the Mādhyamikas (think it is) absolute non-existence (*abhāvabrahman*) and the Pāñcarātrins, unmanifest nature (*avyakta*) while the Sāṃkhya maintains that it is the state of the subject devoid of intellective consciousness (*vijñānakalā*); some Vedāntins (believe that the Self is the) *Īśvara* principle, the grammarians that it is the *Sadāśiva* principle and the followers of the Trika and other (similar schools) that it is one's own nature which both transcends the universe and is at one with it. All these are cheated by Māyā of (their) real (*paramārthika*) freedom and (their consciousness still) resides on the plane of relative distinctions.[9]

* * *

caitanyamātmā

Consciousness is the Self. 1/1

The nature of the Self is consciousness which is proved (*siddha*) to be both knowledge and action. It is unobscured so who can deny its Śiva-nature?[10]

Exposition

Kashmiri Śaivism teaches that at the macrocosmic level consciousness is pure Being, the absolute itself, beyond all specification.[11] Moreover, it maintains that all that is perceived exists as an object of perception because it is perceived as such. This implies that the activity of consciousness is the same for all existing things, whether conscious or unconscious (*sarvasāmānyarūpa*). Thus, neither space, time nor form can divide it, nor can ignorance obscure it, for they are all part of this reality. Moreover, consciousness has the power to make everything it comes into contact with conscious and is free to do all things as it is to know them. In short, consciousness is itself perfect freedom understood as the union of all knowledge and action. Paramaśiva alone enjoys this freedom, as all other beings depend on His autonomous consciousness for their existence. Indeed, the freedom of consciousness specifies Paramaśiva's state more than any other of His divine attributes, for it is on this that they all depend.

According to Kṣemarāja this same consciousness is, in microcosmic terms, the pure reflective awareness of the absolute ego which is the uncreated subjectivity that is the essence of the conceived (*kalpita*) subjectivity attributed to the body, intellect, vital breath and the emptiness experienced in deep sleep. The presence of this universal consciousness gives life to the psycho-physical organism and impels the activity of the senses and mind. It is through this activity that we can discern the presence of consciousness and ultimately experience its true nature.

This means that, from the point of view of practise, there can be no means outside consciousness by which consciousness can be known. All the forms of spiritual discipline through which we come to experience the true nature of consciousness are also ultimately consciousness. In short, consciousness is known by being conscious. Nothing can obscure it. It is free of all means (*anupāya*) and self-illuminating (*svaprakāśa*).

* * *

(Śiva), the Great Lord, spoke (the following) aphorism which defines (the nature) of that obscuration:

jñānaṁ bandhaḥ
Knowledge is bondage. 1/2

The knowledge (based on the notions) 'I' and 'this is mine' arises clothed in speech[12] and consists of the perception (*prathā*) of relative distinctions. It is rooted in the impurity of Māyā and is said to be bondage, whose mark is the obscuration of ignorance.

* * *

The impurity of Māyā (*māyīyamala*) is bondage. It is the impurity of individuality (*āṇavamala*)[13] that obscures one's own sovereign power which is the (lower order of) knowledge. (This knowledge) is the multiple diversified perception that, associated with (the notions) 'I' and 'this is mine', is fashioned from one's own nature. This happens because (the soul's authentic nature) is obscured by the notions of 'existence' and 'non-existence' which arise according to whether there is unity with or division from, the light (of the subject's consciousness). They belong to the Supreme Lord Himself Who, eternal and pervasive, denies His own nature, as does an actor, and assumes the role of an individual soul by taking limitations (onto Himself) by His power of Māyā which can bring about the impossible, in order to make manifest the cosmic drama.

Exposition

Bhāskara equates the knowledge to which this aphorism refers with the discursively represented perceptions that bind the individual soul, based as they are on the ego-sense, centred on the objectively perceivable body, mistakenly identified with the perceiving subjectivity of consciousness. As the form of knowledge that results from these perceptions is based on the relative distinction drawn between subject and object as well as between individual objects themselves, Bhāskara attributes it to *Māyīyamala* which is the impurity that engenders the sense of duality. Kṣemarāja, however, takes a step further back, as it were, and attributes this type of knowledge to *Āṇavamala* which is the metaphysical ignorance through which the universal subject voluntarily limits its own consciousness down to a point source of awareness (*aṇu*) by falsely identifying with the psycho-physical organism with the result that, ignorant of its true identity, its capacity to know and act is severely restricted. This identification gives rise to differentiated perceptions, confused by which the fettered soul (*paśu*) looses sight of the universal nature of its own 'I' consciousness. Again, at the macrocosmic level, it is through such perceptions that Śiva projects onto the emptiness of His own nature all the lower-order subjects and their worlds. Empirical knowledge of a discursive order is thus equated with the incomplete knowledge of the unity of consciousness that binds the individual soul.[14] Kṣemarāja is quick to point out, however, that this state of affairs is entirely self-imposed. When we no longer choose to try and grasp the nature of things in this way and stop seeking to overcome our false sense of incompleteness by clinging to the perceptions of material objects which we misguidedly feel we can possess, the all-embracing reality of consciousness becomes spontaneously apparent.[15]

* * *

(Śiva) spoke (the following) aphorism that defines (the nature) of the powers that delude the fettered soul in order to explain what causes speech to pervade (thought):

yonivargaḥ kalāśarīram
The group of sources constitutes the body of obscuring energies. 1/3.

Know the sources (*yoni*) to be the four powers which are the universal causes of all things. They are *Ambā, Jyeṣṭhā, Raudrī* and *Vāmā* (all of which) are Śiva's forms.

The group or aggregate of these (powers) constitutes the body in the midst of the obscuring energies of (the phonemes ranging) from A to KṢ that give rise to speech (*śabda*). These obscuring energies are variously called "mothers," "powers," "goddesses" and "rays." They manifest the notions (*pratyaya*) of the fettered soul by pervading them with speech. Thus he becomes their victim because the knowledge they manifest invariably deprives him of his power.[16]

* * *

The wheel of obscuring energies consists of (the phonemic energies ranging) from A to KṢ and arises from the four powers that are (collectively) the cause of every power. This wheel of obscuring energies, which consists of the gross phonemes, assumes, by the conjunction of words and sentences, the form of speech in its entirety and diversity, whether that of common or learned parlance (*laukika* and *alaukika*), (and so) generates the notions of the fettered due to which they are deprived of their power and become the objects (of their) enjoyment.

Exposition

Kṣemarāja reads this aphorism along with the previous one and explains that it refers to the remaining two impurities which condition consciousness, namely, the Impurity of Māyā (*māyīyamala*) (including the five obscuring coverings, *kañcukas*)[17] and the Impurity of Karma (*karmamala*). So, from Kṣemarāja's points of view, this aphorism should be translated as follows: *The group of categories associated with the Womb (of diversity) and the body of obscuring energies (which give rise to limited action are also binding).*

The Cave (*guhā*), the Knot (*granthi*), and the Womb of the Universe (*jagadyoni*) are some of the many expressions used to denote Māyā. Here it is referred to as the Womb because it is through it that consciousness creates the world and body of each individual soul by giving rise to an awareness of relative distinctions both directly (*sakṣāt*) between himself and his environment and indirectly between the objects which populate his world. The domain of its binding activity is the so-called impure creation (*aśuddhasṛṣṭi*) ranging from the category Māyā down to that of Earth. It is the basis of the Impurity of Karma (*karmamala*) here called the "obscuring energy" (*kalā*) which is the power that gives rise to limited action equated generically with Māyā. Kṣemarāja writes:

> *Kalā* is that which generates (diversity, *kalayati*), that is, it projects outwards. It is the power of Māyā which differentiates and conditions by limitation. It is due to this that (the individual soul) is deprived of its power. In other words, his sovereign freedom is hidden by his own Māyā.[18]

When an individual is strongly affected by this impurity he feels that he is totally lost and worth nothing as a human being and that he is a helpless victim of the circumstances which in reality he has created for himself as a consequence of his past actions.

Bhāskara's interpretation of this aphorism differs considerably from Kṣemarāja's. According to him, the 'group of sources' (*yonivarga*) refers to the four principle energies of the absolute (*anuttara*), namely, *Vāmā, Jyeṣṭhā, Ambikā* and *Raudrī*.[19] While 'the body of obscuring energies' (*kalāśarīra*) refers to the fifty powers of consciousness represented by the letters of the alphabet that emerge from these four energies and go on to generate the world of words and meanings. These four powers are:

1) *Vāmaśakti*—Also called *Vyomavāmeśvari*,[20] it is the power of bliss (*ānandaśakti*) which, beyond even the supreme energy of the will (*parātitā*), is the source of all the other energies.This is the transcendental awareness (*anākhyā*) of universal consciousness which, beyond time, pervades the three moments of creation, persistence, and destruction to which all phenomena are subject. It is the supreme state of *Kuṇḍalinī* which is Śiva's creative freedom consisting of the union of the three levels of existence, viz., Śiva, Śakti and the individual soul, represented by the powers of the absolute, will and the unfolding of knowledge held together in harmonious union. She is the goddess presiding over those subject to the incessant round of transmigration, creating as She

does for the ignorant the world of diversity and illusion, and also the bestower of Śiva's power to those who have overcome ignorance.

2) *Jyeṣṭhāśakti*—This is the second energy that emerges from the absolute as the power which gives rise to persistence (*sthiti*). For the Well Awakened it is the power through which the pure knowledge and action of universal consciousness is created in them.

3) *Raudrīśakti*—This power is responsible for the withdrawal (*saṃhāra*) of the enlightened awareness created by *Jyeṣṭhā*. It blocks the path to liberation by giving rise to doubts in the aspirant's mind or attachment to the occasional pleasures of *saṃsāric* existence which divert his attention from the ultimate goal.[21]

4) *Ambikāśakti*—Ambikā personifies the powers of consciousness which maintain the state of awareness at a single steady level. Thus *Ambikāśakti* prevents the fall of the elevated yogi to lower states, but at the same time hampers the rise of those less elevated to higher levels.

* * *

Now, are these energies and the knowledge they manifest (supported by any) sustaining ground? In response to this query (Śiva) said:

jñānādhiṣṭhānaṁ mātṛkā
The ground of knowledge is Mātṛkā. 1/4

There are two forms of knowledge, according to whether it is superior or inferior. *Mātṛkā* is the one power which is the ground or support (of both).

* * *

The inferior and superior forms of (this) two-fold knowledge are due to the perception of division and the manifestation of unity, respectively. The power (*Mātṛkā*) is the mother of the universe and sustains and presides over both types. In the case of superior knowledge (She is) the power called *Aghorā* because She manifests both the inner reality (of undifferentiated consciousness) and the outer reality (of the All) as Her own nature. Inferior (knowledge is the domain of the aspect of *Mātṛkā*) called *Ghorāśakti* who directs the consciousness of (the fettered soul) out of himself because of his failure to reflect upon the unity of reality and obscures his Śiva-nature.

Exposition

Kṣemarāja explains that the Impurity of Individuality (*āṇavamala*) which limits the freedom and awareness of consciousness, the Impurity of Māyā (*māyīyamala*), which gives rise to diversity and the awareness of relative distinctions, together with the Impurity of Action (*karmamala*) which binds the individual to the fruits of his action, respectively, obscure the infinite powers of will, knowledge and action of universal consciousness. This obscuration is the basic condition necessary for the emergence of differentiated perceptions (*vikalpa*) out of the body of consciousness. This aphorism goes on to discuss the remaining factor essential for the formation of mental representations and the empirical knowledge which they make possible, namely, speech.

It is a fact clearly proved (*siddha*) by personal experience that speech is invariably associated with thought.[22] It is the vehicle and essence of thought, while thought is the source of speech, they stand and fall together. Mental representation which orders the influx of sensations and presents us with a meaningful, balanced picture of the outer physical environment, memory, the elaboration of ideas and the shifting tide of emotions are all intimately connected with language. Language and the awareness which renders it meaningful serve as the essential connection between the inner world of consciousness and the outer world of material objects. From this point of view, even animals have a language of their own insofar as they respond purposively to their environment and hence must, in some sense, grasp the implications of their situation. One could say that the world we live in as individual perceiving and thinking subjects is a product of language. To grasp the basis of language is to come in touch with the very cause of the world of our daily life. The creative awareness (*vimarsa*) through which language becomes meaningful and by virtue of which we can articulate our intentions and ideas, both to ourselves and to others, is here termed *Mātṛkā,* said to be the unknown mother of all things.[23] As Abhinava explains:

> *Mātṛkā* is the power one with Bhairava in His form as the Mass of Sounds (*śabdarāśi*). The various aspects of objectivity in it are not yet manifest but are yet to come, thus it is called *Mātṛkā* (lit. 'little mother') because (this energy) contains in a potential state (the manifest universe like an expectant) mother.[24]

Thus *Mātṛkā* is equated with Śiva's creative power of action.[25] Born of Śiva's will when He desires to manifest His power as the breath animating all creation, She is the 'unstruck sound' (*anāhata*) heard at the supreme level of speech (*parā vāc*)[26] which is both the vitality (*vīrya*) of Śiva and the power hidden in Mantra. Kṣemarāja quotes the Essence of the Tantras (*Śrītantrasadbhāva*):

> O dear one, all Mantras consist of letters and energy is the soul of these (letters), while energy is *Mātṛkā* and one should know Her to be Śiva's nature.[27]

Mātṛkā as Mantric energy is the source of the higher liberating knowledge of non-duality when She acts as the power *Aghorā* which makes inner and outer manifest as one with Her own nature in the all-embracing experience of liberated consciousness.[28] *Mātṛkā* is also the basis of the lower binding knowledge associated with discursive thought when Her true nature is unknown and functions as the power *Ghorā* which deprives man of the awareness of unity and obscures Śiva's universal activity.

* * *

The Lord spoke (the following) aphorism in order to put an end to the knowledge which envelopes (and obscures the consciousness of the fettered) so as to manifest one's own essential nature (*svasvarūpa*):

udyamo bhairavaḥ
Bhairava is upsurge. 1/5

Śiva is the conscious nature (*cidātman*) which is full (and perfect) in all respects. 'Exertion' (*udyoga*), 'expansion' (*unmeṣa*) and 'upsurge' (*udyama*) are the terms denoting His state of being when He wishes to generate phenomena (*kārya*) without, in this way, abandoning His own essential nature (*svasvarūpa*). This same (state of being) is said to be the universe, Śiva (*śārvatattva*) and Bhairava. Bhairava also abides there in the brilliant radiance of (His) own vibration (*parispanda*). The All-pervasive Lord of Consciousness is called (Bhairava) here (in this aphorism) because (He sustains all things by) filling (them with His infinite consciousness, *bharaṇa*), plays (the game of destruction, *ramaṇa*) and emits them (out of Himself, *vamana*)[29] and also because He perceives His own undivided (*akhaṇḍita*) light (*nijābhāsa*).

* * *

(Certain) individuals are fit to practise the Divine Means (*śāmbhavopāya*) and so, without having to meditate or recite Mantra, etc., are mystically absorbed in the highest Bhairava Whose nature it is to 'fill' (*bharaṇa*), 'resound' (*ravaṇa*) and 'emit' (*vamana*). They have been inwardly purified by an intense descent of the supreme power (of grace) and (so) are fit to be graced with, for example, the vision of those perfected in yoga (*siddha*) or by eating the sacrificial pap (*caru*). By relishing the flow of the aesthetic delight (*rasa*) which is the nectar of (Bhairava's) power of knowledge and action which constantly extends (out of consciousness), they experience absorption (*āveśa*) in their own nature (*svarūpa*) which abounds with the relish of the aesthetic delight (*rasa*) of its ever renewed and life-giving nectar. When the true essential nature (*svabhāva*) of those who exert themselves in this way unfolds, (a state) is attained (in which) the obscuring covering of the light of consciousness is absent.

Exposition

Kṣemarāja comments on this aphorism:

The upsurge (of consciousness) is the sudden emergence of the highest level of intuition (*pratibhā*), the outpouring (*ucchalanā*) of consciousness consisting of the (ever) extending awareness (*vimarśa* it has of its own nature). It is Bhairava because He is full of the entire universe insofar as He is the unity (*sāmarasya*) of all His powers and assimilates into Himself every differentiated perception (*kalpana*). (He appears in this form) to those (yogis) who, devoted to Him, are solely intent on the inner reality (of all things), in order to make their own Bhairava-nature manifest.[30]

The yogi who has reached the highest level of practise (*śāmbhavopāya*) merges with the active effort exerted by the vibrating power of awareness which impels and gives life to the senses and mind. He witnesses it as the outpouring of the activity of consciousness through which his universal nature as Bhairava is instantly made manifest. This aphorism instructs him not to try to grasp his own nature by his personal efforts alone but to let himself be carried along by the innate exertion of his own nature identified with the supreme intuition (*parāpratibhā*) of the freedom (*svātantrya*) of consciousness. This flux of energy, at one with the yogi's true nature, is Bhairava. It contains within itself all the powers of the absolute and spontaneously assimilates all differentiated perceptions (*vikalpa*) the instant it emerges, carrying the yogi in a flash to the highest level of consciousness. Awakened by the grace of his Master, the yogi is absorbed in the highest state of contemplation (*śāmbhavasamāveśa*) on the plane of being beyond mind (*unmanā*),[31] situated in the centre between one thought and the next from whence the world of differentiated perceptions is emitted. *Mātṛkā* operates as *Aghorāśakti* through which the yogi severs the restraints imposed upon him by the three impurities and achieves the supreme knowledge (*parajñāna*) of the enlightened through this all-powerful expansion (*unmeṣa*) of his consciousness.

* * *

The body of consciousness which is the light of one's own true nature (*svasvarūpa*) (never) changes even when the Bhairavic nature that exerts itself in this way expands out (to fill all things with its divine powers, *unmesa*). When the Great Lord had said this, He uttered the following aphorism in order to explain that one's own abiding state of being (*svasthiti*) also remains unaltered when (the powers of consciousness) are withdrawn (back into it, *nimeṣa*):

śakticakrasaṃdhāne viśvasaṃhāraḥ
When the Wheel of Energies fuses together,
***the universe is withdrawn.* 1/6**

The energies are the entire universe[32] and their nature is knowledge and action. (Their) functions have been explained before. (They are said to form) a circle (*cakra*) because they illumine (*cakana*) all knowledge and action.[33] Its fusion is its assimilation into one's own nature engendered by the involution (*nimeṣa,* of consciousness) due to which its withdrawal (*saṃhāra*) and merger (into consciousness) takes place (and it resumes its original) Śiva-nature. Similarly, the same Supreme Soul Who is Bhairava (becomes) Śiva when (He acts as) the impelling cause that engenders the expansion (*unmeṣasaṃbhṛti*) of the knowledge consisting of words, denoted meanings and the rest.

* * *

The point is that when one reflects that the universe, consisting of the powers of knowledge and action, is not separate from the absolute (*anuttara*), which is both the light and reflective awareness (of consciousness), it dissolves away, fusing with Śiva's (divine) fire of supreme consciousness. Thus, as the effect resides at one in this way within its cause, one's own abiding state of being (*svasthiti*) is (never) obscured even in the state of withdrawal (*nimeṣāvasthā*).

Exposition

Kṣemarāja's commentary on this aphorism does not disagree with Bhāskara's but adds a new dimension to his interpretation of it by presenting it from the Krama point of view. Thus he explains that:

> Bhairava Who, as we have said, is this upsurge (of consciousness, *udyantṛtā*), consisting of the emergence of Supreme Intuition, possesses an inscrutable power of freedom which is the supreme (*parā*) and absolute (*anuttara* power of consciousness). In so far as (this power) attends inwardly (to its own nature) while perceiving outwardly (the totality of manifestation), it pervades the successive movement (*krama*) and simultaneous existence (*akrama*) of every (moment of each) cycle of energy and although said to have (also) transcended both succession and its opposite, as well as emptiness and fullness, is not in itself any of these. (This power) manifests the play of the expansion of the cycles of the powers of creation (persistence and destruction) on the screen of its own nature commencing with the Earth (principle) right up to repose within the supreme subject.[34]

In other words, the yogi's experience of the absolute (*anuttara*) is coupled with the emergence within him of the supreme creative intuition (*parāpratibhā*) through which, independent of all other causes, consciousness reflects the universe within its own nature.[35] Bhairava, with Whom the yogi is now identified, is the upsurge of the exertive force (*udyama*) that impels the flux of the power of His infinite freedom which absorbs the entire universe from the grossest category—Earth—up to its resting place in the supreme subject. The inner exertion of Bhairava-consciousness is thus made complete by the consciousness of its power. The two are united together through the practise of *Bhairavamudrā* in which the yogi maintains his inner (*antarmukha*) awareness of the exertion of the Self while its energy flows out through the extroverted (*bahirmukha*) activity of the senses.[36]

Thus, according to Kṣemarajā, the yogi is now instructed to contemplate Anākhyā (lit. 'the Inexplicable'), the power of his own consciousness which pervades the cycle of energies that create, maintain and destroy the universe of perceptions functioning through the subject, means of knowledge and object in three moments of the cycle of cognition. Their simultaneous (*akrama*) as well as successive (*krama*) appearance is recognised to be the creative flow of *Anākhyāśakti* which transcends both the successive movement of the powers of consciousness and their non-successive movement while being at the same time both. Although both full of all things and void of diversity, this power is neither empty not full. In the *Hymn to the Womb of Consciousness* (*Jñānagarbhastotra*) the poet writes:

> I place in the Heart (of my awareness) the Supreme Goddess of Consciousness Who shines radiantly beyond all things and Who, by removing the support of the three sequences (of creation, persistence and destruction), allows one to cross beyond the three changes; She Who is beautiful, Her body one with change and Her nature unchanging.[37]

The yogi who thus contemplates the power of *Anākhyā* which contains and is the circle, or collective whole of all the powers of consciousness, while continuing to sense the world about him, experiences the dissolving away of the universe of duality. Burnt by the fire of consciousness of the universal subject, the diversity of perceptions becomes one with it in the withdrawal (*nimeṣa*) of diversity back into unity.

* * *

The difference that prevails between the waking and other (states)[38] does not obscure the unchanging (*acyuta*) conscious nature because (this diversity of states is the result of) the activity of one's own essential nature (*svasvarūpaparispanda*). The Lord of the gods accordingly spoke (the following) aphorism in order to explain that this is so:

jāgratsvapnasuṣuptabhede turyābhogasaṃvit
The consciousness which is the expanse of the Fourth State (abides constantly in) the various (states) of waking, dreaming and deep sleep. 1/7

The Fourth State is said to be (contemplation, that is) the reflective awareness of the compact unity (and undivided Being) of one's own essential nature (*svasvarūpaika-ghanatā*) because it pervades all (other states) of consciousness. It is consciousness, called the expanse of the Fourth State of the abiding condition in which ignorance has fallen away. It is the (inner) nature of the perceiving subject who thus abides clearly evident and extends (as one) even when division prevails due to the waking and other states.[39]

* * *

States of recollection and others like them and those which involve a loss of consciousness are included in those of dreaming and deep sleep, respectively. Thus, because other states (such as these) are said to be included in the three principle ones (of waking, dreaming and deep sleep) they need not be dealt with separately. These three states unfold in this way, each with their distinctive functions, when the yogi emerges out of contemplation but, because he is aware of his own unique and undivided Being, the obscuration which covers the true nature of reality engendered by these three states does not exist (for him). Therefore, one who attends to his own perfectly integral nature has no need to exert himself to practise contemplation because the precept (to do so) does not apply (to him) (nor is the practise of contemplation possible) for one who attends to that which is incomplete and the locus of limitation because (his doing so) runs contrary to the attainment of fullness.

Exposition

The persistence of an underlying awareness of consciousness experienced as one's own most essential nature which both perceives and acts through its instruments, the body, senses and mind, is central to the teachings of the *Stanzas on Vibration* and is prefigured here in the *Aphorisms* where it is repeatedly referred to as the Fourth State. We have already had occasion to discuss this point in a number of places to which we refer the reader.[40] As we shall see later, the development and maintenance of this awareness, that is to say, the Fourth State, is an important part of the practises taught in the *Aphorisms*.

* * *

Once the Supreme Lord had said this (He went on) to utter (the following) three aphorisms to elucidate (the true nature of) the waking and other (states) so that (all) may attain liberation in this very life.

jñānaṃ jāgrat
Knowledge (born of sensory perception) is the waking state. 1/8

Sensory perception is a product of the intellect, ego and mind (coupled with the sensations) of sound touch, form, taste and smell. The power of knowledge which belongs to the conscious nature (*cidātman*) actively manifests (*sphurati*) in this way in the form of the cognizing subject, means of knowledge and the object of cognition. Here this is (said to be) the waking state which (marks) the loss of the fettered soul's true nature (*svarūpahāni*).

* * *

The meaning here is that the perception born of the external activity of the senses has as its material basis smelling, tasting, seeing, touching, speaking, comprehending, self-arrogation and ascertainment. The waking state, attended by the limitations (*upādhi*) imposed by the subject (object and means of knowledge), obscures the true nature of the fettered but bestows upon those who are free the radiant brilliance of their own nature.

Exposition

The waking state is the form of awareness which prevails when the knowing subjectivity (*veditṛtā*) is totally absorbed in the sensations which come to it through the senses.[41] In this state living beings, gross elements and the words which denote them are made manifest outside the subject[42] and, unlike objects perceived in a dream, are perceptible by everybody (*sādhāraṇa*)[43] . This state arises though the activity of the wakeful body and senses and hence yogis call it "Established in the Body" (*piṇḍastha*). For them it is the state of awareness they experience when concentrating one-pointedly (*dhāraṇā*)[44] on an object.[45] Those who have gained insight into reality (*jñānin*) and express its nature in metaphysical terms, call this state "Everywhere Auspicious" (*sarvatobhadra*) because it represents the state of consciousness manifest as the ubiquitous fullness of objective being (*vedyasattā*).[46]

* * *

svapno vikalpaḥ

Dreaming consists of thought constructs. 1/9

The thoughts of the pervasive perceiver[5] that, constantly renewed, emerge inwardly in the absence of external objects are said (to constitute) the dream state. The liberated condition (*patibhāva*) (makes these) thought constructs firm (and full of divine consciousness) while due to the fettered state, they are, on the contrary, unstable and said to be the covering (which obscures) the Lord Who is the power (of consciousness).

* * *

The dream state obscures the true nature (*svarūpa*) of the fettered soul. It consists of the constantly renewed emergence of thought constructs each of which perform their own function and whose contents are diversely manifest forms such as towns, mountains, forests and groves, generated inwardly in the absence of external objects and independently of them when the (waking) state (in which they appear) ceases.

Exposition

The dream state is one in which the dreamer is unaware of outer sensations and does not perceive external objects.[48] In this state the subject is not a perceiver but one who thinks (*vetṛ*). Turned in on himself, he reflects (*vimṛśati*) on the mental impressions (*saṃskāra*) previously formed in his consciousness by outer objects and orders them into thought constructs (*vikalpa*). The dream state,[49] therefore, occurs not only while we are asleep, but also during the phase of perception in which the external object[50] is inwardly represented mentally. The Impurity of Karma (*karmamala*) persists here only as a latent trace while the objects perceived inwardly are illusory creations of Śiva generated in the individual subject's mind and hence not perceivable by all.[51]

The practise of Dhyāna, in which an object of meditation is repeatedly mentally represented in such a way that the yogi thereby achieves absorption, is said to take place in the dream state.[52] The yogi's vital breath and all his ideas are then drawn together into one place in which his awareness is firmly established. Yogis therefore call the dream state "Established in One Place" (*padastha*). From their point of view it is a higher, subtler level of consciousness than waking and hence it is easier to rise from it to a state of mystical absorption .Those who tread the path of knowledge (*jñānin*) call this state "Pervasion" (*vyāpti*) because it corresponds to autonomous cognitive awareness which, no longer conditioned by the object of knowledge, is free to pervade everywhere.[53]

* * *

aviveko māyāsauṣuptam
Deep sleep is Māyā, the lack of discernment. 1/10

When the power (of consciousness) consisting of cognition and its object does not manifest and, lacking in awareness (*vimarśa*), one fails to discern the conscious nature, the (same power) is said to be Māyā because it nourishes the net of darkness that covers (consciousness). It is the state of deep sleep (in which) memory and its objects (reside in an unmanifest form) in the consciousness which

abides in one's own nature. In so far as (these states may represent degrees) of rest the liberated (enjoys) in his own nature (or else the types of) obscuration which affect the fettered soul, each one of these three (states) is of three types formed by conjoining each to the other, taking one or other as primary or secondary.[54] (All these states) are rightly understood to be those of the conscious nature.

Thus the Lord[55] is here, in the two states (of waking and dreaming), cognition and its object, while in the other (states of) deep sleep and the Fourth, the omnipresent Lord is said to be consciousness.[56]

* * *

The point made in these verses is as follows. (When) the power (of consciousness) which spills out of itself here (in the form of both) sensory awareness (*vedana*) and (its) objects, ceases to be active, withdrawing its rays, as does the sun (at night) and the Self, whose nature is pure consciousness (remains) unmanifest, (this power) becomes the net of darkness (that obscures consciousness), that is, deep sleep which is Māyā. There, objects and all that one recalls (of them) continue to exist only within one's own pure, unobscured nature. And that also exists, otherwise the fact that after waking one recalls having slept well and that one knew nothing could not be reasonably explained. Thus, the inherent nature of the liberated (*pati*) is manifestly apparent in these three states while that of those in bondage is not, as is proved by the very nature of things (*svabhāvasiddha*).

Exposition

The state of deep sleep is characterised by an absence of outer physical and inner mental activity. It is one of silence (*tuṣṇībhāva*) in which there is neither object nor means of knowledge.[57] It is the emptiness (*śūnya*) of the individual subject void of all content who persists, deprived of all support, as the negative correlate of the object.[58] It is a state of potential said to be the "seed of the universe"[59] where everything is merged within the subject in the form of latent impressions (*saṃskāra*) which give rise to the world of differentiated perceptions when he wakes up. As such it is the microcosmic equivalent of universal destruction (*pralaya*)[60] when the categories of experience (*tattva*) in the realm of diversity dissolve away.[61] Although the same cognizing subject present in the waking and dream states persists here also, he appears to be absent because the object and means of knowledge, with which he formerly identified, are no longer present.[62] Only the Impurity of Individuality (*āṇavamala*) continues to operate, contracting consciousness and depriving it of its awareness and freedom. Thus, unsupported by the other impurities, it leaves the subject in a state of emptiness. As the individual living soul (*jīva*), the 'void subject' (*śūnyapramātṛ*) present in this state, is the source from which the powers of the senses and vital breath spring when he rises from sleep.

We can distinguish between two types of deep sleep; one is totally without object (*apavedyasuṣupti*) which we recall when we awake and think, 'I knew nothing at all'. In the second type the Impurity of Māyā (*māyīyamala*) continues to function in a subtle way and so has some objective content (*savedyasuṣupti*), as we know from the fact that when we awake from this state we think 'I slept well'.

For the yogi, deep sleep is closer to the state of universal consciousness than waking or dreaming, for here the subject alone exists. He calls it "Established in Form" (*rūpastha*) because, as the perceiver, the subject is the creator of forms (*rūpayati*) and hence is pure form.[63] So while the average man experiences this state as an absence of consciousness, for the yogi ' deep sleep' is his contemplation (*samādhi*) in which he is in a state of transcendental aloofness (*anudāsīnya*), freed of the awareness of the distinction between subject and object.[64] Those who seek knowledge call this state the "Great Pervasion" (*mahāvyāpti*) because, established in subjective consciousness, they are even freer of the restrictions imposed by the object than they were in the 'Pervasion' (*vyāpti*) of the dream state.[65]

Our account is not, however, complete. A distinctive feature of the Kashmiri Śaiva conception of these states is, as Bhāskara points out, that each one contains the others. In this way there are nine states, which we shall now briefly examine.

1) *Waking in waking (jāgrat–jāgrat)*

This state is technically called "Unawakened" (*abuddha*). The awareness of the individual is here entirely centred on the body and totally given over to objectivity (*prameyabhāva*). Completely unconscious of his own subjective nature, he never asks himself who he is. Whenever he sees an object, he immediately identifies with it and totally forgets himself as the perceiver.

2) *Waking in dream (jāgrat–svapna)*

This state is technically called "Awakened" (*buddha*) and arises when subjective consciousness enters objective consciousness and looses awareness of outer objectivity, while continuing to perceive the mental impressions created by it. We can catch ourselves in this state when we find ourselves staring at something absent mindedly, carried away by our own thoughts.

3) *Waking in deep sleep (jāgrat–suṣupti)*

This is the state we experience when we loose consciousness of both our outer physical and inner mental environment. For a moment we are a complete blank, totally absent from our present situation. The yogi can rest in this state of absorption for long periods of time enjoying the subtle bliss of unity and hence is called "Well Awakened" (*prabuddha*). However, he is only 'Completely Well Awakened' (*suprabuddha*) when he experiences the Fourth State while awake and can continue to perceive and function in the midst of diversity while maintaining an awareness of his true conscious nature.

4) *Dreaming in waking (svapna–jāgrat)*

This is the state we experience when we are overcome with grief, passion, fear or madness. In it we mistakenly believe that our own mental projections are actual objects appearing before us. A person in this state is sometimes caught in the flux of objective perceptions and at other times by the waves of his own mental impressions without being able to distinguish between them. He is constantly coming and going from one sphere to the other hence 'Come and Gone' (*gatāgata*) is the name given to this state.

5) *Dreaming in dreaming (svapna–svapna)*

This is the dream state proper and is called "Well Dispersed" (*suvikṣipta*) because the individual's awareness is here carried hither and thither by the mental images which arise within him without his being aware of either their cause or purpose. He is in a world where one thing may be transformed into another without this seeming strange, while he has as little control over what he sees, despite the fact that it is a creation of his own mind, as when he was awake.

6) *Dreaming in deep sleep (svapna–suṣupti)*

This is a state of greater coherence and hence is called "Consistent" (*saṃgata*). Subjectivity (*pramātṛbhāva*) is more intensely felt so the dreamer can get a better grip on himself and examine the situation he finds himself in. Thus, at the time he realises that the objects before him are not really a part of the external world and that he must be dreaming. He, as the subject, is then clearly evident and he is able to experience a subtle touch of universal consciousness while dreaming. However, it is only when he experiences the Fourth State while dreaming, in the 'Atttentive' (*samāhita*) state, that he is completely awake to himself as the dreamer and can rise directly from the dream state to that of contemplation (*samādhi*).

7) *Deep sleep in waking (suṣupti–jāgrat)*

This state is called "Emergent" (*udita*) because the emptiness of deep sleep rises up to obliterate all objective consciousness. When the subject awakes from this state he remembers nothing, only that he was completely asleep and had lost all sense of himself and the world.

8) *Deep sleep in dreaming (suṣupti–svapna)*

This state is called "Extensive" (*vipula*) because here latent impressions begin to proliferate and mature. The subject in this state is more aware of his nature. Like the faint outlines of a picture, subtle traces of perceptions appear within him at one with his own nature and he rises closer to the state of universal consciousness.

9) *Deep sleep in deep sleep (suṣupti–suṣupti)*

This state is called "Peaceful" (*śānta*) because while he is in it, the subject experiences a subtle, yet uninterrupted, awareness of his own subjectivity at rest within itself. When he awakens he remembers this state as being one of spiritual bliss. Every time he regains it, it becomes more intense, until he reaches a state of deep sleep in the Fourth State which is called "Very Blissful" (*suprasanna*), for now he continues to abide in that state fully aware of his own subjectivity and of its blissful nature. Deep sleep becomes for him contemplation (*samādhi*).

* * *

Now (the next) aphorism follows on (from the previous one). Spoken (by Lord Śiva), its sense is that these three states of consciousness correspond to the three qualities (*guṇa*):

tritayabhoktā vīreśaḥ
The enjoyer of the three states is the Lord of the Heroes. 1/11

The three, *sattva, rajas* and *tamas,* are called "qualities" (*guṇa*). They arise out of one's own essential nature (*svasvabhāva*) according to (its three) states and are the obscuring covering (which envelopes the consciousness of) the fettered but is not such for the Ubiquitous Lord Who is one's own fundamental state of being (*svasthiti*) because He pervades every (state).[66] Thus, in this way, the body of consciousness (*cidvapu*) (which supports) the flux of the activity of the qualities (*guṇaspandaniḥsyanda*) is said to be the experiencing subject (*bhoktṛ*) because he appropriates (them) and pervades the unfolding (of this, his divine power). (All this) is one with the activity of his light and so he is the Lord of the Heroes. Thus the arising of the qualities are the rays (of this light) and he who in this universe of thought constructs is intent on emitting and assimilating it, is said to be the Lord of the Heroes for he reabsorbs (into himself the entire process).

* * *

The three states of consciousness correspond to the dominance of one or the other of the three qualities (*guṇa*) thus:

waking	= illumination (*prakāśa*)	= *sattva*
dreaming	= activity (*pravṛtti*)	= *rajas*
deep sleep	= delusion (*moha*)	= *tamas*

The qualities emerge out of *Prakṛti*, the material nature in which they are in a state of balanced harmony, while the states of consciousness are the unfolding of the power of one's own inherent nature. (The subject is the source of these parallel developments and) he who arouses the state of wonder in all these states is therefore called the "Lord of the Heroes."

Exposition

Kṣemarāja interprets this aphorism in a way which seems to us less forced then Bhāskara's interpretation. According to him, the 'three states' are, as one would expect, those of waking, dreaming and deep sleep, while the 'Lord of the Heroes' is the yogi who, having discovered his true divine identity, is master of his senses. The gap between one state and the next through which the yogi catches a glimpse of the Fourth State, expands until he is carried beyond all levels and states in his experience of the oneness of the absolute (*anuttara*). Mindful of the true nature of subject and object in all three states, the yogi is no longer a victim (*bhogya*) of these states but their master and achieves liberation while yet alive (*jīvanmukti*).

The Well Awakened yogi is said to be the Lord of the Heroes because he is full of the bliss of his mastery over the senses and their universal powers that, vibrant with consciousness, create and withdraw the universe of sensations in consonance with their expansion and contraction. The yogi, now full of the creative activity of consciousness, is one with the 'Churning Bhairava' (*Manthānabhairava*) Who is the hyposthesis of the exertive force of consciousness which 'churns' or arouses its own energy to give rise to the cycles of creation, persistence and destruction.[67] But, as Kṣemarāja remarks: "He who is not like this is a victim of the waking and other states and so is just a wordly fettered soul. Even a yogi who has not ascended into this stream (of consciousness) is not the Lord of the Heroes but is merely a deluded soul."[68]

* * *

The (Lord) taught (the following) aphorism the sense of which is that the fundamental state of one's own true nature (svasvabhāva) does not change even when one rises out of contemplation (vyutthāna):

vismayo yogabhūmikāḥ
The planes of union are wonder. 1/12

In this way the enlightened (yogi) abides as if wonder struck,[69] observing this universe sustained by the Lord Whose body is consciousness and is the cause of all (the phases) of creation (and destruction). (A state of) wonder arises (within him progressively) in consonance with the (development) of a series (of yogic states) that begin with a vision of light (*bindu*).[70] These manifestations of contemplation (*samādhi*) are the planes of union (*yoga*).

* * *

By penetrating into his true nature, which is uninterrupted consciousness (*cidghana*), the yogi relishes the life-giving essence (*amṛta*) of the aesthetic delight (*rasa*) born of objectivity. He then perceives the glorious power (*vibhūti*) of his own nature which is ever manifest and (fully) unfolded through his uncreated and expanded senses. And so, because he (now) sees a novel, transcendent reality that inspires (him) with wonder, a sense of awe (arises within him) without his having to meditate on the psychic centres (in the body where) the vision of light (*bindu*) and the rest (occur), or do anything else.

Exposition

According to Kṣemarāja this aphorism explains that the yogi who is absorbed in the dense mass of consciousness of his own nature is not merely suspended in his state of realisation, but is constantly rising for whatever he perceives lifts him up to still higher planes in a fresh wave of aesthetic delight (*camatkāra*). The common man does at times experience a similar state of wonder when he, for example, sees a work of art, but the yogi whose consciousness has become one with the supreme principle experiences everything he perceives in this way because he, at the same time, views his own nature as the ground and universal cause of all things. The circle of the senses pulsates, expanding and contracting, thus repeatedly leading him to new levels of wonder. He is constantly thrown back into the aesthetic rapture of contemplation which he experiences as fresh and marvellously new at each moment. Thus, although he rests in himself full of consciousness, he is at the same time rising (*udita*) in the wonder of the realisation that his own true nature has of itself within itself. In other words, according to Kṣemarāja, this aphorism refers to the yogi who has reached the highest level of consciousness and so, as Kṣemarāja expressly declares, it does not refer even partially, as Bhāskara maintains, to stages in the development of the yogi's consciousness on the way to this realisation. The ever-developing sense of wonder the yogi experiences at this level is, as the anonymous commentator on Bhāskara's commentary also says, independent and beyond the vision of light (*bindu*) that developed yogis experience between the eyebrows or any other experience they may have of the other psychic centres in the body.

* * *

The Blessed One, Śaṅkara, then explained (in the following) aphorism that His universal will (sarvecchā) unfolds in this way unobstructed:

icchāśaktitamā kumārī
The Virgin is the will, the supreme power. 1/13

The will of the Supreme Self is the highest power of all because it is linked with the (universal) agency of every (act of) perception. (This power is called Kumārī, the Virgin) because (through it the yogi) penetrates into the unobscured conscious nature and so She is the one who destroys (*māriṇī*)

the abhorrent (*kutsa*) round of rebirth (*sṛṣṭi*). Thus She is the Ubiquitous Lord's (universal) causal power (*kāraṇa*) which is everywhere one and unchanging (*akhaṇḍita*).

* * *

The meaning here is that (the liberated yogi's) freedom (operates) unobstructed everywhere in this objective universe because he is united with the power of the (universal) will which contains within itself every power (and so) everything manifests as he wishes it to. In this way the totality of all things from the level of unmanifest existence (*anāśrita*) up to the Earth principle shines radiantly as if it were his own body in the form of unobscured and uninterrupted (*ghana*) consciousness.

Exposition

Although Kṣemarāja acknowledges the validity of Bhāskara's reading of this aphorism and comments on it in this form in much the same way, he follows the lead of his teacher Abhinavagupta and adopts a variant reading (i.e., *icchāśaktir umā kumārī*) which translated means: *the power of the will is the virgin Umā.*

Like Bhāskara, Kṣemarāja glosses the word *virgin* (*kumārī*) to mean that she is the goddess who kills (*mārayati*) or destroys Māyā (*ku*), the principle that engenders duality, by preventing its emergence and extension. He adds that her virginity relates to her nature as the pure enjoying subjectivity (*bhoktṛ*) of universal consciousness that, as such, can never be experienced objectively as an object of enjoyment by any alien reality outside her own nature.[71] Likewise, the commentator on the *Mahānarāyaṇopaniṣad* tells us that when the goddess as the supreme power (*parāśakti*) of consciousness presents herself to us as the fecund source of all things, which she emanates out of herself, she is known as Ambikā, the mother of the universe, but when she retracts them back, her name is Umā.[72] Kṣemarāja attributes both these functions to the virgin Umā. From this point of view, the word *kumārī* is derived from the root *kumar* which means to play. Thus this, the power of the universal will, is said to be *kumārī* because she is the creative freedom of Śiva's universal consciousness which delights in playing the game of creation and destruction.

Finally, although Umā is described here as being a virgin, she is also Śiva's consort. Kṣemarāja explains in his commentary on the *Svacchandatantra* that the goddess Umā pervades the universe and is seated in the centre of the inner circle of deities along with Bhairava as the hypothesis of His saving grace (*śaktipāta*).[73] A devoted wife untouched by anyone else, intent solely on the worship and achievement of union with Śiva, Her lord, Umā is an apt symbol for the pure will unsullied by any desire and of the love and devotion which Śiva has for His own nature. Merger with her is what Utpaladeva ardently longed for when he sang: "May my devotion for You be like the Goddess Who is full of infinite bliss, never separate from You and extremely dear to You."[74]

In short, Umā is the power which leads man, the microcosm, to the realisation of his universal nature through merger with the will which, united with Śiva, works equally within him and the entire universe.

* * *

(Now), does (the Lord) Who is (the inner nature of) all things possess (just) one body, as that of the embodied soul, or is it everything? (In response to this query) the Lord of the gods said:

dṛśyaṃ śarīram
The perceptible is (His) body. 1/14

The Lord is (both) the outpouring of all existing things (as well) as the seed (cause) of all (that comes into being). (His) nature is pure consciousness and, because (He) pervades (everything), His body is not (just) one. Nothing exists outside (Him) and every single perceivable thing born of thought is (His) body because (He) pervades (all things) as (He) is the coming into being of everything. (Moreover), every physical body belongs to Him because the conscious

nature (of every living being, various) according to its own particular type, is one.[75] He to whom the object of perception (appears) separate from the body (only in the way an object does) reflected in a mirror, pervades (all that is perceptible) and so is the abode of the wealth of liberation.

* * *

The intended sense of this aphorism is as follows. Paramaśiva Himself bears the form of every perceivable object, even at the contracted (conditioned, *saṃkucita*) level, because He pervades the inner and outer (nature) of all things which, reflected within Him as if in a crystal, are sustained by Him and He imparts existence to them through the light of His (consciousness). If this were not so, it would be impossible to explain why things are as they are; thus He can be said to be the life (of all things).

Exposition

Consciousness pervades and is the seed of all things, and thus has as many bodies as there are external, objectively perceived and mentally represented entities. Plunged in the ecstasy of universal consciousness the yogi experiences, through its pure will, the arising of his own cosmic nature. He knows that he is one with all embodied beings and that his physical body is not his true nature but an externally perceivable form, separate and yet one with him, like a reflection in a mirror. Identification of 'I' consciousness with the limited locus of his body thus naturally shifts to the unlimited expanse of the All which he now experiences as his true body and shares in Sadāśiva's awareness that 'I am this universe'. The 'I', released from the confines of the locus on the which it was formerly projected, is experienced as pervading all things, the border between inner and outer dissolves away, and they blend together in a state of undivided unity like that of the juices of a peacock's egg.[76]

* * *

Having thus declared what the essential nature of cognitive consciousness is, (the question arises) how union (*yoga*) with it can take place. The (Lord) uttered an aphorism the sense of which is that (this union takes place) for one who has entered the temple of his own Heart.

hṛdaye cittasaṃghaṭṭād dṛśyasvāpadarśanam
By fixing the mind in the Heart (the yogi) has a vision of the perceivable and of dreams. 1/15

The mind is said to be fixed in the Heart (of consciousness) which is its sustaining ground when it assumes a stable state (*sthiti*) (there within it). In this way, (the yogi) has a vision of the perceivable and of dreams. The emptiness (*vyoman*) of deep sleep is technically called the "Heart" because it resides in the centre. The contemplation (*samādhāna*) of the Self is here said to be the fixing of the mind because the interconnected patterns (*jāla*) of (mental) activity which emerge from it become one (in this way) within one's own nature. When it dissolves away in that emptiness[77] (all sense of being) a brahmin, *Kṣatrīya* or (even) a murderer (ceases) because (these notions) relate to the body and are associated (with the activity of the mind).

The perceivable is the object of realisation (*upalabhya*), that is, one's own awakened nature (*svasvarūpa*) free of obscuration, the attainment of which is said to be vision. (This) vision takes place here (in the Heart) when the delusion which induces dreams is destroyed and the awakened (yogi) pervades (all things) at all times by penetrating the Divine Gesture (of enlightenment-*divyamudrā*). (The yogi) of unawakened intellect (experiences only) a vision of dreams which for the awakened is the freedom to dream as he wishes (*svapnasvātantrya*) (that he achieves) by drinking the lunar nectar (*soma* of *apāna*, the descending breath). This is the rending asunder of the darkness (of false egoity)[78] and the arising of enlightened intuitive consciousness (*pratibhodaya*).

* * *

The following is, in brief, the sense of the above verses explaining this aphorism. By close attention, that is, by exercising the mind in such a way as to bring it to rest and turn it away from all external things, whether those of the everyday world or those of the world beyond it, the entire objective order dissolves away in the Heart which is the ground consciousness that sustains all the senses and channels (of the vital breath). The 'Heart' is a term used to denote the emptiness of deep sleep as it (marks) the end (*avadhi*) of the upper Pure and lower Impure Paths (of emanation) because the activity (of the mind) is brought to a halt there and so the mind also dissolves away, just as fire goes out when devoid of heat. (The emptiness of the Heart is) a state of transcendental yogic consciousness beyond mind (*nirmanaska*). It is a 'darkness' devoid of all corporeal and other forms of egoity. Thus, (all) work which needs be done to sustain the course of daily life and (is encumbent on those who preserve a sense of ego) such as the study of the Vedas, and here indicated implicitely by the words *brahmin* and *kṣatrīya*, comes to an end. In this, the emptiness of the Fourth State, (the yogi) perceives his true unobscured nature (*svasvabhāva*) and the ignorance rooted in the senseless (*anartha*) world of birth and death (*saṃsāra*) ceases. However, the man of unawakened intellect who happens to enter this state merely experiences sleep.

Exposition

The Heart (*hṛdaya*) has from Vedic times been a common symbol for the reality which both underlies the universe and the core of man's being. It is here that the macrocosm and microcosm, transcendence and immanence meet. The *Upaniṣads* declare that the Heart contains both Heaven and Earth, what is ours here and now and what is not yet ours.[79] In the Heart the ancient sages heard and saw the creative word (*vāc*) of the Veda for it is from here that all of man's ideas and the cosmic thought are hewn out. Thus, it is the creator (*Prajāpati*) and ground (*Brahman*) of all beings as well as the All.[80] It is the vessel and place of rest of all creatures.[81] Pictured as an inverted lotus which turns upwards and blooms when the light of consciousness shines upon it, it is found in the citadel of the body, the 'City of Brahman'.[82] The Self (*puruṣa*) resides there, infinitely great and yet 'no bigger than a thumb', burning like a fire without smoke, it is the maker of past and future and yet eternal and unchanging.[83]

In Kashmiri Śaiva texts the symbolism of the Heart is very rich.[84] Another name for awareness,[85] it represents the true nature of all things and the Self of consciousness[86] as the undivided essence of its light[87] and aesthetic rapture (*camatkāra*). In it resounds the eternally emergent sound of awareness.[88] Active as the dynamics of the egoity of consciousness it is both knowledge and action[89] and, passive, it is the ground or 'great abode' of the universe when it is manifest as the union of consciousness and bliss.[90] It is the universal source of all three moments of creation, persistence and destruction, pervading them all without itself changing. Thus it exists prior to cosmic manifestation as the pure energy which contains all things within itself, as does the banyan seed a tree.[91] In the second moment it is the 'well-established abode' (*pratiṣṭhāsthāna*) and ground (*ādhāra*) of the entire universe. It pervades and gives life to all the categories of existence with their respective world orders, Śiva and all the lesser gods and the powers of every being in bondage, each with their own individual existence even though they all participate equally in the unity of the Heart's essence.[92] Conversely, it is in the Heart of the pure consciousness (*caitanya*) of the universal ego (*ahaṃ*)[93] that the supreme and infinite light of all the categories of existence is established in all living beings.[94] As Abhinava explains:

> Just as one says that the Heart is the undivided light of consciousness and reflective awareness which is the plane of the abode of rest of the body consisting (collectively) of all the categories of existence and its individual parts such as the skin etc., so the body of Lord Bhairava, which is the universe made up of the individual categories and worlds as well as the fifty letters of the alphabet and is the essence of reality, has this same (reality as His) Heart which is the essence of undivided awareness.[95]

The Heart is Bhairava's true state as the absolute (*anuttara*) which pours out of itself as the supreme power (*parāśakti*) of consciousness.[96] Its throb is the pulsing union (*saṃghaṭṭa*) of Śiva and Śakti through which the universe is eternally emitted and reabsorbed as it expands and contracts.[97] At the microcosmic level, its outpouring is the effulgent flow (*sphuraṇa*) of awareness, in the form of the diverse objects of thought (*cetya*) and thinking subjects (*cetayitṛ*) while it itself abides, unaffected by time and space, on the plane beyond mind (*unmanā*). As the source of all energies it is the pure exertion (*udyoga*) of the uncreated egoity of our true conscious nature which is the union of will, knowledge and action[98] and hence is said to be "a triangular vibration which is the incessant expansion and contraction of the three energies at rest in the abode of great bliss."[99]

The great wisdom of the Spanda teachings should be treasured in secret in the cave of the Heart[100] for he who reflects upon the inner nature of the Heart merges in the expansion of the vibration (*saṃrambha*) of his own consciousness and is liberated.[101] Thus he who knows the Heart in truth gains the true initiation[102] which bestows perfect freedom and bliss. Maheśvarānanda teaches:

> The wish-granting tree of contemplation growing, with its many branches, in the heart blossoms as the wealth of universal enjoyment (*bhoga*) and bears the fruit of the light of the festival of undivided bliss.[103]

Accordingly, Kṣemarāja, commenting on this aphorism, says that the Heart is "the light of consciousness because it is the place where all things are firmly established." And so he goes on to explain that "when the restless movement (of the mind) is fixed therein, the perceptible, that is, (all objectivity ranging from outer objects such as the colour) blue (as well as) the body, intellect and vital breath, along with the emptiness of deep sleep in which it is absent is (perceived in the singleness of) vision that, freed of the distinction between subject and object, illumines (it all) in accord with its true nature as if it were one's own body. (In short) the mind, intent upon the light of consciousness, perceives the entire universe as pervaded by it."[104]

Bhāskara's interpretation of this aphorism differs from Kṣemarāja's even though they basically agree that the practise to which it refers involves that of introverted contemplation through which the activity of the mind is brought to a halt and objectivity dissolves away in the Heart of consciousness which is its sustaining ground. But Bhāskara, unlike Kṣemarāja, links this practise with that described in verses 23–25 of the *Stanzas on Vibration* which he combines with that of verses 33–34 that read together teach how the yogi's true nature (*svasvabhāva*) manifests in the states of dreaming and deep sleep when he is absorbed in uninterrupted prayer, intent on following the commands of Lord Śiva. The Heart, in this context, is understood to be the point of contact between the ascending and descending currents of the breath that, in the contemplative absorption which results when the activity of the mind is suspended, are withdrawn into it. Merged in this way in the emptiness of deep sleep, which Bhāskara equates with the Heart, the breathing can now be transformed into the Upward Moving Breath (*udāna*) which leads contracted individualized consciousness out of the confinment of the body and so reveals to the yogi his true unconditioned nature. Then, when the normal movement of the breath resumes, the yogi can share in Śiva's freedom through which he can dream and create whatever he wishes.[105]

Although stanzas 23–25 refer primarily to the state of breath suspension and 33–34 to its subsequent emergence, the yogi who experiences these two moments must be careful of the same possible danger, namely, that instead of attaining to the enlightened consciousness of the Fourth State, he may fall into the abysmal unconsciousness of deep sleep. Thus he must guard against this by maintaining a state of mindful awareness.

* * *

Now the ubiquitous Lord has talked about the inner and the external (nature). He uttered the next three aphorisms the purport of which is that (the realisation of) one's own nature which, because it is free of both (inner and outer aspects), is perfectly full and forms the undivided circle (of totality), is easily within one's grasp (*karasthita*). (He does this by explaining) how the permanence (of eternal consciousness) abides in the domain of Śiva, Śakti and the Self and (how) the Light of one's own nature may (never) diminish.

śuddhatattvasaṃdhānād vā
Or (the yogi can realise Siva) by contemplating the Pure Principle. 1/16

The pure unconditioned Principle is the Light called Śiva. The contemplation of that (principle) is the reflective awareness (*vimarśa*) of one's own identity with it by virtue of which the obscuring darkness (of false egoity) may also be rent asunder because it is the one perfectly full reality. (Thus), by abandoning one's external (limited) egoity, one's own authentic state (*nijasthiti*) (abides) unbroken (*akhaṇḍita*).

* * *

Here the means (to realisation) is explained along with a description of Śiva-consciousness which is called the "Plane of Rest" and is Supreme Bliss (*parānanda*).

Exposition

In Kṣemarāja's recension this aphorism is lengthened by the addition of an extra element while the aphorism which follows in Bhāskara's recension is modified. Kṣemarāja reads what for us are aphorisms 1/16 and 1/17 together thus: *Or by contemplating the Pure Principle (the yogi) becomes one who is free of the power which binds* (*śuddhatattvasaṃdhānād vāpaśuśaktiḥ*). Kṣemarāja comments: "The Pure Principle is Paramaśiva. When (the yogi) contemplates the universe within it, realising that it is one with (Paramaśiva) then, free of the power which binds (the fettered), he, like Sadāśiva, becomes the Lord of the universe."[106]

According to Bhāskara the yogi is not to contemplate the oneness of the universe with Śiva but fix his attention directly on the pure light of consciousness shining within him and reflect on it as being his own nature. In this way the yogi's extroverted ego is established in the fullness of his true nature. This is the experience of 'rest' (*viśrānti*), a state of tranquility devoid even of the excitement of bliss (*nirānanda*) which characterises Śiva-consciousness (*śivacaitanya*).

* * *

svapadaśakti
Energy established in its own abode. 1/17

not in Kshemaraja

(Śakti's) own abode should be understood to be the place of Being (*sat*) called Śiva. (Śiva's) vitality (*vīrya*), which is knowledge and action, is said to be (His) energy. (Energy's) abiding state is (its) absorption (*līnatā*), that is, penetration into the agential aspect (of consciousness). That same (state) is the light of intuition (*pratibhā*) which is the solitary churner of the light of consciousness (which thus aroused issues forth as the universe and enlightens the yogi).

* * *

Here (Bhāskara) explains what is meant by empowered consciousness which is called the "Plane of Attainment" and is Supreme Bliss.

* * *

vitarka ātmajñānam 1.17
Right discernment is the knowledge of the Self. 1/18

The discriminating insight which (operates) in the midst of (the many and) diverse limiting conditions (*upādhi*) is the right discernment of the single uninterrupted awareness (*vimarśa*) of one's own true nature (*svasvabhāva*) which serves to attain the recognitive insight (*pratyabhijñā*) that the Self is Śiva. Know this to be the highest means to realisation in which one experiences the true Self (*satyātman*) directly. Therefore, (this is) the supreme unfolding of the intuitive awareness of the pure Self.

* * *

This (aphorism) describes the means to attain the light of one's own nature while implicitely refering to the consciousness of the Self called the "Plane of Unfolding" (*prollāsabhūmi*).

Exposition

Kṣemarāja simply writes: "Right discernment is to deliberate that: 'I am Śiva Who is all things'. This is one's knowledge of the Self."[107]

* * *

(The preceding) three aphorisms described the consciousness of Śiva, Śakti and the Self. They are the Blissless (*nirānanda*), Supreme Bliss (*parānanda*) and the Great Bliss (*mahānanda*) (respectively) and are called the planes of "Rest," "Attainment" and "Unfolding." Now (Śiva goes on) to explain how the oneness of the Light (of consciousness) which is the unity of the bliss of self-realisation, shines when the intuitive realisation of this (three-fold consciousness) dawns.

lokānandaḥ samādhisukham
The bliss of the Light is the joy of contemplation. 1/19

The supreme, pure light of consciousness which is as if inwardly and externally manifest (*udita*) is the eternal and Ubiquitous Lord (*vibhu*) Who is all things and their essential nature as well as their arising (*sarvabhāvodbhava*). Know that to be the Light. It is that which is said to be Bliss. This radiant, unconditioned nature which shines at one with the light of consciousness is called the "joy of contemplation" because it attends onepointedly solely to its relish.

Or else the joy of contemplation is said to be the delight inherent in one's own nature (*svapramoda*) (present) in the two states,[108] subject and object which unfold together as one.

* * *

The joy of self-realisation of the yogi for whom the radiant energy of his own nature is fully manifest is the radiance of the oneness of the light (of consciousness which shines) everywhere in (all) things. It manifests in an instant by practising the aforementioned means to realisation.

Exposition

The Sanskrit word *loka* can mean three things, namely, "light," "world" or "people." Bhāskara opts for the first of these meanings and so understands *lokānandaḥ* to mean "the bliss of the light of consciousness." Kṣemarāja, however, chooses the latter two meanings and so explains that *loka* is both that which is illumined by the light of consciousness, i.e., the field of objectivity and the light which illumines it, i.e., the perceiving subject. It is the pure Act (*sphuraṇa*) of consciousness which, undivided either into inner or outer, subject or object, flows continuously between these two poles as the incessant transformation of the one into the other. The yogi merged in this movement is freed of the distinction between subject and object and rests in the centre between them even as he observes both in the abode of universal subjectivity where he experiences the 'joy of contemplation' as the inner aesthetic rapture of its innate bliss. As Maheśvarānanda explains:

> Just as in the analogous case of the wings of a jay which are the same on both sides, how can one say that (this) yogi is either introverted or extroverted?[109]

Again, Kṣemarāja suggests that this aphorism means that the joy of contemplation that the yogi feels when he reposes in his own nature can be transmitted to others who are fit to receive it. The receptive subject who sees the yogi immersed in contemplation, and is aware of his state, experiences its bliss within himself as well,[110] for as a passage from the *Candrajñāna* declares:

> Just as the moon, (beautiful) as a flower, shines all around, and by its pleasing form brings joy to everyone in an instant, so, O Goddess, the great yogi wandering about on the face of the earth brings joy to the whole universe from

hell to Śiva by the all pervading rays of (his) consciousness.[111]

* * *

The Blessed One spoke the (following) aphorism that explains that when the natural fruit (of Yoga) arises the agency of autonomous being (acts) in this way according to its own free will. (However, this does not appear to be so) because the power of action is binding when (operating) in the fettered.[112]

śaktisaṃdhāne śarīrotpattiḥ
The body comes into being when the energies unite. 1/20 1.19

Consciousness and Being is the nature of the possessor of power for without any material cause He illumines externally by (His own) will alone the phenomena which reside within (Him).[113] Five are (His) powers beginning with those of the will, knowledge and action. They are: *Īśānī, Apūraṇī, Hārdī, Vāmā* and *Mūrti*. The other (energies) said to be associated with them are called the "Body of Consciousness."[114] The formation of the Body of Action (*prakriyādeha*) is said to be the union of these (powers). The way the body comes into being when this happens is not at all like that of man, god or beast. Thus the (universal) agency it possesses (operates) everywhere and is imperishable and undivided, while the product of (its) activity (*kārya*) is described as perishable even in the world of the gods.

* * *

The meaning here is that the possessor of power, whose nature is consciousness, displays the phenomena that abide within Him in unity with (His) light according to His own free will. He does this in order to illumine (the universe of) phenomena, (all of) which are (His) powers, on the screen of His own nature without taking recourse to material or any other causes. Therefore, the yogi who contemplates (the

Lord's) power of freedom, referred to previously as one with his own nature is himself free and fashions a body (for himself) at will (which, imperishable and omnipotent) differs from (and is superior to that of all other living beings) including even the gods.

Exposition

The five powers to which Bhāskara refers are as follows:

1) *The Power of Mastery (Īśānī)*

Also called *Vaiṣṇavīśakti*, this is the power of the universal will, unsullied by any object of desire.

2) *The Power Which Fills (Apūraṇīśakti)*

This is *Kaulikīśakti* or the pure emissive power (*visargaśakti*) of the innate bliss of the absolute (*anuttara*). Also called "the Mouth of the Yoginī" (*yoginīvaktra*), it is the womb of the universe from which flows the flux of creation.

3) *The Power of Bliss (Hārdīśakti)*

This is the energy which issues from the union (*melāpa*) of the illumined senses (*siddhas*) and their objects (*yoginīs*) that gives rise to the aesthetic rapture and power (*sāhasa*) of the bliss of cosmic consciousness (*jagadānanda*).

4) *The Power of Emanation (Vāmāśakti)*

This is the energy which flows from the expansion (*unmeṣa*) of consciousness as the will to know and create all things emanating from the union (*yāmala*) of Śiva and Śakti.

5) *The Power of Form (Mūrtiśakti)*

This is the highest form of the energy of action in which the powers of the absolute, will and knowledge co-operate to stimulate the ebb and flow of energies from universal consciousness.

By contemplating these energies in the movement of his introverted awareness and gathering them together, the yogi creates a new body for himself through which he acts in the world (*prakriyādeha*), free of the constraints that his former mortal body had to suffer. Through it the yogi can create and know all things.

Kṣemarāja again understands this aphorism in a different way. He takes *śaktisaṃdhāne* to mean not 'the union of the energies', as Bhāskara does, but the 'contemplation of power'. Thus the teaching here, according to Kṣemarāja, does not concern the generation of a new transfigured yogic body, but the contemplation of the will. Initiation, the practises leading to the attainment of lesser yogic powers (*siddhi*), Mantra, continued Mantric practise and Yoga are all fruitless if we fail to contempalate the innate energy of our own consciousness. The source of all the gods and their powers, it is the vital energy that animates the breath and issues out of itself as both knowledge and action. Thus the yogi can make use of the flow of energy he experiences in the course of his contemplation to create whatever he may desire both within himself while dreaming and externally in the waking state. Thus, Kṣemarāja understands the practise taught here to be that outlined in verses 33–34 of the *Stanzas* which explain how the individual will is coupled to the universal and the fruits of this union.

* * *

Again the Blessed One uttered (the following) aphorism which explains (the nature of His divine) manifestation said to be the game He spontaneously plays by virtue of (His) freedom:

bhūtasaṃdhāna-bhūtapṛthaktva-viśvasaṃghaṭṭāḥ
The union of the elements, the separation of the elements and the union of the universe. 1/21 1.26

The gross elements, ether (air, fire, water and earth) are fashioned by (their corresponding) constituent (energies), namely, the powers of sound (touch, vision, taste and smell respectively). This is said to be their union.

The separation (of the elements) is said to be the isolation of each element from the unity of its essential being (*sattā*) (which consciousness brings about) with the inten-

tion of (indicating in a manner amenable to) discursive representation the difference between the form (*mūrti* of each one).

(When) the agential aspect (of consciousness assumes a) dominant role it becomes, through its activity, a pure experience (devoid of thought constructs) called "light" and a (subtle, inner) tactile sensation which is bliss (*āhlāda*). (These two aspects combine with two others), namely, the Sun and Moon (which symbolize the powers of) knowledge and action of the sacrificer, the all-pervasive Lord of Consciousness. The union of the universe which is such is said (to take place) by means of (these) four (united together).

The universe which is the coalescence of the group of eight is the shining of the all-pervasive Lord of Consciousness in association with every form and each action.

* * *

The aggregate of the powers of consciousness, bliss, will, knowledge and action (when) clearly manifest serve as the material basis for the Pure Path of the conscious nature. They are the mainstay of the progressive downward evolution of the principles (*tattva*) (which manifest) in groups of five on the lower (Impure) Path. In this way the conscious nature (descends to) the level of the principle of individual consciousness (*puṃtattva*) through its own contracted power that assumes the state of Māyā when the plane of nothingness (*akiñcanya*) becomes manifest. The group of (five powers), for their part, become the obscuring factors (which envelope the individual soul, *kañcukībhūta*) so that (it) can experience the conditioned state of manifestation proper to that level. Subsequently, this (same energy), taking its support from the three energies (of will, knowledge and action) unfolds as the transformation of the qualities (*guṇa*) in order to generate the continuing succession of the lower network of principles. The subtle body (*puryaṣṭaka*) is produced by this (power) established on the level of the material nature (*prakṛti*) in which the (three qualities) are in a state of equilibrium. The basis of the principles of mind, intellect and ego are the three (powers) of will (knowledge and action). The (five) cognitive senses come into being when, in assocation with (all) five powers, the power of knowledge assumes a dominant role, while the organs of action arise due to the predominance of the power of action. This same process of generation takes place in a gross form externally also along with the objects (of the senses). All things are variously deployed in this way. Thus, the one reality which is the universal light (of consciousness) pervades these principles in such a way that it remains undivided in the midst of diversity and differs from it. Assuming the role of the subtle body (*puryaṣṭaka*), the conscious nature acts out the cosmic drama which is described as the radiant manifestation of (its) free and spontaneous play.

Exposition

The anonymous author of this note clearly interprets the coalescence of the 'group of eight' which corresponds to the 'bringing together of the universe' as the formation of the subtle body or 'City of Eight' (*puryaṣṭaka*). The process by which manifestation in space and time (Form and Action) takes place is here interpreted as the formation of the subtle body or, rather, as the assumption of this form of limitation on the part of consciousness and all the conditions which attend its occurrence. Torella, however, maintains that "Bhāskara's interpretation, which is complex and not entirely clear, revolves on the conception of the eight *mūrti*, according to which Śiva pervades the universe by differentiating Himself into eight forms (cf., e.g., *Liṅgapurāṇa* 2/13): the five gross elements (earth, water, fire, air, and ether), the Sun, Moon and the Self (*ātman*) frequently called the "Sacrificer" (*yajamāna*). The freedom of the yogi to act, which derives from his identification with consciousness, manifests as the possibility of effecting the universe by acting on these, its essential components. *Bhūtasaṃdhāna* is understood to be the 'union of the elements', that is, the construction of the various gross elements such as ether, etc., by putting together the various parts which constitute it represented by the various qualities (i.e., powers of the qualities) such as sound, etc., *Bhūtapṛthaktva* takes place when the elements are separated from one another and circumscribed in their own nature. The Sun and Moon are understood to be the powers of knowledge and action of the Sacrificer, that is, of the consciousness which experiences these elements.[115]

While Bhāskara understands this aphorism to refer to one of the processes through which Śiva's universal consciousness manifests in and as the phenomenal world of individual subjects and objects, Kṣemarāja sees it as refering to three yogic powers (*vibhūti*) the yogi acquires if he manages to unite his consciousness with the universal will. In this perspective the 'elements' are the constitutents of the psycho-physical organism, together with the vital breath and the general state (*bhāva*) of mind and body. The union of the elements is the power the yogi acquires to nourish and harmonise all the parts of his physical and mental constitution by permeating it with the health and vigour of his spiritual essence in the way described in verse 38 of the *Stanzas on Vibration.*

The yogi who has overcome the ignorance which cuts him off from the fullness of his nature by expanding his consciousness (*unmeṣa*) severs at the very root the cause of all disease and mental unrest as taught in verse 40 of the *Stanzas*. This is his second power, namely, 'the separation of the elements'.

The yogi's third power, through which he brings together the universe, is the all-embracing vision of the state of consciousness he attains by becoming master of the innate exertion (*udyoga*) of the power of his true nature (*svabala*). Penetrating into the furthest corners of space, discerning events far in the future and in the distant past, it unites all things together as elements of the yogi's universal experience as described in verses 36-37 of the *Stanzas.*

* * *

(The Lord) spoke (the following) aphorism the purport of which is that the (universal) cause of all things is the powers of the Self which (collectively constitute) its divine sovereign nature (*prabhutva*):

śuddhavidyodayāccakreśatvasiddhiḥ
(The yogi) attains mastery of the Wheel by the
arising of Pure Knowledge. 1/22 1.21

The unconditioned light (of consciousness) which illumines every manifestation (*ābhāsa*) is 'pure'. 'Knowledge' is the enlightened consciousness that 'I am all things'.[116] It is said to be the awareness (*vedanā*) of that (light) which, because it emits (all) the countless things (that exist), possesses the highest possible degree of freedom (*parasvātantrya*). The vision (*prathana*) of that (light) is the arising of (Pure Knowledge) through which (the yogi) attains the perfection (*siddhi*) which is the expanding development of the sovereign power (of consciousness) and the mastery of the Wheel of Energies.

* * *

The yogi achieves mastery over the circle of goddesses representing the eight yogic powers of atomicity (*aṇimā*) etc., by acquiring the power that comes from the expanding development of the highest degree of divine sovereignty (*paramamāheśvarya*) once he achieves both the supreme and lower levels of creative autonomy (*svātantrya*) by directly perceiving (*sakṣātkāra*) that his own nature is Paramaśiva Who is absolute, uninterrupted consciousness and the nature of all things.

(The yogi) can, by the power of atomicity (*aṇimā*), reduce the size of his limbs at will in an instant and thus, by making (his) body small, enter even (tiny) atoms. By (the yogic power) of lightness (*laghimā*), the gross body (can) move on the trail of breezes like the tip of a reed. By the (power) of greatness (*mahimā*) (the yogi can) make (his body) big (at will). By (the power of) attainment (*prāpti*) (he can) extend his limbs and so, by the length of the tips of his fingers, touch the moon even while he stands on earth. By the power of forbearance (*prākāmya*), the elements do not affect (the yogi's) basic state (*rūpa*) either when they emerge (and are present) or are submerged (and are absent) because they cannot obstruct his determined intentions, like water (that remains the same) even when on the ground. By the power of control (*vaśitā*) all beings follow (the yogi's) commands. By (the power of) lordship (*īśitā*) (the yogi can) bring groups of gross elements together or disperse them at will and freely change the nature of the elements as he pleases.[117]

Again, if by this Wheel (we mean) the Goddess of Consciousness Who is the Wheel of Brāhmī and the other energies, then by mastery (of this Wheel) the highest forms of knowledge arise well known in (Patañjali's) treatise on Yoga, namely, enlightened intuition (*pratibhā*) and the rest. The point being that this is the way in which the Lord of the Wheel Who is replete with the unconditioned power of sovereign freedom (*aiśvarya*) appears.

Exposition

Kṣemarāja basically understands this aphorism as Bhāskara does, however he approaches the practise that it teaches from a different point of view. According to Kṣemarāja, this aphorism describes what happens to the yogi who, at this level of consciousness, does not seek limited yogic powers but contemplates instead the power of the universal will inherent in his own consciousness in the first moment of perception which, still brilliant with the light of consciousness, is the pure awareness (*vedanā*) that marks the cognitive intent which precedes the formation of thought constructs as described in verse 43 of the *Stanzas*. Thus, solely intent on realising his universal nature (*vaiśvātmya*), the yogi achieves lordship over the Wheel of Energies and is liberated by the inward emergence of the Pure Knowledge that 'I am all things'. Kṣemarāja quotes the Svacchandatantra to explain what this knowledge is:

> As there is no other knowledge but this, it is supreme and it attains (for the yogi who aquires it) omniscience and (all) the highest attributes (of consciousness) here all at once. It is called "knowledge" because it is the awareness (*vedanā*) (of Siva's) beginningless nature and is consciousness of the Supreme Self in that it eliminates all that it is not. Established there, it manifests the Supreme Light (of consciousness) and the ultimate cause (of all things), and once the Supreme Light is made manifest (the yogi) established therein attains Śiva's nature.[118]

* * *

Well, if this is so (the question then is) how does the consciousness which is the vitality of Mantra (arise)? Thus, (in reply the Lord) spoke (the following aphorism which explains what the vitality of Mantra is:

mahāhradānusaṃdhānānmantravīryānubhavaḥ
(The yogi) experiences the vitality of Mantra by
contemplating the Great Lake. 1/23

The form of the conscious nature, supreme and pure, is that of the power of its possessor. It is emission (*sṛṣṭi*) and when phenomena emerge (from it), it is the supreme state of Being as the undivided flux (of universal consciousness) free of the diversification (*kalanā*) of time and space. (This reality) is called the "Great Lake" because it is like a vast lake (on the surface of which play the waves of cosmic manifestation). It is said to be the uncreated force (*bala*) present both there (in pure transcendental consciousness) and in the Self. (This) force is called the "state of empowerment" which consists of the expanding unfolding (of consciousness) (*vikasvaronmiṣattā*) through which (the awareness of the yogi) becomes firmly fixed in the Lunar aspect (of the flow of the vital breath which, coupled with the cognitive act, corresponds to *apāna* and the object of cognition). (This state) is marked by the innate aesthetic delight (of the Self, *svarasa*, experienced) in the centre between the essence (*sāra*) of the (two) dynamically interacting polarities (*araṇi* of consciousness), namely, cognition (*dṛk* which is equivalent to *prāṇa*). and bliss (*ānanda* also known as *āhlādaśakti* and equivalent to *apāna*). This entry into the Upward Moving Breath (*udāna* which rises as *Kuṇḍalinī*, the power of enlightened consciousness) is (true) contemplation. When by this (practise the yogi's awareness) abides there (without wavering), his fundamental state of being assimilates into itself the form of objectivity (he) desires and (thus full of its potency) swells (like a ripe seed), out of which emerges, like a sprout, an expanded state of consciousness (*pronmeṣa*) con-

sisting of the subtle (inner) speech (of enlightened insight full of) the phonemic (energy hidden) unmanifest (within it). (Thus), uniting with the (inner) activity of (*Kuṇḍalinī* technically called) the "Half of Ka," he experiences clearly and distinctly the Dawning of Mantra (*mantrodaya*). This is the experience of the vitality of Mantra which bestows perfection on the adept.

* * *

The union of (Śiva), the possessor of power, and (His) energy is figuratively called the "Great Lake" because it is the unfathomable ground of the emergent flow of the emission (*visarga* of consciousness). It is the abode of rest, (the ultimate) goal and the highest level of Speech (*parāvāc*) which has assimilated into itself all the infinite numbers of words and what they denote. It is the jewel of the Great Mantra which, independent and free of thought constructs, is the reflective awareness of the (universal) ego (*ahaṃparāmarśa*), perceivable only to itself, as well as the wealth of the inner essence (*sāra* of all things). Great yogis who possess that blissful experience (*upabhoga*) savour, through the contemplation explained previously, the unique vitality (of Mantra) which is the (universal) 'I' (consciousness) that sustains all things.

Exposition

The similarities and differences between Bhāskara's and Kṣemarāja's interpretation of this aphorism illustrates an important development in Spanda doctrine. Thus Bhāskara, like Kṣemarāja, understands the Great Lake to be pure consciousness and this is what it generally symbolizes in Kashmiri Śaiva works. Consciousness can indeed be fittingly compared to a vast lake that, full to overflowing, is fed by underground streams for in this way, explains Abhinava, consciousness unfolds spontaneously by the force of its outpouring[119] and, one could add, it flows down to fill and contain all three levels of existence, viz., Śiva (unity), Śakti (unity-in-difference) and the individual soul (diversity).

Bhāskara takes consciousness to be the power which he equates with the force (*bala*) of the power-holder's divine energy in the Self of every living being. Similarly, Kṣemarāja thinks of it as the supreme power of consciousness (*parāśakti*) which he understands to be the immanentalization of consciousness manifest as the entire universe through the emanation of its fifty aspects. These are symbolized by the letters of the Sanskrit alphabet constituting the Wheel of *Mātṛka*, while its movement towards transcendence, in the process of cosmic withdrawl, is symbolized by *Mālinī*.[120] Kṣemarāja equates this dynamic consciousness, understood as the collective whole of its energies, with the vitality that empowers Mantra. This vitality, which is the inner urge of consciousness to emanate all things (*visisṛkṣā*),[121] is the reflective awareness that constantly pours out of the Heart of consciousness and resounds within it as the highest form of speech (*parāvāc*) and all-embracing 'I' consciousness.[122] "I" consciousness (*ahaṃ*) is itself the Great Mantra manifest as the wonder inspired by the light of consciousness.[123] From it are created all Mantras and to it they return.[124] Thus Mantric energy gives life to all living beings, indeed it is the very essence of all consciousness which is increasingly, manifestly apparent to the degree in which it perceives itself in the pure awareness of "I am." Kṣemarāja explains this aphorism accordingly:

> The supreme mistress of consciousness (*parā bhaṭṭārikā saṃvit*) emits the entire universe (out of Herself) beginning with the power of the will right up to the gross object of perception. (She is) the Great Lake because She is endowed with (countless divine) attributes, thus She stimulates the activity of the Wheels of *Khecarī* and all the other currents (of energy) and is pure, unobscured and deep. (The yogi) experiences the vitality of Mantra which is the reflective awareness of supreme I-ness (*parāhantāvimarśa*) consisting, as will be explained latter, (of Śiva as) the Mass of Sounds (*śabdarāśi*) , by contemplating (the Great Lake), that is, by constant introspection through which he reflects upon (his) identity with it and it manifests as his own nature.

Thus, Kṣemarāja identifies Spanda, the pulse of consciousness, which in the *Stanzas* is portrayed as the strength inherent in one's own nature (*svabala*) that empowers the senses and Mantras, with 'I' consciousness. That this is his intention is evident insofar as he quotes verse 26 of the *Stanzas* which declares that the source of the power of Mantras is this inner strength and says that this is how the Spanda teachings explain it. Again, he sees the practise as consisting of the direct experience of this energy attained by identifying one's own true nature as the universal ego. Bhāskara, however, following more closely the original Spanda teachings, does not admit the existence of this noumenous egoity but thinks of the experience of Mantric energy as one the yogi achieves through the rise of *Kuṇḍalinī* which is stimulated by the power (*bala*) inherent in consciousness.

The practise Bhāskara teaches here can be summerized as follows. The yogi must first repeat his Mantra mentally in conjunction which the breath, for unless it is in harmony with the breathing movement it can bear no fruit. He must then seek to fix his attention on the centre between the two breaths where they, along with the Mantra, arise and fall away. In this way the two breaths work against each other like two firesticks made of consciousness and bliss, to generate the fire of consciousness which rises as the ascending breath (*udānaprāṇa*) in the central psychic channel (*suṣumnā*) that leads upwards to the supramental plane (*unmanā*) of the universal vibration (*sāmānyaspanda*) of consciousness. The lunar current of the descending breath, corresponding to object-centred awareness (*prameyabhāva*), is fixed in one place by uniting it with the ascending solar breath, representing awareness centred on the means of knowledge (*pramāṇabhāva*), and this in its turn is made one with subjective consciousness as the Upward Moving Breath (*udānaprāṇa*) rises. The ascent of this breath is in harmony with the unfolding of the centre (*madhyavikāsa*) at the individualized (*āṇava*) level of consciousness and takes place by virtue of the strength (*bala*) or power of the Self (*ātmaśakti*). The vibration of its movement is the true arising of Mantra (*mantrodaya*) technically called *uccāra*.[125] It is the spontaneous recitation of Mantra which occurs in contemplation (*samādhi*) through the union of the Upward Moving Breath and the resonance or silent sound (*nāda*) of consciousness that marks the merger of the vital breath with the mind (*prāṇacittātman*). As 'mind' (*citta*) is the union of consciousness and awareness (which is the supreme level of speech), *uccāra* unites the three aspects of Mantra, namely, consciousness, speech and breath. Bhagavadutpala quotes the *Haṃsaparameśvara* as saying:

> Mantras (recited) in a fettered state (of consciousness *paśubhāva*) are nothing more than mere articulated sounds, but those recited in the Central path (*suṣumnā*) become all-powerful (*patitva*).[126]

This Mantra cannot be uttered in the normal way and hence is called *Anacka* (a pure consonant without any vowel sound and hence unutterable) or *Kakārārdha* (lit. "half of Ka," i.e., the pure consonant 'K') as it is the pure energy (*śakti*) symbolized by the consonant series.[127] Bhāskara explains that it is a subtle form of inner speech (*sukṣmavāgrūpa*) the phonemes of which are unmanifest, representing the first sprout of pure consciousness which arises from the state of the perfected potency of awareness (*samyagucchūnatā*). When the energy of *Anacka* is conjoined with the expansion (*pronmeṣa*) of consciousness in the Centre the yogi experiences the vitality of Mantra which is Śivahood endowed with all knowledge and action and thus achieves perfection (*siddhi*).

* * *

Thus ends this, the first section of the *Aphorisms of Śiva* which expounds the one unique nature of the light of universal consciousness.

In the next section (Śiva) will describe the highest nature of Mantra and the arising of knowledge.

Thus ends the first chapter of the *Śivasūtravārtika*, written by the venerable Ācārya Bhaṭṭabhāskara, the son of the venerable Bhaṭṭadivākara, called the "Description of the Light of Universal Consciousness."

Now Begins the Second Light Called

THE ARISING OF INNATE KNOWLEDGE

Now that the Blessed One has established in the stated manner that the omniscient Self that does all things is Śiva and what the vitality of Mantra that (resides) there is, the Unborn One then went on to explain what needs to be explained, as He did the innate nature of Mantra, namely, what the Mantra is to which this vitality belongs:

cittaṃ mantraḥ
The mind is Mantra. 2/1

Know that the mind itself is Śiva, the unconditioned subject who, free of the diversifications (*kalanā*) of time and space, is endowed with omniscience and (every) other divine attribute. It naturally experiences itself directly and so is said to be Mantra.

* * *

The means taught (in the previous section) can be easily grasped by those who have been (blessed) with the most intense degree of grace (*śaktipāta*). But those who have received only a weak degree of it must resort to a different means to acquire the vitality of Mantra. (This means basically involves) attentive concentration (*nibhālana)* on a number of things, including Mantra. This is done by purifying thought by, for example, repeatedly hearing and recalling to mind (the teachings) (so that insight into the truth) may develop progressively (from the initial stages), in which it is only dimly apparent, to that in which it becomes more so, until it is finally attained. In this way, when the notion of duality ceases by means of the direct intuitive awareness (*saṃvedana*) of the supreme radiance (of consciousness), the knowledge innate (in one's own nature) emerges. (This section deals with this other means so that those less graced) may attain the goal.

The mind (*citta*) is consciousness (*cit*) that, desiring to play the game of cosmic (manifestation), initially descends from its own eternal conscious nature to the lower level and becomes intent on perceiving the finite object of thought (*cetya*) that emerges (out of consciousness) when it assumes a limited, conditioned state of being. When (the mind) seeks to rise (again) to its original state (*svapada*), it ascends successively step by step, as one does along a ladder, (progressively) abandoning its limited condition, (and ultimately) attains Śiva's (universal) nature (*śivatā*) which is the free (*īśānaśīla*) and uninterrupted light of consciousness. Thus that mind (*manas*) can reflect on its own glorious energy (*mahat*) because once it has withdrawn the object of awareness (into itself), it becomes introverted and so is free (to do so). Thus mind and Mantra are figuratively said to be one because they inherently possess that (same) awareness.

Exposition

From the Kashmiri Śaiva point of view, the mind is not a misconceived abstraction made by working back from thought to a mind which presumably thinks it. Although there is no mind apart from thought, even so, the reverse also holds good, namely that, without mind, there can be no thinking. The mind is at once a screen of awareness onto which thoughts are projected and held together, a vessel in which latent traces of past sensation and thoughts are stored and the active principle which generates them. It is in fact consciousness itself which initially contracts itself down to the level of an object of thought (*cetya*) to then assume the form of the mind (*citta*) when intent on reflecting on its own objectively perceived nature through the medium of thought.[1] As pure consciousness manifests as the thinking subject (*cetayitṛ*), the mind, free of all limiting conditions both spatial and temporal, is endowed with all its attributes. To state the matter another way, one of the many ways in which we can understand the nature of consciousness is as a single universal mind which generates the world of thought constructs that rise and fall from it like waves in the sea. Each wave (*ūrmi*) or vibration (*spanda*) on the surface of consciousness as it rises reaches its peak and falls away,traces the history of a single chain of thought which threads through and constructs the events of a lifetime.

This happens when the mind is intent on the objective world which includes not only the domain of physical objects perceived by the outer senses but also the subtler sphere of abstract notions and feelings, in short, all that is in any way conceivable (*caitya*). However, when it turns in on itself to examine its true nature as consciousness, it resumes its basic, higher state in which it reflects not on the profane world but on the supreme reality of deity and so shares in the nature of the Mantra that evokes it. As Kṣemarāja says, referring to verse 27 of the *Stanzas:*

> Mantra is that which (the adept) reflects upon inwardly in secret as one with the Supreme Lord.... The mind of the adept intent on reflecting on the deity of the Mantra, becoming thus one with it, is Mantra. (Mantra) is not just a mere aggregate of various letters.[2]

* * *

But how can yogis achieve this? The Supreme Lord explained that:

prayatnaḥ sādhakaḥ
Effort is that which attains the goal. 2/2

Excellent is said to be the effort (exerted) to penetrate the nature of the mind. It is the function (*vṛtti*) of the vitality we have spoken of before and is (generated) by repeated meditation (*nibhālana*). This is said to be the most excellent means, which attains the goal. (Through this effort, exerted)

in the way we are about to explain, (the yogi) realises the conscious reality (*cittattva*) of the Self. Śiva Himself described it in the Essence of Trika (*Trikasāra*) of six thousand verses (where He says):

> **Mantra is said to be the inherent nature (*svasvabhāva*) of the power of consciousness, for by concentrating (*manana*) on it constantly the yogi abides well established on Śiva's plane of being. It is by virtue of this that those yogis who apply their minds to Yoga know (the true nature) of ultimate reality (*paramārtha*).**

* * *

The point here is that this (effort) is the greatest possible aid to attain the goal. Heralded by the cessation of the diversified awareness that subject (object and means of knowledge are distinct), (attained) by withdrawing (the mind) repeatedly from its extroverted activity, (this effort) is the flow of one-pointed concentration (*pratyayaikatānatā*) centred on the identity (*tādātmya*) between the Self in the form of the object of meditation and the essential nature of Mantra as described above.

Exposition

Kṣemarāja explains that effort, in this context, means the spontaneous force of awareness the yogi applies to catch hold of the initial moment in which he is intent on contemplating Mantra. The initial unfolding of his thought, charged with the power of Mantra, is the point where he can achieve oneness with the deity it symbolizes as verse 31 of the *Stanzas* teaches. To do this he must attempt to catch this fleeting moment in a single, swift movement of awareness. To illustrate this point, Kṣemarāja quotes the *Essence of the Tantras* (*Śrītantrasadbhāva*):

> O dear one, just as a bird of prey, glimpsing in the sky a piece of meat (flung to it), quickly catches it with the speed

natural to it, so should the best of yogis catch hold of the light of consciousness (*mano bindu*).[3] Just as an arrow fixed to a bow and drawn with great force flies forth, so, beloved does *Bindu* fly forward by the force of awareness (*uccāreṇa*).

* * *

Now the Blessed one has explained in this way what the nature of Mantra (*vācaka*) is, the next aphorism He utters sheds light on the question as to whether or not Mantra (*vācaka*) and what it denotes are one:

vidyāśarīrasattā mantrarahasyam
The secret of Mantra is the Being of the Body of Knowledge. 2/3

By *knowledge* we mean the unfolding of one's own inherent light; it is the sudden expansion (*unmeṣa*) of the thrill of energy (*sāhasa*) that takes place within the Pure Principle by penetrating (*āveśa*) (and becoming one with) pure consciousness (*cinmātratā*). This is the Being (*sattā*) of the body of the one who recites Mantra and the supreme secret.

* * *

Mantra denotes (*vācaka*, essential metaphysical principles). It manifests initially as diverse (and cut off from the adept's consciousness but) once it has performed its function and the adept seeks to discern its inner vitality (*vīrya*), it becomes one with its denoted object, namely, the pulsing radiance (*sphuraṇa*) of the essence of the reflective awareness of perfect 'I' consciousness (*pūrṇāham*) which is the oneness of the entire universe. Essentially what this means is that the cycle (through which a) Mantra passes (as it emerges from consciousness and returns to it) is one with the supreme reality which it denotes. For if it were not so it would be impossible to account for its manifest existence (*prakāśamānatā*) insofar as each stage of its development (out of consciousness) proceeds from the previous stage. (This happens as follows):

First, *Bindu,* that is, the energy of Supreme Speech (*parāvāc*), unfolds as the Voice of Intuition (*paśyantī*) which is still free of the sequence (and distinction) that obtains between words and their denoted meaning. This happens when the light of consciousness, replete with the supreme resonance (*paranāda,* of reflective awareness), comes to prominence after (the energy of *Bindu*), that is, the resonance (*nāda,* of awareness) in the form of the unfolding power of action penetrates (and assumes the nature) of the subtle (inner) being of the vital breath according to the manner described in the saying: "the vital breath is the first transformation of consciousness."

After this comes the Middle Voice (*madhyamā*) (the inner speech of thought), the basis of which is the intellect and the other (faculties of the mind). (It is so called) because (at this level) the succession (of words and meanings) is indistinct (insofar as it is not yet articulate speech) and yet clearly apparent (as thought constructs).

The Corporeal Voice (*vaikharī*) develops after this. The organ (of speech) is its basis and (it consists of words articulated) in a clearly apparent sequence.

Exposition

According to Kṣemarāja, the knowledge referred to here is supreme non-dual awareness (*parādvayaprathā*). Śiva, as the essence of all possible words and meaning (*śabdarāśi*) contained in a potential form in the fifty lettters of the alphabet, possesses this 'Body of Knowledge' the essence of which, as the secret power of Mantra, is the pulsing radiance (*sphurattā*) of the light of consciousness identified with the reflective awareness of perfect 'I' consciousness (*pūrṇāhaṃvimarśa*) that consists of the oneness of the entire universe.[4]

Kṣemarāja, like the anonymous commentator on Bhāskara's commentary, explains how the formation of this body takes place by describing the progressive development of speech from its highest level down to that of articulate sound. It is through this process that all speech and thought are vitally linked with absolute consciousness and so is Mantra of which it is, therefore, the 'secret'. More specifically, Kṣemarāja sees this process as the development of *Mātṛkā*, the goddess who contains the fifty energies symbolized by the letters of the Sanskrit alphabet that, by their development, generate the universe of words and that which they denote.

This development finds a parallel in the progressive rise of *Kuṇḍalinī*, the spiritual power that lies latent in the restricted consciousness of the fettered soul. From this point of view, the 'secret power of Mantra' is *Kuṇḍalinī* in its supreme form (as *Parā Kuṇḍalinī*). This energy is one with Śiva as His innate bliss (*ānanda-śakti*). It is the heart of consciousness that contains the entire universe within itself[5] as the pure awareness (*pramitibhāva*) which encompasses and transcends subject, object and means of knowledge. It is the bliss of cosmic consciousness (*jagadānanda*) the yogi experiences when he attains liberation. As such, it is the universal vibration (*sāmānyaspanda*) of the union of Śiva and Śakti (*rudrayāmala*) through which the universe is created and destroyed. In its creative aspect, Śiva veils His own nature and manifests as the absolute (*anuttara*). In its destructive aspect, Śiva reveals His divine nature as the Highest Lord. The destructive power of *Parā Kuṇḍalinī* withdraws diversity into the unity of consciousness and thereby creates a universe at one with consciousness. This function is carried out by *Parā Kuṇḍalinī* in Her aspect as *Mālinī*,[6] the highest state of which is the experience of the undivided light of consciousness present in all the letters and phases of the cosmic process they represent. The creative form of *Parā Kuṇḍalini* is *Mātṛkā* which, as the *Essence of the Tantras* (*Śrītantrasadbhāva*) explains, is full of the supreme effulgence of consciousness that, established in the absolute (*avarṇa*), pervades the entire universe of letters.[7] As *Kaulikīśakti*, She is the supreme emissive power (*visarga-śakti*). of consciousness which arouses Śiva from the rest He enjoys in His own nature and unites with Him to give rise to the body of letters.[8]

In this form *Kuṇḍalinī* is described as the supreme resonance (*paranāda*) of reflective awareness eternally manifest as the single phonemic power (*varṇa*) which is the undivided essence of the energies of all the letters.[9] This is the unstruck sound of *Anacka*,[10] the supreme form of *Haṃsa*,[11] said to be the essence, source and resting place of the life of every living being as *Varṇakuṇḍalikā*, the

Kuṇḍalinī of letters.[12] It is in this form, otherwise known as *Śakti Kuṇḍalinī*, that *Parā Kuṇḍalinī* rests in a potential state in the body. She sleeps in *Mulādhāra*, the 'Root Support', which is situated at the base of the genital organs, coiled like a snake around Śiva's seed (*śivabindu*) and awakens due to it. This is the form in which cosmic energy resides in the body. When *Kuṇḍalinī* awakes, individual consciousness unites with universal consciousness and man discovers his cosmic nature. The world of diversity is withdrawn and a new world of unlimited blissful experience is emitted. *Kuṇḍalinī* is thus the vital link that unites the microcosm with the macrocosm. Permeating both levels of being, the power of consciousness makes the transition from individual to universal consciousness possible and, conversely, the creation of the finite from the infinite. The awakening of the letters makes speech possible in man and also brings the universe into being. Thus the *Svacchandatantra* explains how *Kuṇḍalinī* creates all the gods, worlds, Mantras and categories of existence and concludes by saying that it is found in the *Mulādhāra* within man.

The rise of *Kuṇḍalinī* from *Mulādhāra* where it rests as the supreme form of speech (*parāvāc*) is the movement from the supramental (*unmanā*) level of pure consciousness to that of articulate speech (*vaikharī*). Although this is a process that is constantly repeated whenever we speak, only the yogi is consciously aware of it. Moreover, this movement in all its phases is, for the average man, the spontaneous and universal deployment of emanation while for the yogi it occurs through the agency of his will. The unconscious rise of *Kuṇḍalinī* marks the emanation of the energy of the letters as the forces which bind individual consciousness. The conscious rise of *Kuṇḍalinī*, on the contrary, marks the dissolving away of these binding forces and the creation, through the realisation of their true nature, of these same energies as aspects of the freedom (*svātantrya*) of the reflective awareness of pure consciousness. Thus the passage below, quoted by Kṣemarāja from the *Essence of the Tantras* (*Śrītantrasadbhāva*), is at once an account of the creation of the body of letters which mark the phases of the development of *Mātṛkā* that, as the manifestation of the supreme form of speech, is Bhairava's divine power (*śakti*) identified by Kṣemarāja as the "Being of the Body of Knowledge," as well as the phases of the awakening and rise of the *Kuṇḍalinī:*

O Goddess, that Divine Mother (*Mātṛkā*) Who is filled with the supreme effulgence (of consciousness) pervades this entire universe from the highest form (*Brahmā*) to earth. O beloved Goddess worshipped by all the gods, just as the all-pervading phonemic energy (*varṇa*) (of the letters) is present in the letter 'A'[13] so is that which is pervaded (by *Mātṛkā*) ever established there (in that power). So I will clearly explain to you the sense of the final conclusion (the scriptures have reached concerning Her nature). That subtle and supreme power is said to be beyond the bounds of scriptural injunction (*nirācāra*).[14] O well-formed Umā, wrapping itself inwardly around the *Bindu* of the Heart,[15] it slumbers there in the form of a sleeping serpent and is aware of nothing at all. That goddess, placing in her belly the Moon, Fire, Sun, stars and fourteen worlds, (sleeps) like one affected by poison.[16] O beloved, She is awakened by the resonance of supreme awareness and churned by the spontaneous rolling (*bhramavega*) of Śiva's seed (*bindu*) within Her.[17] Pierced (in this way), that subtle power of *Kuṇḍalinī* is aroused, accompanied initially by brilliant sparks of light. O beloved, the all-powerful divine (*prabhu*) four-fold seed[18] in the womb of (that) power straightens by the union of the churner and the churned. (*Kuṇḍalinī*) is then called the power *Jyeṣṭhā* manifest between the two points (*bindu*, of objectivity and subjectivity). The immortal *Kuṇḍalinī* (now) straightened (and further) agitated by (Śiva's) seed is called *Rekhinī* Who absorbs both points (*bindu*, of subjectivity and objectivity and reconverts them into their true nature as Śiva and Śakti). (In the next phase, *Kuṇḍalinī*) is said to flow in three channels and is called *Raudrī* or *Rodhinī* because She blocks the path to liberation.[19] (To overcome this obstruction, *Kuṇḍalinī* assumes) the form of a crescent moon as *Ambikā* (otherwise known) as the "Half-moon."[20] In this way that one supreme power assumes three forms.[21] By the union and separation of these (powers) the nine classes of letters are born and (*Kuṇḍalinī*) is then said to be nine-fold as the nine classes. O Goddess, she then assumes the form of the five Mantras beginning with (*Sadyojata*) the first,[22] in due order. One should know, O mistress of the gods, that She is then said to be five-fold. O goddess, when She is manifest as the twelve vowels, She is said to be twelve-fold and divided fifty-fold when manifest as the letters from 'A' to 'KṢ'. In the heart She is said to have one point; in the throat, two; and She should be known to have three points at the root of the tongue. Articulate words are formed on the tip of the tongue, there can be no doubt that this is the way speech is formed and that the moving and unmoving world is pervaded by speech.

* * *

Now if this is the secret reality (*artha*) of Mantra, how can embodied beings bring about the desired Arising of Mantra (*mantrodaya*) which is the Supreme Emergence (*paramodaya*, of ultimate reality). In reply to this question, the ubiquitous Lord uttered the following aphorism:

garbhe cittavikāso viśiṣṭo'vidyā svapnaḥ
The expansion of the mind in the womb (of consciousness) is the slumber of (all) particular forms of ignorance. 2/4

By the force of withdrawal from the objects of sense into the essence of consciousness and bliss, the mind, intensely content, abides as pure consciousness. This is the supreme (state of consciousness). (This is) the cosmic nature inspired with bliss by the flood of the nectar of divine power which, flowing (from the moon of consciousness), fills it to the full. Through this (expanson of consciousness), the slumber of ignorance which extends itself in the form of the network of principles starting from Earth onwards is, by being assimilated into consciousness, brought to an end. When this takes place, (the yogi) grasps knowledge (*vidyā*) itself as it truly is (in its most essential being). This (knowledge), therefore is the means to realisation and the essential nature of every Mantra and *Mudrā*.

* * *

The means to realisation (*upāya*) (described here essentially involves) an extremely elevated ascent (of consciousness to the level at which it can) penetrate (*āveśa*) into the supreme plane (of existence). This takes place when (the true nature of) Mantra dawns (within the pervasive awareness of expanded consciousness) by destroying the the mind's material nature (*prākṛta*) by bringing the three states (of happiness, sadness and delusion) engendered by the *guṇas* to an end. When (the yogi) has acquired the vitality (of one Mantra) in this way (he can) use it to empower other Mantras, (all of which) derive their vitality (from that same energy), and so heighten their efficacy. (Mantras find their proper application through this power of awareness) because if they are applied (when the yogi has already attained) Śiva at the higher level, they would serve no purpose, while at the lower level of individualized consciousness, they are (merely) lifeless (sounds) and so in either case would be useless.

Exposition

The previous aphorism explained, according to Bhāskara's interpretation of it, how the yogi engaged in the practise of reciting his Mantra penetrates and becomes one with the universal cosciousness which is the source of all Mantras and the entire order of manifestation they mystically represent and denote. This takes place, as Bhāskara says, when the divine light of the yogi's true and universal nature suddenly expands, extending its brilliance throughout the infinite expanse of the pure conscious nature which the yogi now realises is the marvellous extent of his infinite Being and his true body, one with the deity, his Mantra thus evokes. Now, as Bhāskara sees it, this aphorism goes on to elaborate what happens when the yogi experiences this expansion of consciousness and how this wakes him up from the sleep of ignorance to realise the true, absolute nature of consciousness and hence that of all Mantras and *Mudrās*.

Kṣemarāja reads this aphorism quite differently. According to him it means: *The expansion of the mind in the womb (of illusion) is the knowledge common (to all men)—(a mere) dream.* According to Kṣemarāja this aphorism serves to warn the yogi that he should not make use of the power of Mantra to develop any petty yogic powers he may obtain through it. Nor should he be attached to the visions or other experiences that may come to him but should seek instead to merge with the universal will of Śiva, the Supreme Lord of consciousness. Thus he writes:

> The womb is *Mahāmāya,* which is ignorance. The expansion of the mind that takes place within it is the (foolish) satisfaction (the ignorant yogi) feels with the limited yogic powers Mantra gives rise to. This impure, limited knowledge is common to all men and is (a mere) dream, that is, the confusion of diverse thought constructs grounded in relative distinctions.[23]

Kṣemarāja accordingly refers to verse 47 of the *Stanzas* which makes much the same point.

* * *

When Lord Śaṅkara had explained the nature of Mantra's vitality, the awareness (*vimarśa,* the Yogi has of it) and (the manner of) its arising, he went on to say the following in order to explain the nature of the vitality of *Mudrā:*

vidyāsamutthāne svābhāvike khecarī śivāvasthā
When the knowledge innately inherent in one's own nature arises, (that is) Śiva's state—(the gesture of) the one who wanders in the Sky of Consciousness. 2/5.

Pure Knowledge is said to be the light of one's own nature (*svāloka*) which dawns when (the yogi) emerges from the higher stages of contemplation (*samutthāna*). (At the same time) It is the uncreated and innate (*sahaja*) power (*bala*), rightly described before, inherent in one's own nature. As it is such, the vitality of *Mudrā* expands within it. It is Śiva's state, called (the gesture of) "the one who wanders in the Sky of Consciousness" because it is risen

(*udita*) in the sky of Śiva and because (it is the power of awareness) which moves (*caraṇa*) in the expanse (*ābhoga*) of the firmament of one's own consciousness. It is the dawn of realisation (in which the yogi perceives) his identity with (Śiva), the object of (his) meditation. And so, (this gesture) that possesses the contemplative absorption (*āveśa*) which penetrates into one's own nature, is Śiva's state.

* * *

The gesture of the one who wanders in the Sky of Consciousness (*khecarīmudrā*) is Śiva's state itself, directly apparent (*sakṣāt*). (By making this gesture) the yogi moves (*carati*) through the Sky of Supreme Consciousness. The state of the vital essence of Mantra and *Mudrā* (which develops) by quelling all the agitation engendered by Māyā is the same (for both), namely, the emergence of one's own nature which is consciousness. We think them to be different only because, in terms of (our) perception of outer reality, their products (*kārya*) are distinct.

Exposition

In a non-technical sense, the word *mudrā* in Sanskrit means a number of things, of which three are relevant here. First, a *mudrā* is any instrument used for sealing or stamping as well as the stamp or impression made by the seal. Second, *mudrā* is the gesturing of the hands and posturing of the body in dance which is assigned a meaning and forms a part of the mime enacted in the dance. Third, *mudrā* is a ritual gesture usually made with the hands in the course of worship (espescially Tantric), conveying a symbolic meaning and thought to be charged with spiritual energy. Corresponding to these three common meanings of the word we can distinguish at least three distinct levels of meaning accorded to this term by Kashmiri Śaivites. Firstly, *Mudrā* is both the seal of pure consciousness which stamps its cosmic form on the background of its own nature and the image or reflection of consciousness thus created. The original form (*bimba*) and its reflection (*pratibimba*), the seal and its impression, pure consciousness and cosmic consciousness, both are *Mudrā*.[24] The first meaning leads naturally to the second. As an attitude or posturing of awareness, *Mudrā* is the state of awareness which makes its impression on all the contents of consciousness. *Mudrā*, in other words, is the stance the subject assumes in relation to himself and the world which he thus experiences accordingly. Our experience is a reflection of our inner attitude. This third use of the term indicates that *Mudrā* is not only the way we see or know things but the actions we make in accord with our understanding. *Mudrā* is not only the world of our making, it is also the means through which it arises. *Mudrā* is action. Thus, although the power of *Mudrā* and Mantra are at root identical, *Mudrā* is fuller of the power of action (*kriyāśakti*) than Mantra, which is primarily a channel for the power of knowledge (*jñānaśakti*). The outer movement of the hands and body, the inner movement of the vitality of *Kuṇḍalinī*, speech and mind are the basic forms of *Mudrā*, ranging from gross to subtle.[25] Through *Mudrā*, microcosm and macrocosm are united in the harmony of a single universal act. Abhinava explains:

> The word *Mudrā*, as its etymology indicates, means that which bestows (*ra*) bliss (*mud*), that is, the realisation of one's own nature and, through the body, that of the (universal) Self.[26]

The bliss of *Mudrā* is the act of self-awareness (*parāmarśakriyā*), the aesthetic rapture of resting in one's own nature. According to another popular etymology, *Mudrā* means that which bestows bliss and dissolves away (*drāvayati*) bondage[27] by fusing together (*dravaṇa*) all the categories of existence to form a single compact mass of consciousness.[28] The vitality of Mantra is the emergence (*sṛṣṭi*) of this universal consciousness,while the vitality of *Mudrā* is the power which seals it with the stamp of the Fourth State and maintains the yogi in it. Hence, it corresponds to the persistence (*sthiti*) of this consciousness. Thus, he in whom both have arisen achieves the peaceful state (*ātiśāntapada*) of liberation and no longer falls from it.[29]

Khecarīmudrā is Śiva's true state in which the power (*bala*) of His awareness arises and wanders (*carati*) in the Sky (*kha*) of His consciousness as the effulgence or flow of His innate bliss (*svānand-*

occhalattā).[30] To course in the Sky of Consciousness is to follow the Path of Totality (*kulamārga*), it is the liberating experience that any one thing contains within itself all things and that all things are contained in one reality. *Khecarīmudrā* is thus the highest level of awareness (*parasaṃvittirūpā*)[31] and hence the essence of the power which unifies all other *Mudrās*.[32] Whatever movement of the body or gesure of the hand one who is established in the wholeness (*kula*) of this attitude makes is *Mudrā*.[33]

> For the yogi (established) in *Kula*, vibrant (*ghūrṇita*) with the supremely (intoxicating) juice of Bhairava which abounding (pervades him), every position of his body is *Mudrā*.[34]

The yogi in *Khecarīmudrā* is intent on devouring time (*kālagrāsa*). To do this he first withdraws all the energies of his senses and mind, establishes them firmly in his own nature and frees himself of all sense of past and future. Plunging through the centre between these two times, seeking to grasp the fleeting instant (*tuṭimātra*) of the present, he is eventually freed of the present as well, in the timeless fullness of the incessant expansion and contraction of his own consciousness, at one with which he instantly and spontaneously becomes a 'wanderer in the Sky of Consciousness' (*khecara*) and is liberated.[35]

* * *

Thus the vital essence of *Mudrā* and Mantra are essentially the same. They differ from the point of view of outer reality because their functions are different. Therefore, in order to explain how (the yogi can realise) the (true) all-pervasive (nature of) Mantra and *Mudrā* (the Lord) said:

gururupāyaḥ
The Master is the means. 2/6

Here the Master is the power (of consciousness) said to be the supreme means to realisation because Śiva's power (*śāmbhavīśakti*) is always graceous. Protected by its arising,

it frees man from his longing for the world of fettered existence (*bhāva*). It leads the man whose corporeal nature (*deha*) it sustains to a true Master who, taking his support from the plane of being (the disciple) seeks to realise (*upeyapada*), speaks of matters concerning ultimate reality and so directs (him) on the path which leads to repose in the abode beyond the mind.

* * *

The Master is here the power of grace, the Supreme Goddess Who leads (the yogi) to the plane (of Being) he seeks to realise once he has attained the power of Mantra, etc. Through Her, devout souls enjoy rest in the absolute, the plane beyond mind (we) call Paramaśiva.

Exposition

Popular etymology derives the word *guru* from two words, namely, *gu* which means "darkness" and *ru* which means "remover." The Master (*guru*) is therefore he who removes the darkness of his disciples ignorance.[36] In other words, as Kṣemarāja explains, he teaches him the true nature of reality and reveals to him the pervasive oneness of consciousness (*vyāpti*).[37] It is he who reveals to the disciple the true nature of Mantric power.[38] The disciple, however, must take care to select the right Master, for only he is able to lead others to higher levels of consciousness who has himself realised them.[39] Although not all Masters have attained the highest level of consciousness, and the seeker may not be fortunate enough to have found one who has reached perfection in all respects, he should test his teacher and be sure that he has indeed achieved a higher level than himself, for a bad teacher is not only unable to grace others but will obscure and cloud their consciousness with doubts even further.[40] In the quest for self-realisation we may be led from one teacher to the next. If we profit by each encounter and grasp each Master's instructions, there is nothing wrong in this. Indeed this is what Kallaṭa and Abhinava himself did. For as the Tantras declare:

> Just as a bee, desirous of nectar, goes from flower to flower, so a disciple, desirous of knowledge, goes from teacher to teacher. If he has a Master devoid of power how can he ever attain knowledge and liberation? O Goddess, how can a tree without roots bear flowers or fruit?[41]

The true Master (*sadguru*) can only be one who has attained perfect freedom and this through identification with Śiva.[42] Such a man is Śiva Himself in human form,[43] so it is in him that the disciple sees the goal of his endeavour.[44] His sandals (*pāduka*) are said to be the light of consciousness and awareness.[45] The master of the five cosmic functions,[46] his feet are said to move everywhere (symbolizing the cosmic creative activity of consciousness) and absorb everything into his nature, (representing the Master's knowledge which annuls multiplicity by merging it into the unity of consciousness).[47] Two verses from the *Haṃsabhedatantra* describe the true Master:

> Many are those Masters who are honoured and served, resplendent with consciousness and discrimination. But, O Goddess, it is hard to find that Master who (himself free of ego) can destroy the egos of others. It is through him that revelation is communicated, through him that all things are accomplished, through him that, freed of ego one recognises oneself in one's essential purity (*kevala*).[48]

The essence of the Master's nature is grace. As the Master, Śiva graces mankind with the power that flows through him and leads his devotees to find rest in the supramental abode of the absolute. It was the Master's grace, as *Śāmbhavīśakti*,[49] which led the disciple to him in the first place and then frees him of craving for the world of transmigration.

In the end, the disciple discovers that the Master is none other than himself and that he, as the disciple, is the reflective awareness of the enquiring consciousness (*prāṭṣṛ saṃvit*) of the Light which constantly responds with ever-deepening revelations of its own nature. Abhinava explains:

> One's own nature is of the nature of all things and knows itself. It is one's own nature itself at one with itself that,

> through question and answer, is contemplated as 'Iness' which gives rise to a sense of wonder by (assuming the) form of the questioner and replier.[50]

The one Lord assumes the form of both Master and disciple.[51] The dialogue between them is always held within consciousness. It is the inner dialogue the Self has with its own nature, enlightening itself through itself:[52]

> The undivided freedom of consciousness shines on the plane of distinctions. It emanates the state of teacher and taught. It is one's own nature alone that is the Lord and teacher and (yet) one thinks that he is other (than oneself). One thinks that the words one's Self utters are those of another. That which is to be understood as well as that by which it is understood, all is of the nature of Self, (although) one believes them to be different.[53]

At the highest level of practise the Master infuses this awareness into the disciple directly and he rises in an instant to the recognition that he and the Master are one.[54] At the lower levels of practise, on the other hand, the sense of difference is almost total. Thus the Master and disciple, cut off from each other by the objective constituents of their being, their relationship assumes the form of that between an enlightened sage (*ṛṣi*) and another human being.

* * *

Then He explained what happens when the Master is pleased:

mātṛkācakrasaṃbodhaḥ
The awakening of the Wheel of Mātṛkā. 2/7

One should know *Mātṛkā* to be the light of one's own nature (*svābhāsa*) and the Lord's supreme power of action. Her Wheel, it is said, is the aggregate of Her powers and the complete and correct knowledge (of its true nature) is its

awakening. When this happens the diverse (world of) apparent change consisting of words and the objects they denote is, by virtue of this (awakening), always (one and) undivided (*abhinna*) because the power of action has emerged (out of consciousness and operates).

(This transformation takes place in stages) the first of which is the body of the light (of consciousness) that is ever manifest and never sets. (Then), by being intent on (its inherent) vitality, the power of the Lord's will (*icchāśakti*) emerges, followed by a pure awareness (*saṃvedana* free of thought constructs which heralds manifestation) and a subtle tactile sensation (*sparśa*, which corresponds to the direct vision of supreme consciousness). Then comes the universal manifestation of all things (*sarvārthapratibhāsa*) followed by the unstruck resonance (*anāhatadhvani*, of awareness). After this comes the activity of the vital breath which contains within itself the meaning of (every) word and sentence and speech (*vāc*) that contains (all) fifty letters (of the alphabet). Thus all things come into being.

Therefore, the one root of (all) Mantras and every existing thing is also said to be *Mātṛkā*. This, Śiva's power of action, unfolds in this way. If the awakening of the Wheel of *Mātṛkā* has taken place in this way, then (the yogi thus) awakened is Lord (of all and) whatever he says becomes the king of Mantras.

* * *

Paramaśiva is the form (*mūrti*) of the absolute, His power of action, at one with Him, is *Mātṛkā*. It is the reflective awareness of His own nature and the first pulse (*spanda*, of His being which takes place) when He, out of His own free will, desires to emit the universe. (This power) generates the four energies, *Ambā, Jyeṣṭhā, Vāmā* and *Raudrī*, and having done so, generates the Pure Path that consists of (the powers of the vowels) which are the seeds (*bīja*, of all things), by their combining with one another through the expansion and repose, etc., of the absolute (symbolized by the letter 'A'), the will (corresponding to the letter 'I') and the unfolding of consciousness (*unmeṣa*, which is the letter 'U') and the other energies (of the vowels). (*Mātṛkā*, the power of action) then generates *Bindu*, which is the pure awareness of their oneness (*abhedavedana*, that precedes the manifestation of diversity) and when this pours out of itself, (*Mātṛkā*) manifests *Visarga* which is the inner impulse of consciousness to emit (*visisṛkṣā*) the lower emitted plane of existence. Thus, it goes on to generate the Impure Path consisting of the upsurge (*ullāsa*) of the energy (of the consonants) which are the womb (*yoni*, of the principles of individualized consciousness) in which (*Mātṛkā*, the power of action) gathers together within Herself all the wheels of energy. Thus, when the power of the will descends (to the lower levels of existence) in the form of the vital impulse (*prāṇana*) (that gives life to the body), heralded by the transformation of the unstruck resonance (*anāhatadhvani*, of pure awareness), the activity of the vital breath (*prāṇakriyā*) which contains within itself every word and sentence, is set into operation. Therefore, *Mātṛkā* alone generates this universe of words and the things they denote and is the principle and primal cause of (all) Mantras.

Whatever (the yogi) who is thus awakened and enlightened may happen to say, whether nonesense or just common everyday talk, is like a Mantra that (unerringly and) without restraints effects his task.

Exposition

Although Kṣemarāja's commentary differs from Bhāskara's it does not disagree with it but, one could say, develops a point that Bhāskara does not go into, namely, the structure and contents of the Wheel of *Mātṛkā*. This is basically because Kṣemarāja understands the awakening of this Wheel as the conscious assimilation of its energies that seemingly emerge and become active one by one as the Wheel rotates. As these energies are the sources of the constituents of all manifest (i.e., immanent) and unmanifest (i.e., transcendent) reality, this effectively means that when the Wheel is awakened and the yogi is fully conscious of its potencies and activity as that of absolute consciousness, and hence of his own true nature, he too awakens and reclaims his own inherent power. This is none other than *Mātṛkāśakti* which is, as we have already noted, the supreme power of speech as the reflective awareness (*vimarśa*) and creative autonomy (*svātantrya*) of universal consciousness and hence the vital energy of Mantra.

The fifty letters of the Sanskrit alphabet, arranged in their usual order, make up the Wheel of *Mātṛkā*. Each one represents a phase in the 'counting out' (*kalanā*) or differentiation of the universe and its projection onto the screen of consciousness. The vowels symbolize phases of the 'pure emanation' (*śuddhasṛṭi*). This is the movement and transformation of energy within Śiva's transcendental and all-embracing consciousness through which the universe is emitted externally while it abides at the same time within it in the form of this process itself. The consonants symbolize the kingdom of Śiva's power (*śakti*) when actively engaged in and manifest as the 'impure', i.e., external creation. Thirty-four is the number of consonants and thirty-four are the categories of existence below Śiva (excluding Śakti which pervades them all). Each letter corresponds to a category. The order of emergence is, however, reversed. Thus, 'K' (the first consonant) corresponds to Earth (the last category). The reason for this is that Śakti is the reflection of Śiva on the plane of phenomena and, as such, is as if turned upside down, like a mountain reflected in a lake.[55]

Pure 'I' consciousness (*ahaṃ*), as we have already seen elsewhere, contains and unites all the letters in itself as the unbroken flow of awareness from 'A' to 'Ha', which are the first and last letters of the alphabet, respectively. The rotation of the Wheel of phonemic energies marks the arising and subsidence of the universe in harmony with the incessant movement of the creative power of awareness within 'I' consciousness.[56] Through the Master's grace the disciple awakens to this, the eternal flow of *Mātṛkāśakti* by penetrating into the consciousness and bliss of his own nature that contains the entire aggregate of powers making up the fifty aspects of Mantric energy. The unconscious movement of the Wheel now becomes a conscious process of creation and withdrawal, *Kuṇḍalinī* rises and all that the yogi thinks, utters, hears spoken or reads is experienced as a liberating Mantra.[57] Thus, *Mātṛkāśakti* which is Śiva's power of action (*kriyāśakti*), now known, no longer binds the yogi but, on the contrary, sets him free.[58]

* * *

Lord Śiva (then) explained that the body of *Karma*, which is the cause of bondage (*bhava*), burns away in the radiant power (*tejas*) of Mantra that has been inflammed in this way:

śarīraṁ haviḥ
The body is the oblation. 2/8

In the blazing fire of consciousness, at one with Mantra, the body abandons the gross, phenomenal bonds of *Karma* and, as an oblation (in this fire), it assumes the form of a divine body. This is the supreme body of the all-pervasive Lord of Consciousness Who is the Sacrificer Who constantly offers the body and other phenomena in the great, eternally blazing and unfettered fire of Great Being (*mahāsattva*).

* * *

The meaning here is this: the sacrificer sits, taking up his place in the divine body of Mantra, and performs the fire sacrifice which makes all things one with the fire of consciousness. As he does so, the *Karmic* impurity which is the cause of his physical bondage (*dehabandana*) is destroyed through the stilling of his conditioned, illusory subjectivity (*māyīyapramātṛtā*) once he attains the Body of Mantra consisting of the supreme vitality of universal 'I' consciousness.

Exposition

Kṣemarāja merely stresses that what is meant here by offering one's own body as an oblation is the abandonment of all false identification with it. For, as Kṣemarāja points out referring to verse 9 of the *Stanzas*, once the notion of oneself as the body (*dehādyahaṃpratyaya*), which agitates consciousness with countless thought constructs, ceases, the awakened yogi can realise the highest state. Kṣemarāja writes:

> The body gross and subtle, etc., that everybody (generally) consecrates with (a false sense of) subjectivity is the oblation the great yogi offers in the supreme fire of consciousness. (He can do this) because he is constantly centred on the subjectivity of consciousness by quelling the subjectivity (centred) on the body.[59]

Appropriately, Kṣemarāja goes on to quote the *Vijñānabhairava*:

> (To perform the true supernal) oblation one must offer, with the ladle of awareness (*cetanā*), the elements, the senses and their objects, along with the mind, into the fire which is the abode of the Great Void.[60]

* * *

What is the supreme food of one who resides in this way in the Body of Consciousness (*jñānakāya*)? (The Lord) said:

jñānam annam
(This yogi's) food is knowledge. 2/9

The knowledge (meant) here is the supreme (knowledge of ultimate reality) correctly explained in these two sections. Know that to be like food which satisfies (the yogi) fully, for by reflecting on it (*nibhālana*) repeatedly, (one achieves) the perfect plenitude (*paripūrṇatā* of consciousness).

* * *

Attending to the expansion of the glorious power of his own nature in the supreme state (of being) this (yogi) is completely free of craving because he (abides) full (of the plenitude of consciousness) everywhere in this world (which is itself nothing but) the internal and outer radiance (*visphuraṇa*) of his own nature. When, in the course of daily life, he happens to reside on the plane of corporeal existence, he is like an alert actor. Infusing his inner nature with wonder (*svātmacamatkaraṇa*), he prepares himself to play his role and acts out his part. As he does so, he draws towards himself the objects of sense drenched with the supreme nectar (of self-awareness) by means of the senses and deposits them within his own nature. He is not like the fettered soul who, attached to the objects of sense and forgetful of the radiant pulse of his own nature, assumes the lower state of being.

Exposition

Kṣemarāja says that this aphorism can be interpreted in two ways according to how we understand the nature of the 'knowledge' to which it refers. If we take this knowledge to be, as Bhāskara does, the dynamic consciousness of ultimate reality, then it corresponds, as Kṣemarāja says, to "the reflective awareness of one's own nature which is (the enlightened yogi's) food that, because it satisfies him perfectly, causes him to rest in his own nature."[61] In other words, it is pure awareness that, preceding the formation of thought constructs, operates in the first moment of perception with which, as Kṣemarāja points out, verse 44 of the *Stanzas* instructs the awakened yogi to scan the field of perception. In this way he realises that all things are one with Śiva, his own universal consciousness.

The second interpretation is purely Kṣemarāja's suggestion. He couples the knowledge to which this aphorism refers with the limited knowledge that binds the individual soul described in the second aphorism of the first section. It is this lower, conditioned knowledge of reality that the awakened yogi assimilates into his consciousness and with it all thought constructs, perceptions, conflicting views, time and space, in short, all that exists in the realm of the awareness of relative distinctions that to the unawakened appears to be separate from him as the individual perceiving subject. All this is his food in the sense that he engulfs and digests it into his true conscious nature, thus making all things one with it.

* * *

When this is the case, ignorance is destroyed. (Śiva), Who is worshipped by (all) the gods, uttered the (following) piece to explain what happens due to this:

vidyāsaṃhāre tadutthasvapnadarśanam
The withdrawal of knowledge heralds the vision of dreams that arises from it. 2/10

The knowledge which perceives the world of birth and death (*saṃsāra*) is described as common (*aviśiṣṭa* to every fettered soul). It is withdrawn when the light of one's own nature dawns. When it is destroyed (the yogi's) perception of phenomenal existence that arises from ignorance and deludes (the ignorant) is said to be the vision of dreams. This is how the Supreme Lord has described (this insight) in brief:

> **The waking state (of enlightenment, *prabuddhatāvṛtti*) is, when it dawns, one of permanent freedom from all constraints, eternal contentment and oneness with (Śiva), the object of meditation and the manifestation (*kalanā*) of the light of one's own nature.**

* * *

When the knowledge common (to all fettered souls) marked by limited understanding is merged (in consciousness) by thus contemplating the reality (made manifest) by the aforementioned technique, the yogi perceives the (many) phenomenal and imagined things (*bhāvābhāva*) of the world that arise from it and consist of the thought constructs that manifest things devoid of an essential nature of their own, as if (they were) a dream. (He perceives) them arise and fall away in the pure mirror of awareness (*saṃvedana*) (manifest there) without the material aggregate of causes by the power of his own freedom as the wonderful diversity of groves, towns and mountains, etc., disassociated from the essential being of consciousness. (Perceivings things in this way, the yogi) is like Śiva, endowed with the eternal power of omniscience and the rest and, free of constraints, sports on the plane of the arising of innate knowledge.

Exposition

Kṣemarāja takes the knowledge to which this aphorism refers as being the Pure Knowledge (*śuddhavidyā*) that corresponds to the insight that: "I am this (universe) and this (universe) is me" (*aham-idam-idamaham*). Accordingly he says that:

> When the Pure Knowledge which is the expansion of consciousness (*jñānasphāra*) is withdrawn and recedes (*nimijjana*), there emerges a clear vision of the extending chain of thought constructs that constitute duality (*bhedamaya*) and is the dream that arises through the gradual dwindling away of (pure) knowledge (impressed upon the yogi's consciousness).[62]

What Kṣemarāja means to say is that if the yogi is unable to maintain a steady, continuous stream of awareness, he falls from the contemplative absorption he experiences through the awakening of the Wheel of phenomic energies, into the dream state. The pristine purity of his consciousness is thus seemingly marred and its unity broken up by the flood of images that pour into the yogi's mind to distract him and carry him away from the authenticity of universal consciousness. In failing to exert himself to maintain his awareness of this higher state of consciousness, he ceases to be a true yogi and is no better than an ordinary man. Thus, Kṣemarāja, quoting verse 21 of the *Stanzas,* instructs the yogi to be constantly aware of the universal activity (*spanda*) of his consciousness in order to realise his true nature through the vigilant wakefulness of awareness.

It is always the 'I' which maintains awareness of itself and of its projections. The minute 'I' forget myself I am lost in 'this'. Cut off both from my own autonomy and the grace of a higher, more universal level of consciousness, and so no longer awake to myself, I am at the same time no longer awake to the direct experience of reality. This is the fall from the perpetually renewing awakening of self-awareness to the dream of thought constructs and projections.

For the yogi this means resting content with the minor yogic accomplishments and powers (*siddhi*) which come in the wake of the traces (*vāsanā)* of the self-awareness left by his contemplative absorption (*samādhi*). But, however exalted these powers may seem to the ordinary man, the yogi who is distracted by them fails to persevere in maintaining his awareness and so, as verse 35 of the *Stanzas* declares, the generation of images that takes place in the states of waking and dreaming reverts to its natural spontaneity as happens normally with the worldly man.

* * *

Here ends the second section of the *Aphorisms of Śiva* which describes the arising of innate knowledge. What remains to be discussed is the vibration of the powers for the attainment of the power of the Yoga of Knowledge is a veritable wish-granting gem.

Now the Third Light Commences Called

THE VIBRATION OF THE POWERS

The powers (*vibhūti*) we are about to describe are generated either by the spontaneous (*sahaja*) arising of Mantra or by the recognition (*pratyabhijñā*) of one's own nature.

Supreme, unconditioned bliss arises spontaneously through the expansion of the awakened consciousness which develops by reflecting on the beginning and end (of the arising and subsidence of the breath, perception and thought). One's own natural and unconditioned power of creative freedom (*svātantryaśakti*) becomes clearly apparent through (this bliss) and one perceives the glorious power (*vibhūti*) (of one's own conscious nature).

This section is devoted to this topic (and so the Lord) began by saying (the following) to explain what the true nature of the mind is:

ātmā cittam
The mind is the Self. 3/1

The mind, also known as the mental faculty of mentition (*manas*), is consistently represented in the teachings as an organ of sense and as such (essentially consists of the) intent (*saṃkalpa* which directs the synthesis of perceptions and the formation of thought constructs). That is said to be Mantra. One should know that the Self itself, when devoid of verbal constructs (*vāc*), etc., is Mantra that follows the directives of intent and by that (all of one's) wishes are fulfilled by contemplating (*nibhālana*) (mind's) essential nature.

* * *

Discursive intent (*saṃkalpa*) (is the form of) awareness (*parāmarśana*) when the mind is extroverted. When (the mind) is introspective it is Mantra, which is the contemplative awareness (*manana*) of one's own nature. When introverted, it is undistracted and so the contracted (conditioned) state of the mind is abandoned and it then assumes its natural (*sahaja*) condition which is its inherent conscious nature. (Now when the mind is thus) pervaded (with consciousness) it is not dependent, at the level of practise, on the activity of the senses and so (all its) knowledge and action is free of impediments. Thus, by laying hold of its (inherent) power (*bala*), it can, like Śiva, manifest externally, as it wishes, the desired object without recourse to earth, water, fire or any other (physical element), (in such a way that) all people can see it. The intentions, etc., of one who is not dedicated to the practise of Yoga (*ayukta*) are not apparent to anyone (but himself) and cannot be made externally manifest. While, on the contrary, the Mantras, etc., of one who is intent on the practise of Yoga (*yukta*) and possesses Śiva's unique qualities can, for this reason, make any phenomenon manifest, however hard this may be.

Exposition

As the reader will recall, the first aphorism taught that the Self is pure, dynamic and universal consciousness. This is true for the yogi who has awakened to his true nature at the highest (*śāmbhava*) level of consciousness. At the individual (*āṇava*) level, however, the situation has changed. In this sphere of consciousness, where attention is directed to the external world and the flux of awareness is coloured by the sensations and perceptions generated by the contact between subject and object, the analytic and synthetic activity of the mind assumes the status of the subject in relation to sense objects. When consciousness is extroverted and directed to the objects of the senses, the intermediate process of discernment, analysis and classification of perceptions, which bridges the gap in the flow of awareness from the universal subject to a specific object of knowledge, appears, at the individual level, to take over the status of the perceiving subjectivity which underlies it. The universal Self recedes into the background as a pure, undefinable awareness and the individual ego, consisting of the perceptions, thoughts and emotions generated by the contact between the perceiver and the perceived, emerges in the juncture between them.

The lower-order subject created in this way is a pin-point (*aṇu*) of awareness which emerges when consciousness freely limits itself to adapt to, and focus down on, externally projected objectivity. This is the Self, which moves (*atati*) from one state of being to another, from one body to the next. At the empowered (*śākta*) level, enlivened by the direct intuition (*pratibhā*) consciousness has of its own nature, mind ceases to function in a paradigmatic, formative manner to generate mutually exclusive mental representations but appears instead in the subtle form of Śakti,[1] i.e., reflective awareness (*vimarśa*). This, as we have seen, is the essence of Mantra. Independent of the activity of the senses, the mind's powers of knowledge and action are no longer conditioned in any way and so the mind is able, like Śiva Himself, to emanate at will, without need of material cause, whatever it may desire. At the individual level, the creative powers of consciousness reflected though the extroverted mind are greatly attenuated. All that remains is the power to create thoughts and determined resolutions (*saṃkalpa*) which go on to issue, through the body, into outer action, at which point the private creations of the mind become apparent to others. The next two aphorisms go on to explain the nature of the forces which bind and contract consciousness at this level.

* * *

Now why are the mind's intentions unfulfilled? He explained:

jñānaṃ bandhaḥ
(Empirical) knowledge is bondage. 3/2

(Empirical) knowledge relates to the objects of the senses and so is (a form of) cognitive awarenes (*jñapti*) (sul-

lied) by attachment, etc. This is bondage, the veil which obscures the mind's essential nature. Practising detachment from internal and external objects, the perceiving subject is liberated from (his) thoughts (*mantavyatā*) whenever (they arise).

* * *

The mind that is not free of the impurities of passion (*rajas*) and ignorance (*tamas*) is distracted by its interaction with objects of the senses because of its attachment, etc. (to them). The veil which obscures the light (of consciousness) has not been removed and so one does not gain the power (*bala*) inherent in one's own nature, (the acquisition of which) is penetration into its original authentic nature. In this situation it is incapable of creating (the object of its conscious) intentions (in a manner) commonly perceivable to everybody. Thus the root cause of all the impediments that prevent one from creating what one desires is attachment to the objects of the senses.

Exposition

In this context *knowledge* does not refer to the pervasive limiting power of the impurities of Māyā and individuality (*māyīya* and *āṇavamala*) as it did in the second aphorism of the first section, but to individual sensory perceptions and the mental activity which accompanies and processes them. Bound by its knowledge of objectivity and out of touch with its essentially subjective nature, the soul wanders from life to life, state to state, carrying with it the subtle traces left behind by sensory and mental activity. Together these are said to constitute, and be caused by, the subtle body (*puryaṣṭaka*) with which consciousness is identified and due to which it is subject to the constant alternation of pleasure, pain and delusion which are the qualities (*guṇas*) of its material nature.[2]

Thus when one practises detachment from inner and outer objects, the perceiving subjectivity (*draṣṭṛ*) is liberated from the limitations imposed upon the inherent omniscience of its consciousness and the yogi is not only freed from them, but is also actively free to do whatever he wishes.

* * *

So what is it that obscures the eternal perceiver? (The Lord) explained:

kalādīnāṃ tattvānām aviveko māyā
Māyā is the lack of discernment of the principles
beginning with Kalā. 3/3

The principles (that obscure the individual soul) form a group that ranges from *Kalā* to Earth. (They are called) "principles" (*tattva*) because the entire universe is pervaded (*tata*) by them.

Kalā is said to be (the individual soul's) limited power of action. Similarly, the principle of (impure) knowledge (*vidyā*) is said to be (the soul's limited) power of knowledge. The fetter of attachment (*rāga*) is of the sort (exemplified in the notion) "this is desirable" and is (a form of) bondage. The time (*kāla*) which is present in this, the temporal condition of the present, is also said to be (a form of) bondage. Necessity (*niyati,* is) the condition of constraint (which determines according to fixed principles) the fruits of one's own actions. *Pradhāna* (the substantial ground of the remaining physical, mental and sensory principles) consists of an inner equilibrium between the perceptions of pleasure and pain (discerned at this level in all the lower) principles. The qualities (*guṇa*) are pleasure, pain and delusion. The intellect is pure intelligence (*mantṛtā*) while the ego is the stir (*saṃramba,* of limited self-awareness) and the mind is (the principle) which directs the senses. The cognitive senses (*buddhīndriya*) are said to be (a form of) cognitive consciousness determined by (the activity of) the senses while the organs of action, are (the form in which) agency is individualized by these same (senses). The subtle elements consist of the manifest condition of the (pure sensation) of sound (and the rest perceived by the senses) while

the group of five gross elements is the outpouring brought about by sound and the other individual (sensations).

Māyā, which deludes (the fettered soul, is his) failure to discern (the true nature of these principles and distinguish between them), while (right) discernment is established here in Pure Knowledge and the other (principles of the Pure Path). Therefore the wise who know reality (*tattva*) call them the "Pure Principles."

Śiva is the principle which corresponds to the light of one's own nature (*svajyotiṣṭva*) while Śakti is said to be (Śiva's) knowledge and action. Sadāśiva is the omniscience and universal activity (of consciousness), while *Īśvaratattva* (corresponds) to the (inner) impulse (inherent in consciousness) because the impulse (which stimulates the perception of diversity arises) through it. Pure knowledge is here said to be the enlightened understanding of the Śaiva and other scriptures.

The principles are conceived in this way within the Self through these states. (But) this, the state of the principles we have just described, does not contaminate the reflective awareness (*vimarśa*, of one's own nature) because, pervading all things, it is supreme.

* * *

Māyā veils the true nature, that is, the perceiving subject (*draṣṭṛ*) who is the self-luminous and ever-manifest light of those individual souls who, gripped by the false notion of conditioned subjectivity (*parimitapramātṛbhāva*),[3] reside in bodies consisting of the gross elements, the subtle body (*puryaṣṭaka*) and the (five) obscuring coverings (*kañcuka*) fashioned by the series (of thirty-one impure) principles, starting with *kalā*. Those who persist in the practise of discrimination and have transcended the plane of Māyā are grounded in Pure Knowledge and so the light of their own nature is (never) obscured. And so, because the bonds (which condition their consciousness) have been removed, the Mantras, etc. (of these enlightened souls) become, as explained before, fit to carry out their task.

Exposition

This aphorism goes on to explain why the individual fails to recognise that all perceptions and mental representations are essentially forms of awareness and hence cannot condition consciousness.

The thirty categories of existence belonging to the Impure Creation (*aśuddhasṛṣṭi*)[4] envelope the remaining category, i.e., *Puruṣa*, the individual soul, in three layers or bodies. The five obscuring coverings (*kañcukas*) of limited action, knowledge and desire and the limitations of time and space which condition the individual by contracting his consciousness directly, form the innermost body. Together these five represent aspects of the deluding power of Māyā. Next comes the subtle body (*puryaṣṭaka*) consisting of the intellect, mind and ego together with the five primary sensations. Finally, the third and grossest body consists of the ten organs of knowledge and action together with the five gross elements. While Māyā, the psychic cause of diversity and *Prakṛti*, the material nature, pervade the other categories.

These categories are in reality emantions of, and at one with, the freedom (*svātantrya*) of consciousness. The soul in bondage, however, fails to discriminate between them and his true nature when this same power operates as Māyā. The lower order categories are not realised to be one with the higher order (of the Pure Creation) and so become aspects or energies of the binding power of Māyā. Thus the universal vibration of consciousness (*sāmānyaspanda*) appears to break up into countless individual motions of consciousness (*viśeṣaspanda*) that manifest as the pleasure, pain and delusion of the soul's material nature which, as verse 20 of the *Stanzas* quoted by Kṣemarāja explains, cast him down into the world of transmigratory existence (*saṃsāra*).

* * *

Now once (the (Lord) had thus described the expansion (*prasara*) of the Self consisting of the forces which constitute the principles of existence, He want on to explain what arises due to its contraction:

śarīre saṃhāraḥ kalānām
The forces are withdrawn in the body. 3/4

The forces are said to be the specific functional capacities of (each of) the principles of existence. The body is made up of the union of these (forces) and so consists of the multiple aggregate of energies (*sakala*) which are (the corporeal) support of the Self. The withdrawal of the forces there (in the body) is said to be the progressive penetration (and absorption, *anupraveśa*, of each of them) into their respective causes. This continues until (the yogi) attains a body of pure awakened consciousness (*bodhadeha*) and there (experiences) the Supreme Arising (*parodaya*, of ultimate reality).

Or else, (the yogi) may attain *Śivatattva* through a (single) act of transcendence (*ullaṅghanavṛtti*). This also involves the withdrawal of the forces due to which (the yogi experiences) the arising (*udaya*, of universal consciousness).

* * *

The supreme body of awakened consciousness arises within one's own nature by the realisation brought about by contemplating the successive penetration and merger of the principles into their respective causes (by withdrawing them back into one another) in a manner contrary (to their original successive manifestation). (The process takes place) in the body, which (is itself) made up of the union of these principles, (and continues) until (the yogi) reaches their end (and original source), which is one's own nature consisting of the pure consciousness that sustains them all.

Or else (the yogi may achieve the same result and) attain the level (on which he can realise) the sovereign power of (his own) pure conscious nature which is devoid of (all) thought constructs by a single act of transcendence that withdraws all the (lower) functions (*vṛtti*) in an instant directly (*haṭhāt*) once he has attained a state of one-pointed concentration which annuls thought. The sprout of perfection thus emerges free and vigorous (*pallavita*) by withdrawing the extension of the forces which (the ignorant) consider to be (their true) subjectivity (but is in fact) the repository of (their) bondage and the veil (which obscures their own nature).

Exposition

Bhāskara suggests that the diversity of the multiple principles of existence can be fused into a unity either gradually, in successive stages, or at a stroke, all at once. Kṣemarāja however rejects the second possiblity in this case insofar as, according to him, practise operates here at the individual (*āṇava*) level where diversity prevails and realisation takes place gradually and not suddenly as it does at the higher levels of practise.[5] Even so, he explains that the gradual assimilation of diversity into universal consciousness can take place in two ways, namely, either by a process technically called the "contemplation of dissolution" (*layabhāvanā*) or else by meditating on the fire of consciousness (*dāhacintā*). Although I have already touched upon these methods in my *Doctrine of Vibration*,[6] I should add here some further details concerning the first one which is important for both Bhāskara and Kṣemarāja.

The 'contemplation of dissolution' (*layabhāvanā*) is a form of contemplative awareness through which the outward movement and progressive differentiation of consciousness from its causal, pre-cosmic form to its phenomenal manifestation is reversed in successive stages. Kṣemarāja quotes a verse from the *Vijñānabhairava* instructing the yogi in this practise:

> One should meditate on the All in the form of the Paths and the world-orders, etc., considered successively in their gross, subtle and supreme forms until, at the end, the mind dissolves away.[7]

Consciousness becomes objectively manifest in two streams or sequences (*krama*) of appearances (*ābhāsa*) as aspects of the wave or pulse of creative energy[8] flowing through consciousness. Projected outside it by a process of successive differentiation (*kalanā*), it appears as the deployment of experience in the flux of time and space.[9] The diversification of outer activity (*kriyāvaicitrya*), such as the movement of the sun or the alternation of the seasons is the medium through which the Path of Time is externally apparent, while the Path of Space corresponds to diversity of form (*mūrtivaicitrya*) and relative distinction between objectively perceived entities.[11] Abhinava explains:

> Thus, all this Path rests in consciousness. The Path of the Great Lord is the manifestation of all-pervasive, and hence inactive and formless, consciousness, as actions and forms. The word *Path* (*adhvan*) is chosen to denote this reality (i.e., the universe) because, for those who have not overcome duality it is one, in the sense that it is the cause of the gradual attainment of the plane to be achieved, while for the awakened it simply represents an object of enjoyment to be devoured.[12]

The Path of Denotation (*vācakādhvan*), corresponding to the Path of Time, is represented in its outer supreme, subtle and gross aspects by letters, Mantras and sentences, inwardly grounded in pure perception (*pramā*), the subject and the means of knowledge, respectively. The Path of Denoted Meaning (*vācyādhvan*), corresponding to the Path of Space, consists of the five Cosmic Forces (*kalā*),[13] thirty-six categories of existence (*tattva*) and the 118 world systems (*bhuvana*). These constitute the sphere of objectivity ranging from supreme to gross. Thus, the Path of the Cosmic Forces (*kalādhvan*) represents the state of objectivity while it is still manifestly a part of the act of perception associated with the mental representations of the object perceived. The subtle state, represented by the categories of existence (*tattva*), corresponds to the pure object denuded of all specification, while the world-orders (*bhuvana*) represent the gross manifest object with all its specifying particulars.[14]

The configuration of the All is thus the deployment of consciousness as it emerges from itself through the flux of perception (*pratīti*) ranging from the level of pure awareness to gross objects. This movement constitutes the essence of universal consciousness (*caitanya*) as Pure Act, identified with which the enlightened make all things one with their own nature.[15] At the same time, mediated by consciousness, the All rests on what is emitted from it, namely, the void (i.e., the subject present in deep sleep), the mind, vital breaths, psychic nerves, senses and the external body.[16] Thus the yogi visualizes the objective sphere of the All as arising successively in his own body. Starting with the 118 world systems, he imagines that they are all present within him from the lowest hells at his feet to the highest heavens in his head. The same process is then repeated with the thirty-six categories of existence and the five cosmic forces, each containing the grosser aspect of the Path within it.

The elements of each Path are ordered in a graded hierarchy such that the higher, being closer to consciousness, assimilates the lower. Thus as the yogi ascends along it, the higher element acts as the purifier for the lower ones.[17] Again, the higher is the support (*ādhāra*) of the lower, supported (*adheya*) elements, while the whole is sustained by the supporting power (*ādhāra* or *dhārikāśakti*) of consciousness which is identified with the power of the universal will (*icchāśakti*). Present at the very source where Śiva and Śakti unite as the first phase (*prathamāṃśa*) in the flow along the cosmic Path, this sustaining power is both the screen (*bhitti*) of perception onto which the All is projected and the pervasive space (*vyoman*) in which it is suspended. Abhinava writes:

> Thus, perception (*pratīti*) alone is the creatrix and sustainer identified with Śiva. From it are born all beings, in it they are grounded. Thus, it is this power which supports all things. One should contemplate the All on the analogy of an imagined object which, though devoid of support, falls not, resting as it does on a power which sustains itself.[18]

The yogi ascends along the Path he visualizes in his body, absorbing the lower elements into the higher as he does so, thus strengthening and extending his unifying awareness (*anusaṃdhāna*) of the configuration of the Path. Thus moving from the gross elements constituting the outer physical body, to pure sensations (*tanmātra*), then to the senses and mind, etc., back to their primordial source, the yogi rises from the embodied subjectivity of the waking state of the Fourth State where he is one with the all-pervading intent that initiates the creative vision of consciousness.

The second method Kṣemarāja teaches, namely, meditation on the fire of consciousness (*dāhacintā*) involves, as I have already explained in the *Doctrine of Vibration*,[19] the visualisation of the fire of consciousness which is made to traverse the body in which the adept imagines the presence of the entire cosmic order arranged in layers from the lowest hells at the bottom of the body to the highest divine worlds at the top. As the fire rises from below, the microcosmic body burns and so is transformed into that same fire which, once it has burnt its cosmic fuel, leaves behind the emptiness of the pure, undifferentiated light of consciousness.

* * *

Once Śiva had explained how, by transcending (the lower) function (*vṛtti*, of consciousness) in this way, one's own true nature (*svasvarūpa*) dawns within the Self which consists of the outward extension (*prasara*) and withdrawal (*saṃkoca*) of the principles of existence, he went on to explain how the accomplishment of the elements (*bhūtasiddhi*) arises:

nāḍīsaṃhāra-bhūtajaya-bhūtakaivalya-bhūtapṛthaktvāni
The withdrawal of the vital channels, the conquest of the elements, freedom from the elements and the separation of the elements. 3/5

Just as the householder is master in (his own) house (similarly) by virtue of its freedom, the Self (is master) in this body which consists of the five elements and is the support of consciousness. The vital channels are withdrawn there (within it) by merging in the Sky of Consciousness for (consciousness) is everywhere said to be the opening (*mukha*, at the extremities) of all the vital channels.

The breaths are the supports of the vital channels while their support is the ubiquitous Lord of Consciousness. The highest function (*vṛtti*, of consciousness) possesses six qualities (and is set into operation) when the activity (of consciousness which operates when the breath moves through the vital channels) is merged in the centre. (These qualities are) *stability, flow, heat, movement, emptiness* and *reversal*.

Or the awakened lord (of yogis) can conquer the elements by contemplating the essential nature of the princi-

ples individually in their corresponding centres (in the body) where they can be perceived.

By renouncing (the power that comes from this practise the yogi) attains unconditioned freedom (from the elements). (Thus the yogi) though (his) contact with (his) own (inner) strength (*bala*)[20] separates the elements one from the other (while each continues) to possess the power of (all) thirty-six principles. (Thus the yogi who is identified with) the ubiquitous Lord can, by changing (His own apparent) transformations, alter (anything at will), be it a single incomposite entity (*ātmastha*) or one which consists of an aggregate of constituents (*saṃghaṭastha*). Thus the power of one's own freedom (*prabhuśakti*) is nowhere obstructed.

* * *

(The yogi) who desires yogic powers (*siddhi*) must first pacify *iḍā* and the other vital channels by withdrawing the inhaled and exhaled breaths (*prāṇa* and *apāna*) into either the internal or external twelve-finger space and practise concentration for the perscribed time on the Earth and other elements, each of which has it own characteristic shape, be it triangular or round, etc., is marked with its own seed-syllable and is located in the Root or its corresponding centre (in the body), as described in the methods (*prakriyā*) taught in the Tantras. In this way the elements come (under the yogi's) control and so entry or exit from the midst of the five gross elements or the abiding among them, etc., does not affect him. (The yogi) who practises in this way and does so without being attached to the powers (he has gained thereby) also attains , without any (extra) effort, the power (*siddhi*) to abide in his own nature, which is pure, uninterrupted consciousness and bliss unaffected (*anuparakta*) by the elements. In this way, he can also unite and separate at will (any) entity formed by the conjunction of the principles of existence. Thus, he has the power, by virtue of his unimpeded freedom, to give rise to, alter and even radically change the various states to which phenomena are subject, (each of which are anyway) transformations of his own nature.

Exposition

Kṣemarāja's interpretation of this aphorism largely agrees with Bhāskara's, although not entirely. Thus, Kṣemarāja, like Bhāskara, equates the first two practises, namely, that of the withdrawal of the vital channels and that of the conquest of the elements, with the regulation of the breath (*prāṇāyama*) and concentration (*dhāraṇā*) on the elements, respectively, these being the first two stages in the practise of Yoga. However, while Bhāskara understands that the yogi is freed from the elements by renouncing the yogic powers which he attains by meditating on them, Kṣemarāja couples this with the next stage in the practise of Yoga, namely, the withdrawal of the senses from their objects (*pratyāhāra*). The yogi withdraws the flux of awareness travelling from the Heart of consciousness through the senses to outer objects and fixes it in the navel by attending closely, as it rises and falls, in accord with the movement of the breath.[21] Again, while Bhāskara takes the practise of the separation of the elements to refer to the yogi's freedom to control the gross physical elements, Kṣemarāja understands this as refering to the detachment of the mind from the elements that the yogi achieves through the unsullied purity and freedom of the consciousness of his true nature in which his mind participates by gradually raising his awareness to the level beyond thought constructs (*unmanā*) when his practise reaches maturity. This is the final stage of Yoga and corresponds to that of pure contemplation (*samādhi*).

* * *

Now even if this is so (a question still arises) as to whether (the yogi) does or does not in fact realise his own nature (in these conditions, that is,) while the illusion with its countless forms (*bāhuśākhā*, that obscures) the Self (still persists and so Lord) Śaṅkara said:

mohāvaraṇāt siddhiḥ
(The yogi attains) perfection through the obscuring veil of delusion. 3/6

When lust, anger, greed, or fear arise or when one feels happy, experiences a sudden fright or even when intensely joyful, delusion extends its sway everywhere. This alone should be known to be the obscuring covering (of consciousness) because it shrouds one's own nature. Therefore, as this is the cause (of delusion, the yogi can attain) the perfections (*siddhi*) of the Self, namely, omnipotence and omniscience, by reflecting (*vimarśa*, on his own unsullied consicousness) at the initial stage (just before these states lay hold of his mind).

* * *

If we consider matters from the standpoint of ultimate reality, the yogic powers, etc. (yogis acquire) arise at the lower levels (of practise) where (one still) perceives relative distinctions (and so) belong to the sphere of Māyā and obscure the yogi's own nature. Therefore, in order to perceive it in this state he must, when feelings (*vṛtti*) of intense pleasure or passion, etc., arise (within him), fix his attention either on the initial phase (when they are just about to arise) or on the final phase (when they wain away) for they (in themselves) obscure his own nature. In this way (he attains) the supreme perfection (*parasiddhi*), namely, (the power of) omniscience and the others (inherent in his true nature).

Exposition

Bhāskara clearly couples the pratice taught in this aphorism with that taught in verse 22 of the *Stanzas* to which the reader is referred. Kṣemarāja's interpretation is quite different. According to him, the word *siddhi* in this aphorism doesn't mean the supreme perfection (*parasiddhi*) of liberation but the inferior, limited yogic accomplishments (*aparasiddhi*) the yogi may acquire on the way to his ultimate goal. According to Kṣemarāja, each stage of the practise of Yoga whether that of posture (*āsana*), breath control (*prāṇāyama*), withdrawal of the senses (*pratyāhāra*), concentration (*dhyāna*), meditation (*dhāraṇā*) or contemplation (*samādhi*) can by itself lead to absorption in the highest reality (*paratattvasamāveśa*). At the same time the yogi can also acquire yogic powers through them or other benefits, such as improved health or a prolonged life, but these, warns Kṣemarāja, are of secondary importance and the pursuit of such things leads the yogi astray for they are a product, not of his enlightened consciousness, but of the residue of the ignorance which deludes him.

The practises taught in the previous two aphorisms find application in the material (*bhūta*) realm of consciousness. The yogi cannot reach the supreme level of consciousness through them, for he is still subject to the power of Māyā. The Master points out in this aphorism that he is in fact concerned with manipulating the forces of matter. His pursuit in this respect is magical or manipulative. Although the ultimate goal of Yoga is mastery over oneself through the insight vouchedsafe by enlightenment, even so, the first major milestone on the path is the achievement of mastery over the elementary world and body. Here, the yogi is warned of the dangers and incompleteness of his attainment, once he has reached this stage. The results may be extraordinary, but they are still nonetheless limited. The yogi must press on beyond them to the higher realms of the spirit. In order to do this his practise must take on a new and more elevated form.

* * *

(Once having explained) that (the yogi) attains perfection (*siddhi*) in this way while delusion prevails, (the Lord) went on to say what happens by overcoming it:

mohajayād anantābhogāt sahajavidyājayaḥ
(But) by conquering delusion and by (his) infinite expanse (the yogi) achieves Innate Knowledge. 3/7

Delusion, they say, has countless aspects and its conquest is the full awakening of the unconditioned (*asaṃkucita*) and eternal activity (*gati*) of consciousness that takes place by the light of one's own nature (*svāloka*). The light of one's own nature (*svaprākāśa*) dawns in a clearly evident manner out of this infinite expanse and (the yogi's) victory

knows no bounds, for countless are its aspects. This is said to be (true) bliss for it is completely full and perfect. Innate knowledge is, as explained before, the light of one's own nature and by its arising (the yogi beholds) the supreme light of the Self.

* * *

The fully awakened (yogi, *suprabuddha*) (experiences) the dawn of uncreated knowledge said to be the consciousness which is the reflective awareness of the absolute ego (*pūrṇāham*), by the unconditioned and perfect plenitude (that arises) by (his) conquest of delusion, that is, by stilling duality (*bheda*) in its countless forms.

Another interpretation is the following. By conquering delusion and attaining the plane of pure knowledge governed by the Rudra-subject (*rudrapramātṛ*), otherwise known as the Infinite Lord (*anantabhaṭṭāraka*), (the yogi) acquires the wealth of the innate light (of consciousness, *sahajāloka*) and, on the plane of pure knowledge, he, as the Rudra-subject called the "Infinite Lord," enjoys (the expanse of his cosmic) empire everywhere around him.

Exposition

Kṣemarāja reads this aphorism to mean: *(But) by conquering delusion completely (the yogi) achieves Innate Knowledge. Ananta,* which Bhāskara takes to mean "infinite" or "endless," Kṣemarāja glosses as "up to the stilling of (all) latent traces (of ignorance)."[22] Thus, from Kṣemarāja's point of view, the expression *anantābhogāt* qualifies *mohajayāt* so that read together the entire phrase literally means "by the conquest of delusion which extends up to the end," that is, which is so complete that no trace of delusion remains.

Kṣemarāja bases his interpretation of this aphorism exclusively on the *Svacchandatanta,* which he considers to be a major authority and from which he draws frequently, thus adding elements to the interpretation of the aphorisms Bhāskara ignores, even though this may at times, as happens in this case, somewhat stretch the meaning of the aphorism beyond its immediate sense. Kṣemarāja understands this aphorism in this way also in view of his interpretation of the previous one. In order to achieve perfect enlightenment, which can only come by acquiring the pure unconditioned insight that, inherent in the very nature of reality, reveals it, the yogi must not only overcome the immediate ignorance which prevents him from perceiving the underlying unity of reality but every trace of it that may still remain latent within him, if he is to be no longer liable to fall prey to the delusion of duality. Thus, basing himself on the authority of the *Svacchandatantra,* Kṣemarāja distinguishes between two stages of realisation at the highest level of spiritual development. The first is that of the pervasive nature of the Self when ignorance ceases and the second is that of Śiva's pervasive nature (*śivavyāpti*) when the latent traces of ignorance are also eliminated.

The subtlest forms of practise operate at the universal level of Śiva's nature (*śāmbhava*) and lead directly to the attainment of Śivahood through a sudden and total merger of individual consciousness into the universal consciousness of Śiva by an immediate realisation of their oneness. The lower, grosser forms of practise that function at the individual (*āṇava*) level, are gradual and centered on individualized consciousness. They are designed to free it from the constraints imposed upon it by the power of Māyā due to which it is subject to duality and the play of its own thought constructs. In other words, they work within the domain of diversity in order to raise the soul above it and aim to bring the mind to rest (*cittaviśrānti*). But while this state of repose is blissful and is one of self-realisation, consciousness is still individualized. In this state the yogi breaks through Māyā to the extent of realising himself to be a centre of living vitality, intrinsically free of the impurity and ignorance which limited him to the body and mind. Unaffected by time and space, the yogi experiences the eternal all-pervasive nature of the Self (*ātmavyāpti*). This realisation takes place, as the *Svacchandatantra* explains, when the yogi ceases to perceive the net of binding forces and factors that condition his consciousness and, abandoning the obsessive vision of them which leads him inevitably to identify with them, he attends instead to his true and most essential nature (*svarūpa*). Even so, slight traces still remaining of the effects of Māyā influence the yogi in such a way that he continues to sense a difference between himself and Śiva. He must press on beyond this level and no longer experience himself as an individual soul, even if all-pervading, but be aware instead that he, as Śiva, pervades all things (*śivavyāpti*) and that there is no break anywhere in the all-embracing fullness of his nature. To do this he must rise to the supramental (*unmanā*) level which is the knowledge and insight (*vidyā*) that is an instrinsic property of universal consciousness. Freed of the laborious and successive operations of the mind, he simultaneously gains the omniscience and other attributes of consciousness. Firmly established on this plane beyond mind (*unmanā*) which is that of the innate knowledge through which the supreme light of consciousness appears to him, he realises that he is Śiva, the Supreme Soul (*paramātman*), and not the lower, individual soul.[23]

* * *

The Unborn (Lord then) explained that (the yogi) who has attained perfection in this way should remain well awake and tirelessly deposit all things in one place:

jāgrad dvitīyakaraḥ
Waking is the second ray (of consciousness). 3/8

The waking state is said to be the knowledge (born of sensory perception). Observing the field of his (awareness) with it the lord of yogis should gather together all things into a unity and thus eliminating delusion should remain awake at all times and free of duality. The ray (*kara*, of sensory awareness) is like a hand (*kara*) because it has the power to gather together the waking state in this way and so is said to be the second (ray) because of its wonderful nature.

* * *

According to a preceding aphorism, "knowledge (born of sensory perception) is the waking state." Thus, what is meant by the waking state in this case is the power of knowledge. (When we commented on this aphorism) before, our concern was to explain the basic term predicated (i.e., the *waking state*) now, conversely, our main concern is the second term which predicates it (i.e., *knowledge*). This is fair enough because the aphorisms refer equally to all their terms of reference.

Observing whatever happens to lay (on the path of) the rays (*kara*, of his) power of knowledge and is made manifest by virtue of its form, the light which illumines it and the activity of the mind, the awakened yogi gathers it together as one would pick something up (with one's hand, *kara*) by seeing that it is one with the supreme light (of consciousness, although seemingly) obscured by the notions (*vikalpa*) of unity and diversity. In this way he realises that the inner and outer world, all of which is his own nature, reposes in the one pure awareness (*saṃvedana*) and so, possessing the wealth of liberation and behaving in everyday life as one who is liberated, he sports in his true nature.

Exposition

Bhāskara understands this aphorism in the light of verse 44 of the *Stanzas,* which teaches that the yogi should always maintain a state of alert awareness even as he observes the field of objectivity. Similarly, Kṣemarāja explains that this aphorism describes the state of the yogi who attains the Innate Knowledge (*sahajavidyā*) which is the inherent attribute of his own conscious nature. The object-centred perceptions of the waking state no longer militate against the pure subjective awareness of contemplative absorption. The yogi is active in the world and continues to be aware of himself as the perceiver contrasted with the object perceived but, grasping the fullness of his universal 'I' consciousness, he realises that it is the source from which objectivity emanates. He alone of all men is truly awake and so recognises that everything is an extension of his own nature, a second ray of light from the source of which he is the first ray. Thus whatever he perceives through the senses makes the universal consciousness of Śiva apparent to him and he realises that he and it are two aspects of the same reality.

* * *

How does the Self, constantly inebriated with the juice (*rasa*) of supreme bliss, behave when it resides in the body of one who is liberated in this life and, the mass of his delusion long since burnt away, is always well awake? (Śiva), the One Who Bears the Crescent Moon as His Crestjewel, spoke this aphorism to explain:

nartaka ātmā
The Self is the actor. 3/9

The experienced actor, who knows about (the forms) of sentiment (*rasa*), emotive states (*bhāva*) and acting, and who possesses the correct state of mind (*sattva*), speech, physical appearance and dress, is said to act his part well. Similarly, the Self manifests itself in accord with its own inherent nature everywhere (as every living being) by penetrating into the sentiment (*rasa*) of each emotive state (*bhāva*, it express) and playfully behaving accordingly. (Thus the Self) is said to be an actor because it assumes every state of being.

Inebriated with the juice of supreme bliss, (the Self sports) in this way in the world of daily life (*vihṛti*) like an experienced actor who, knowing well the (various types) of sentiment (*rasa*), the states of being which evoke them and their semblances, etc., assumes the role of a limited subject. Manifesting the sentiments and emotive states, etc., that his part demands (*anukārya*) by the gestures, etc., of his limbs without (however) forgetting his identity, imitating each state through the signs which express sentiment (*vibhava*), etc., he is transported to the plane (of Being) in which he savours (the joy of the beauty of consciousness) and so acts out the cosmic drama through the activity of the senses, desiring neither to gain some desired object or avoid the undesireable. Thus he delights everywhere with the light of his own nature, his mind filled with contentment by the power of his ever-persisting (*avilupta*) consciousness.

Exposition

Śiva, the true Self of every living being and the essence of all existing things, dances to the rhythm of creation and destruction, now appearing in this form and now in that. Projecting the waking and other states of consciousness onto the screen of His own nature,[24] He unfolds the cosmic drama with its varied and constantly shifting sentiments. He has no purpose and follows no fixed plan. Drunk with the savour (*rasa*) of supreme bliss, Śiva's dance is the game He plays out of the sheer delight of the blissful vibration of His own nature.[25] Śiva alone is awake and active in a universe asleep to its true nature. He is the director of the drama of life and the sole actor:

> Śambhu, Who is pure consciousness alone, is the actor in the cosmic drama and it is He Who is the individual soul, (for) His undefinable state consists of assuming (all the) roles.[26]

Śiva is free to conceal His own nature at will[27] and don the garb of the bodies of creatures. The bodies He assumes are commensurate with the planes of reality; similarly, the mental habitus He assumes is commensurate with the bodies. As a game, He even takes on the form of the bodies residing in the depth of hell![28] Somānanda writes:

> Just as a king over the whole earth, in the joyous and startled intoxication of his sovereignty, can play at being a simple soldier, imitating his behaviour, so, in His beatitude, the Lord amuses Himself by assuming the multiple forms of the whole.[29]

Through the pulsing activity of the senses of each spectator, Śiva enacts His play, enriching it with all the varied sentiments of the different states of consciousness. Neither an illusion nor simply an imitation (*sādṛśya*), the audience views the performance as being as real as consciousness itself[30] .The actor himself, however, never forgets his true identity, he deceives others but is never himself deceived.[31] The perfected yogi, at one with Śiva, constantly reflects upon his own nature. Detached (*tatastha*) from the outer show, he sees its inner essence and recognises that his life is merely the spontaneous acting out of the role consciousness has assumed in the drama of universal manifestation:

> Although I have changed my form and act out all the important junctures in the plot (sandhi) of the drama of man's life through birth, infancy, youth, adulthood and old age, I (remain) Śiva, the great actor.[32]

* * *

The Self (turned actor) dances (and so requires a stage) to serve it as a fitting support. Thus (the Lord) said:

raṅgo antarātmā
The stage is the inner Self. 3/10

The Self which unfolds externally is said to be the actor; the inner Self is its internal contraction. It becomes the subtle body (*puryaṣṭaka*) and so is called the "stage." Here the ubiquitous Lord of Consciousness dances as it were (to the rhythm) of creation, persistence and destruction.

* * *

The stage (*raṅga*) is where (the actor) makes his appearance (*rajyate*) with the intention of exhibiting the (delightfully) various and extensive sport of the drama (in which he performs). It is the inner self, the subtle body (*puryaṣṭaka*) where (the Self) assumes each of its wonderful and varied (*vicitra*) roles. Basing itself on that as its support, the conscious nature assumes (various) roles according to whether it takes up its residence in the body of man or beast, etc., and by setting the senses into operation performs the five (cosmic) functions of creation (persistence, destruction, obscuration and grace).

Exposition

The stage, with its scenery and lighting, is the ground on which the drama is enacted. It is there that the actor portrays the part allotted to him. Analogously, the 'inner soul', which is the vehicle that transports consciousness from life to life, is where Śiva enacts the cosmic drama for each individual soul.

* * *

Thus, the senses do not obscure (one's own nature). (Lord Śiva) the Divine Androgene spoke the following aphorism to explain this:

prekṣakānīndriyāṇi
The spectators are the senses. 3/11

The supreme conscious nature is free and fully awake and the senses perform their functions by its power;[33] like spectators (they view) the ubiquitous Lord of Consciousness here as He dances and cannot obscure His true nature.

* * *

The conscious nature is free and makes the senses and (all else) manifest. It is the light of all things for they all shine (manifestly apparent). All this universe would be as if blind, dumb and insentient were it not to draw its life from the shining (radiance) of that (light). And so the senses, enlivened by it, directly perceive, like aesthetically sensitive spectators, the inherent nature (*svarūpa*, of all things) which is free of the split between subject and object and is full of the extraordinary delight the performance of the cosmic drama (inspires within it). (In this way, the senses) inspire the introspective yogi with the wonder that comes from the aesthetic delight (*rasa*) which is the supreme nectar (of universal consciousness). When this is missing *Khecarī* and the other energies obscure the aesthetic delight of the nectar (which flows from) the perception of oneness (*abhedaprathā*) and impel the wheel of the senses along the universal path of suffering. Thus, the true nature (*svarūpa*) of the conscious nature (that turned actor) dances, is not obscured.

Exposition

When the senses of the Well Awakened yogi are directed to the outside world they view it within the universal Self. Through them the Lord of the Dance appears in His many forms. Free of the division between subject and object, the yogi delights in the aesthetic rapture that comes from perceiving the wonderful diversity (*vicitratā*) of the spectacle which unfolds within Śiva's all-pervasive nature. Captivated by the beauty of the cosmic outpouring of his own nature, the yogi is the most sensitive of aesthetes (*sahṛdaya*). Never deluded by the mistaken notion that there is any other reality but this, he perceives his own nature directly through the senses as full of the delight of the sentiments elicited by the drama of transmigratory existence.

* * *

The Lord then uttered an aphorism to explain that when this is so the boldest of men prevails (over all) by the (power of his) intellect:

dhīvaśāt sattvasiddhiḥ
The pure state is achieved by the power of the (illumined) intellect. 3/12

When the activity (*vṛtti* of the senses), which has sound and the rest as its object, is established in the conscious nature the intellect determines (its nature) there within it. Thus, because it precedes (sensory perception), it is pure and it is this that is said to be the power of the intellect. Free as it is of (all latent) tendencies (that can distract and obscure it), it is said to be the screen and ultimate limit of pure being (*sattva*) through which one can achieve the pure state (*sattva*) and so is described thus.

* * *

Given the presence of the senses which are naturally always active, sound and the other objects of sense are reflected in (their) activity and are, for the reasons given in the scriptures and elsewhere, essentially one with consciousness. The intellect which determines (their nature) is, because all other latent traces (within it of past action) have been destroyed, unsullied by the states (induced by the inordinate activity of) *rajas* or (the dullness of) *tamas* and, perceiving everywhere the Supreme Light (of consciousness) which is its own inherent brilliance, it makes of the yogi an abode for the light of pure Being (*sattva*) which is the pulsing radiance (*sphurattā*, of consciousness).

Exposition

As the drama of life unfolds, each new moment represents a fresh scene in the plot. But while each man has his part to play, and is at the same time a spectator, the best actor is he who plays his role full of the brilliance and deep feelings of *sattva*. Cast for the hero's part, every movement of his body and every word he utters is an inspiration for all who come in contact with him. This is how the true yogi lives in the world. For as the intellect of each man informs him of his situation so does he perceive and react to his environment and those around him. The intellect (*dhī*) of the average man is either dull or over excited, constantly affected by the shifting, changing forms projected onto it. The yogi's attention, however, is fixed on the centre between different moments in the plot. It is from here that each scene is illumined with the brilliant and unsullied light of consciousness and from here that the yogi draws the power of his illumined understanding (*dhīśakti*) which directs him to act out his role with the ease and genius of perfect mastery.

* * *

As this is so, the Self is free, thus (the Lord) said:

siddhaḥ svatantrabhāvaḥ
(Once this has been achieved) freedom is achieved. 3/13

The freedom (the yogi) has achieved in the way explained above is that of the Self.

* * *

The innate (*sahaja*, capacity inherent in the Self) through which it knows and does (all things) is (the yogi's) freedom which commands all and by virtue of which the entire universe from Śiva to Earth is sustained, perceived, made manifest and brought under his control. Just as by the magical power of an alchemical herb, everything it touches turns to gold, similarly, all things sanctified (*bhāvita*) by contemplating Śiva's innate nature come under (the yogi's) control.

Exposition

The yogi thus continues to play the part of a limited individual, all the while enjoying the omniscience and omnipotence of universal consciousness.

* * *

Now, do the omniscience and power to do all things (the liberated yogi possesses) extend everywhere as they do in this body or not? (In response to this question, Śiva) the One Adorned with the Crescent Moon said:

yathā tatra tathānyatra
As it is here, so is it elsewhere. 3/14

When the body is sustained by the Self one knows everything that happens within it,[34] similarly, (the same powers of omniscience and the rest) manifest everywhere by virtue of the force inherent in the ground of one's own being (*svādhiṣṭhānabala*).

* * *

Just as (the liberated yogi) is endowed with omniscience and the power to do all things by contemplating His own Śiva-nature in the body over which he presides, similarly (this same) omniscience is made manifest freely in the bodies (one normally) considers to be those of others by the power (he acquires) by laying hold of the energy latent in his own nature.

Exposition

While Bhāskara's commentary is virtually a paraphrase of verse 39 of the *Stanzas,* Kṣemarāja quotes verses 6–7. These verses can indeed be read together, thus verses 6–7 explain that the pulsing (*spanda*) principle of consciousness is free to operate everywhere and so impels the senses of all living beings, while verse 39 teaches that the yogi attains the omniscience and hence freedom of consciousness by grounding his awareness in his true nature. The awakened yogi experiences this freedom not only within his own body but also outside it, for he realises that the source of his own freedom is the same power which drives the entire universe with the spontaneity of its outpouring.

* * *

Now if (the yogi who realises his true nature to be that of the universal) agent who is free in all respects, transfers his consciousness into other bodies, etc., he (must be) affected by their qualities, so how can he abide in a state beyond time (*akālapadasthiti*)? (In reply to this question Śiva) the Enemy of Time spoke the following aphorism:

not found in Kṣemarāja

visargasvābhāvyād abahiḥ sthitestatsthitiḥ
The nature (of consciousness) is emission and so that which is not external abides as such. 3/15

Time is the recurrent pulse (of consciousness, *spanda*) produced by the progressive differentiation of the ongoing

course of phenomenal action (*pravṛttikalanā*), while perpetual emanation (*sṛṣṭi*) is the essential state of being (*svabhāva*) of the conscious nature and so (time) never arises on the plane of consciousness because (origination) takes place by the differentiation of the product of intent (*saṃkalpa*). External entities do not exist independently outside (consciousness) and so those who are devoted to the path of contemplation (through which they realise) the oneness of the light (of consciousness) with the object of its illumination never fall from the abode of their own nature because of their mindful practise of union (*yoganibhālana*). That is itself born of the eternal creative urge (of consciousness, *akālakāmaja*) because it resides on the plane of eternity.

* * *

The Supreme Lord is full of desire to emit (*visisṛkṣāśīla*) and that which is to be emitted and has emerged (out of Him) He contemplates within His own nature, its sustaining ground, as one with Him and so supports its existence. But even as He does so, He never forgets His own true nature. Now, the manifestation of objectivity is, even on the plane of Māyā, really at one with the Supreme Light (of consciousness) and because this is so (it is in fact pure) Being which abides (within consciousness) that (consciousness), by virtue of its freedom, manifests externally. Therefore, once one has realised the true nature (*tattvikasvarūpa*, of all things) one is never conditioned again (by the split) between (the phenomenal world of) qualities (*dharma*) and (consciousness, the absolute substance) in which they inhere.

Exposition

This aphorism (which is not found in Kṣemarāja's recension) amplifies and extends the previous one. From the vision of the essential unity of outer contents and inner consciousness, the next step is the realisation that nothing is external. Those who contemplate the unity of the light of consciousness are aware that that which is made manifest never exits from the abode of their own nature. One with the freedom of consciousness which emanates all things, they realise that it projects itself into itself from itself.[35] The yogi rests on the plane of eternity (*akālapada*), for although the power of time is the creatrix of all things,[36] the outpouring of consciousness is free of temporal succession.[37] The birth of manifest creation is due to the association of objectivity with time. But while the power of time is essentially the unfolding on the plane of Māyā of the cause of past, present and future which orders the rhythm of cosmic activity, it can in no way affect the pure light of consciousness of which it is an expression.[38] Time is an attribute of the object while, despite the fact that the object can only be made apparent through contact with the subject, the pure subject is never conditioned by time.[39] The cyclic creative activity of the yogi's freedom is in reality the pulsing rhythm (*spanda*) of consciousness. It does not entangle him in the web of time nor is he conditioned by its products.

* * *

Thus the Lord explained the best means to attain the plane of eternity, namely:

bījāvadhānam
Constant attention to the seed. 3/16 3.15

The supreme seed of all the universe is said to be the conscious nature (*cidātman*). The attention (the yogi) pays to it with an alert mind[40] is the reflective awareness (inherent in it). The clutches of delusion and the rest destroyed, it is the attainment of the plane of eternity.

* * *

The means to realise the inherent nature (*svarūpa*, of all things which abides) unaffected by time is an attentive mind (*cittāvadhāna*), (which develops) once (the yogi) has eliminated the limited ego through continuous and assiduous practise at the empowered level of being which is the (universal) cause of all things.

Exposition

According to Kṣemarāja the "seed" is "the supreme power (*parāśakti*) which is the pulsing radiance (of the light of consciousness) and the cause of all things."[41] But basically both commentators agree that this aphorism teaches that the yogi must continue to sustain his state of awareness at all times even when he has reached the highest level of consciousness. He must repeatedly plunge back into his realisation of the divine nature of all things and his own being to thus reabsorb the finite mind (*citta*), directed at outer objectivity and hence set in time, into the eternity of the creative movement of the energy of consciousness.

* * *

How can (the yogi) penetrate again into the conscious nature (out of) which all things arise by the practise of Yoga? (In reply to this question) Śaṅkara said:

āsanasthaḥ sukhaṃ hrade nimajjati
(Confortably) seated (the yogi) sinks effortlessly into the lake (of consciousness). 3/17 3.16

The seat wise yogis take by (stimulating) the Movement of the Fish (*matsyavalana*)[42] is the Central (upward moving) Breath, (called) the "Purifying Fire" (*pavamāna*), the Radiance (*śuci*) and Wrath (*caṇḍa*). (The seat is) also (the Seed) mentioned before and the one established there sinks effortlessly into the lake (of consciousness). (Universal consciousness possesses) the lake-like quality mentioned above[43] because it is the source of all things and so is described as the seed-like quality of the conscious nature.

Attentive concentration (*avadhāna*) is said to be the means to conquer time and contemplative penetration (*anupraveśa*), passion so that one can attain the state free of birth and death.

* * *

Wise yogis apply themselves to practise by means of the applied persevering application of the technique (*vṛtti*) which can be achieved by means of the effort proper to the Yoga which serves to penetrate into the conscious nature. When coupled with the practise of breath retention through which both currents of the breath are (suspended), the 'radiance' which is a synonym for the fire of the Ascending Breath (*udāna*) that is to be generated by the union of the Solar and Lunar (breaths) is projected upwards as the current of the exhaled breath. In this way it gradually traverses all the lower levels from the base (*ādhāra*) upwards until, reaching the Twelve-finger Space, repose (within consciousness) is produced. The Ascending Breath thus burns the fuel of duality and so is "wrathful." It also brings about the highest form of purification and so is the purifying fire. By penetrating into it (one) plunges completely into the nectarine ocean of Śiva-consciousness in the Twelve-finger Space out of which pour the waves of cosmic diversity (*viśvavaicitrya*). Those intent on savouring the aesthetic delight of incessent sexual union (*nirantarasaṃbhogarasa*) by practising the above means, attain the absolute and eternal plane of power and (their attainment) is unconditioned freedom unaffected by either inner or outer diversification (*kalanā*).

Exposition

According to Bhāskara, the yogi's seat is the flow of the Upward Moving Breath (*udānaprāṇa*) which emerges in the centre between the inhaled and exhaled breath (*prāṇa* and *apāna*). As it rises, it burns away all duality and purifies the yogi's consciousness until, carried along by it, he merges with the source of all the breaths and attains the supreme plane of divine power beyond time where he becomes master of the unobstructed freedom of consciousness.

Kṣemarāja's explanation is different. According to him the time comes when the yogi constantly reflects inwardly on the oneness of his true nature and so no longer needs to exert himself. His seat and constant support is the supreme strength of the power of consciousness (*paraśāktabala*). The practise of meditation and the higher levels of contemplative absorption are abandoned and there is nothing more for him to do. Enjoying the ease and bliss of the higher levels of practise the yogi has simply to relax and feel all the limitations imposed on his awareness by his body and mind dissolve away as he plunges into the great lake of consciousness which, full of the nectar of immortality, is the primordial source of all things, and so becomes one with it. Kṣemarāja quotes the *Netratantra* as saying:

> One must not meditate on anything above, below, in the centre, in front, behind or to either side. One should not contemplate anything within the body or outside it. Do not fix your attention on the sky nor below (on the earth). Neither close the eyes nor gaze fixedly. Think not of the support, the supported or the supportless, nor of the senses or of the gross elements or sound, taste, and touch, etc. Having abandoned (everything) in this way be established in contemplation (*samādhi*) and become one. That is said to be the supreme state of Śiva, the supreme soul. Having attained to that unmanifest (*nirābhāsa*) plane, one no longer falls from it.[44]

* * *

(Śiva), the One Whose Sign is the Bull, said the following to explain that repose in this way in the agential aspect (of consciousness) is unconditioned freedom through which He (and the liberated yogi) has the power to do (all things, *kartṛtva*):

svamātrā nirmāṇam āpādayati
(Śiva) fashions the world by means of His mother. 3/18 3.17

The Supreme Lord's capacity to know and do (all things) is His (inherent) power, for it is His (inner) strength and vitality, the cause of the origination of phenomenal existence. And so She is the power holder's supreme (power) and the mother of the universe. Through Her, His own

mother, the all-pervasive Lord fashions (all things) as He wishes in an instant (*aśu*) by that power of freedom.

* * *

(The yogi attains) repose on that (higher) plane (of consciousness) by assiduously practising the means described above, namely, attentive concentration and contemplative penetration (into the conscious nature). By his omnipotent power which can make manifest things that have never been made manifest before and reposing on that plane, he can fashion whatever he wishes, whether manifest as subject or object. (Thus his) creation serves as a sign that he reposes in the abode of freedom.

Exposition

Kṣemarāja takes this aphorism to mean: (*The yogi*) *fashions the world by an aspect of his nature.* Essentially, however, the commentators agree that this aphorism refers to the divine creative power the yogi acquires when, as Kṣemarāja explains, through his practise at the individual (*āṇava*) level he conquers delusion and attains the energy (*bala*) of the empowered (*śākta*) state of Pure Knowledge to reach the level of Śiva-consciousness (*śāmbhavapada*). Now, through his fully expanded and pure consciousness, the yogi can generate the world of diversity as he likes by separating a part of his universal nature off from himself in such a way that it condenses down to the level of objectivity.[45] Thus, as he emerges from the unmanifest state to that of manifestation, girted about by the limiting conditions of finitude, he carries with him the inner consciousness of the subject which flows out into the moulds of outer objectivity. He realises, in other words, that the objective world is nothing but an outer objectivized projection of Śiva, the one universal subject, and that each particular object is a tiny, gross fragment of the infinite, supremely subtle consciousness which is the yogi's true nature. Thus the yogi who realises, as verse 30 of the *Stanzas* declares, that the whole universe is, in this sense, nothing but the play of consciousness, is liberated in this very life, even as he perceives the world of diversity.

* * *

This, (the individual soul's true) nature, is shrouded with impurity due (to his limited) intellect. By the destruction (of this impurity) rebirth ceases. (So the lord) went on to say:

vidyāvināśe janmavināśaḥ
Once (limited) knowledge is destroyed, rebirth is destroyed. 3/19 3./8

Conditioned, empirical knowledge is termed "impure knowledge" and is the cause of rebirth. The destruction (of impure knowledge) is consonant with the contemplative awareness (*nibhālana*) that the innate knowledge (*sahajavidyā*) (inherent in consciousness) is dawning. When this happens, it engenders the supreme manifestation of the freedom of the Self. And so, by grounding (awareness) in the power inherent in one's own nature (*svabala*), rebirth ceases. This perfection (*siddhi*) is liberation in this very life (*jīvanmukti*) which bestows (upon the yogi) the timeless state of being (*akālapada*)

* * *

Impure knowledge is defined as empirircal knowledge (*vṛttijñāna*) which, because it is inlaid (*khacita*) with the form of the things (of this world), serves as a means to obtain objectively perceivable results. This (form of knowledge) is binding. By reflecting on the pure knowledge (of self-awareness) which is its opposite, one realises (one's own) innate consciousness (*sahajasaṃvit*) through which one acquires the vitality inherent in one's own nature (*svavīrya*). When this takes place, the bondage of *karma* consisting of the aggregate of the body, senses (and mind), etc., fashioned by the coupled (effects) of the two impurities, *māyīyamala* (which engenders the notion of duality) and *āṇavamala* (which contracts consciousness), is destroyed.

Exposition

Kṣemarāja understands this aphorism to mean: *Due to the continued existence of (pure) knowledge, re-birth is destroyed.* But despite the divergence, Kṣemarāja makes much the same point as Bhāskara, namely that the awakening realisation of enlightenment is a constantly renewing and renewed process. The wisdom and insight inherent in consciousness is constantly emerging afresh. When this happens, the conditions of mind and body which give rise to the suffering and troubles of transmigration have no time to form. Viewing all things as the harmony of Śiva's consciousness, there is no space for conflict and the limiting knowledge of the finite.

* * *

(Impure) knowledge is intent on that which is objectively perceivable because it is sullied by the limitations imposed by external objects. The Unborn Lord said the following to explain what impels it:

kavargādiṣu māheśvaryādyāḥ paśumātaraḥ
Māheśvarī and the other mothers of the soul in bondage reside in the gutterals and the other classes of consonants. 3/20

The aggregated totality of speech (*śabdarāśi* which reposes in consciousness at one with it) is the universal nature of all things.[46] To it belongs the (binding) power (*kalā*), whose nature has already been explained, (that obscures) the fettered soul which, pervaded by speech (*śabda*), gives rise to mental representations (*pratyaya*).[47] (This power) is said to possess two forms according to whether it is a seed (*bīja*) or matrix of generation (*yoni*). The seed is Śiva Himself while the matrix of generation is the power called Māyā and consists of the eight classes of phonemes that range from 'K' to 'KṢ'. The eight (mothers) *Māheśvarī*, etc., bestow the higher fruits (of Yoga) and the lower fruits (of *karma*) and reside there so that the fettered may gain knowledge of outer things. (Every one of) the eight mothers possesses three aspects in each one of the

classes (of consonants). (The first is represented by) the power *Ghorā* which engenders attachment to the fruit of mixed (good and bad) action. The power *Ghoratarā* throws down those whose mind is attached to sense objects to increasingly lower levels (of consciousness), while the power *Aghorā* bestows Śiva. It is in this latter aspect that Bhairava's eternal Being (*bhairavatā*) resides.

* * *

The supreme power of speech is one with Śiva. It generates three powers, namely, those of will (knowledge and action) and, having done so, engenders within each individual, fettered soul (the power of) *Mātṛkā* (which operates) on the level of discursively conceptualizing consciousness (*savikalpa-saṃvedana*) and consists of (the energies of) the phonemes and those of the classes to which they belong. (Thus) it gives rise to the reflective awareness of inner subtle and gross speech. (*Mātṛkā*) induces the spread of attachment, aversion, passion and greed, etc. (in the minds of the fettered) through (the divine power of) *Māheśvarī* and the other (mothers) who preside over the classes (of consonants) and so engenders (the mistaken sense of) oneness (the fettered feel) with their body, etc. Thus extending their activity in this way through the senses, the mothers, *Māheśvarī* and the rest called *Ghorā*, etc., cast down the fettered who do not attend to their own nature (to lower levels of consciousness) by the attachment they feel for the objects of the senses. (Things, however, are different for those who) have mastered (these forces, *pati*, and are no longer their slaves, *paśu*). They do not engender the perception of duality (*bhedaprathā*, in them) but inspire them with a sense of wonder initially and then fill them with the aesthetic delight of the expansion of their own nature (*svātmavikāsarasa*).

Exposition

This aphorism goes on to warn the yogi of the potential dangers of getting lost in the realms of thought forms. The pure power of awareness functioning at the supreme level of speech spontaneously issues forth from itself and moves down to the sphere of thought and articulated speech. As we have seen, this descent coincides with the diversification of the power of consciousness as the letters of the alphabet, then to the formation of words and finally to that of sentences through which thought constructs are created. The classes of consonants are thus represented as the mothers or wombs (*yoni*) of diversity and the vowels as the seeds (*bīja*). When these two unite, the world of speech is made manifest.

The unenlightened cannot follow this process consciously and so are caught in the welter of emotions which words, whether thought or uttered, inspire in him. The enlightened yogi, however, is established in the introverted awareness of subjectivity represented by the vowels and so is master of the energies of the consonants and is not bound by them. Thus, the eight powers presiding over the eight classes of consonants can either elevate the soul, in which case they are called *Aghorāśaktis*, or throw him down, in which case they are called *Ghoratarāśaktis*. They manifest as *Ghorāśaktis* when the individual is caught halfway between these two extremes and is attached to the mixed fruits of his actions.

* * *

These are the three aspects of the Aggregate of Words (*śabdarāśi*) each of which is born of the eight classes (of consonants). (It is similarly threefold) in the case of (any) aggregate of phonemes (which happens to constitute a word or Mantra), each aspect corresponding to the beginning, middle or end of its utterance. (The Lord then) explained how (the yogi realises his own) Śiva-nature (*śivatā*) by the union (of these three).

triṣu caturthaṁ tailavadāsecyam
The Fourth should be sprinkled like oil
into the three. 3/21

The remaining reality that abides within the three energies (*Aghorā, Ghorā* and *Ghoratarā*) mentioned above and in the phonemes, here (called) the Fourth, is Śiva, the

supreme reality (*para*). (The yogi) should contemplate Him and sprinkle Him in the three like oil in water. (Thus the yogi attains) the perfection (*siddhi*) which persists constantly because (he realises that he) pervades (all three).

* * *

Thought constructs (*vikalpa*) (are verbal mental representations) which consist essentially of gross phonemic sounds and subtle ones (the mind both perceives and produces). Their existence is sustained by *Ghorā*, *Aghorā* and the other energies (which bind) the fettered as described in the previous aphorism. (The yogi) should sprinkle the initial (state when they arise) and the final (when they fall away) with the juice (*rasa*, of the aesthetic delight) of consciousness, that is, with (the consciousness the yogi) perceives as their underlying sustaining ground. (The yogi) should, in other words, first reflect how (thought constructs) are consciousness and then, eliminating the perception of duality by gradually extending the pervasive presence of (the consciousness) which sustains them, like oil (that is soaked up gradually by a cloth), he should contemplate their basic state (*avasthiti*) as being the juice (of the aesthetic delight) of consciousness so that the binding activity of these (energies) may come to a halt.

Exposition

Kṣemarāja's understanding of this aphorism is quite different. According to him, the 'three states' are, as one would expect, those of waking, dreaming and deep sleep. Thus, Kṣemarāja says that this aphorism goes on to explain how the yogi is to maintain his awareness of his own nature in all these three states in order not to loose sight at any time of the Pure Knowledge he has gained through the previous practises.

The yogi is instructed to pay close attention to the moment of transition from one state to the next. He must lay hold of the centre between the cessation of one state of consciousness and the unfolding of another. There, between waking and dreaming, dreaming and deep sleep, etc., he discovers the blissful abode of the Fourth State (*turīya*) brilliant with the light of Pure Knowledge. To the degree in which he manages to attend to the centre, the savour (*rasa*) of consciousness gradually pervades these states like oil sprinkled on a cloth, until all three are constantly experienced by the yogi in the contemplative absorption of the Fourth State.

* * *

Then (the Lord) explained the means by which (the yogi) can penetrate (the energy of each) phoneme:

magnaḥ svacittena[48] *praviśet*
Merged (in his own nature, the yogi) must penetrate (the phonemes) with his mind. 3/22 3.21

The all-pervasive Lord assumes the form of outer reality (*bāhyākāratā*) in the act of moving (out of Himself). He withdraws (His outer form) into Himself when (this outgoing movement gives way to) the emergence of the (opposite) movement which preceded it and so Śiva merges into His own nature when the outward movement ceases. When (the yogi) becomes Śiva in this way by withdrawing (*nimeṣa*, his energies from the outer world) he should use his mind (*cetas*) to enter the phonemes (of his Mantra) as fire does burning coals. Then, by applying *Bhairavamudrā* (*bhairavavṛtti*, through which the power of consciousness expands),"[49] (the yogi's) Mantra becomes supremely vitalized and (he acquires many powers including that of) transfering his consciousness into another's body.[50] When this takes place the Śiva and Bhairava nature of Mantras is clearly manifest (to him) for otherwise why should Mantra, that consists (merely of) phonemic sounds, be the Lord Himself?

* * *

It is because the powers of knowledge and action have been set into operation and are extending their activity that the Lord of Consciousness Who is their possessor and desires to move (out of Himself), is intent on outer objectivity. By withdrawing this activity (*vṛtti*), tinged with outer objects, the yogi should penetrate the phonemes (of his Mantra), as fire does burning coals, through an act of awareness free of thought constructs. When (he) penetrates the phonemes (in this way) he also manages to vitalize (his) Mantra, etc., by means of the *bhairavamudrā* he has accomplished.

Exposition

Kṣemarāja, unlike Bhāskara, sees no special connection between this aphorism and the practise of Mantra and its power but reads it simply to mean that: (*with his limited subjectivity*) *submerged* (*the yogi*) *must penetrate* (*into the power of consciousness*) *by means of his* (*thought-free*) *mind*. Consistent with his understanding of the previous aphorism, Kṣemarāja sees this one as teaching what the yogi must do once the subjective awareness of the Fourth State has pervaded the other states and he has merged the limited egoity associated with the body and mind, etc., into the aesthetic delight of universal consciousness to experience the pulsing vitality of awareness. Rising from the individual (*āṇava*) level to that Beyond Mind (*unmanā*), he becomes absorbed and at one with his true nature through an inner act of non-discursive awareness. The mind, individual consciousness, breath and ego dissolve away[51] and the yogi's individual mental activity is united with the universal activity of consciousness by virtue of which he attains Śivahood and is liberated. Kṣemarāja quotes the *Hymn to the Womb of Knowledge* (*Jñānagarbhastotra*):

> O Mother, having abandoned all mental activity and, no longer bound to pursuing the activity of the senses, the brilliance of which depends (on outer objectivity), those men who by Your grace are established (in their own nature), instantly experience the supreme plane which pours forth untiringly the incomparably blissful nectar (of immortality).[52]

* * *

The Lord then uttered the following aphorism to explain what happens when divested (of the consciousness) which precedes and succeeds it, a phoneme abides alone:

madhye'varaprasavaḥ
The emergence of the lower (plane) occurs
in the centre. 3/23 3.23

Kshemaraja's 3.22 in Baskara's 3.23

A phoneme is, in the course of its utterance, divided into three parts: the beginning, the middle and the end. Śiva's Being (*śivarūpatā*) abides in the first and last of these which correspond to the intent to existence (*udbubhūṣā*) and repose (in universal consciousness), respectively. Emergence in the centre of these two is the fall of the fettered soul (from the awareness of pure consciousness) into the mere (inert sound) of the phoneme (for) the teaching is that (it is at the beginning and the end that) the Lord's empowered (*śākta*) nature is clearly manifest.

* * *

Śiva can easily be realised (while one speaks or intones a Mantra) at the beginning when one intends to speak or at the end (when the utterance) ceases. This is because there the gross aggregates of phonemes (of corporeal speech) and the subtle (inner sound of thought) at the middle level of speech fuse in the undivided unity of the Voice of Intuition (and that of Supreme Speech). In the middle, however, (the phonemes) manifest as aggregates, each with its own diverse form, and so (the yogi's awareness) falls from the presence of consciousness free of thought constructs.

Exposition

As before, Kṣemarāja's explanation of this aphorism differs from Bhāskara's because he understands it with reference to how the yogi can develop and maintain the higher consciousness of the Fourth State (*turīya*) in relation to the other three states of waking, dreaming and deep sleep. Kṣemarāja warns him to be careful because he is liable to fall as he makes the transition from one state of consciousness to the other. When the yogi succeeds in catching hold of the inner flow of the savour (*rasa*) of the Fourth State in all three states, he is led to the unifying consciousness of the state Beyond the Fourth (*turīyātīta*) from which he never strays to lower states. If, however, he merely rests content with the experience of the Fourth State in the gap between the impending outpouring of one state and the coming to rest of the previous one, his lack of awareness at other times inevitably entangles him in the downward flow of the diversity of perceptions in the centre between these gaps, engendered by the latent traces of past experience, and he is thrown out of his contemplative state into the bondage of conditioned consciousness.

* * *

Now given that this is (each phoneme's) three-fold nature, (Śiva), Pārvatī's Beloved, went on to say the following to explain what (their) oneness (*sāmya*) is:

prāṇasamācāre samadarśanam
When the breath moves uniformly one has an equal vision of all things. 3/24

The highest (faculty the soul possesses) is its innate capacity to know and do all things. (This power) which can impart life to all things (*sarvānuprāṇana*) is the vital breath (*prāṇa*) also known as the Supreme Resonance (*paranāda* of consciousness). Its uniform movement is the contemplative penetration (*āveśa*) radiantly manifest in (every) phoneme, word and individual soul and the experience of unity one has through it is the equal vision of all things. No wonder then that by seizing that strength (*bala*) in this way,[53] Mantras and phonemes are endowed with the power of omniscience.

* * *

The point is that (the yogi) attains the supreme vitality which comes from his being well established in the (uninterrupted) flow of his practise centred on the experience of the oneness of every Mantra and word, etc., that emerges (from the highest level of consciousness) down to that of corporeal speech by the unifying contemplation (*samāpatti*) that (he experiences) in the autonomous light (of consciousness) known as the Supreme Resonance (*paranāda*, of awareness), which is the life of all that manifests (*sarvaprakāśa*).

Exposition

What Bhāskara is saying here basically is that the yogi who manages to maintain a constant flow of awareness in harmony with the rhythm of the breath in the moments of its emergence, movement and cessation, experiences the pure vitality (*prāṇana*) of consciousness which creates and knows all things. All the letters, words and sentences he utters or thinks then become equally empowered with the innate strength of the yogi's nature and a means by which he can penetrate, instantly and without effort, through the veil of thought.

Kṣemarāja reads this aphorism differently. According to him, it means: (*The yogi*) *views all things equally when he exhales slowly and correctly*. The yogi, once merged in pure transcendental consciousness where all his thoughts, perceptions, mind, senses and breath have dissolved away, must rise from his internal absorption (*nimīlana samādhi*). His aim is to maintain this pure state of awareness, that is, consciousness of the Fourth State (*turīya*), when he returns to the usual fluctuations of the three states of waking, dreaming and deep sleep. The breath, which was drawn in and arrested when he turned inwards has thus, as Kṣemarāja puts it, been "purified by the fragrance of (God's divine power) which is the supreme radiance (of consciousness)."[54] Now he must slowly let it out as his consciousness flows out to the outer world of experience. If this is done correctly, the yogi does not feel that the breath exits from his essential conscious nature. The flow from inner to outer, which at the individual level is represented by the exhalation of the breath corresponds, at the empowered (*śākta*) level, to the flow of awareness from subject to object and, at the level of Śiva-consciousness (*śāmbhava*), to the movement of the power of the will to that of action. All three aspects of this flow are now experienced as one internal movement. The yogi's awareness is recognised to be a single, compact mass of consciousness and bliss, present on all planes. All relative distinctions between good and evil, high and low social status, bondage and liberation, etc., now loose all meaning for him for he sees all things as being equally the bliss of universal consciousness even when his senses and mind are actively engaged in the activities of normal mundane existence.

* * *

Having explained how the phonemes are vitalized, Śambhu accordingly went on to explain how the body of phenomena (*bhāvaśarīra*), etc., are given life:

mātrāsvapratyayasaṃdhāne naṣṭasya punarutthānam
That which was destroyed arises once more in the course of the unifying awareness of one's own perception of the individual units of experience. 3/25 3.24

The functional energies (*kalā*) of the group of categories ranging from Māyā to Earth are the individual units of experience (*mātrā*) (understood as) the manifestations of each category in its own specific field (of manifestation). One's own perception of each one is the cognitive awareness (*jñāna*) which fills it (with its vital presence and in so doing functions) as the unifying awareness (that connects them together) and rests in the (one) acting subject (*kartṛ*, engaged in the act of perception). When this takes place, the phenomena (and other functions which concur to generate the objective world) that were destroyed, manifest once more. Thus the (diverse) perceptions of the individual elements of experience are unified by penetrating into the (underlying) acting subjectivity (which generates and hence connects them all together). Wherever this occurs the (conscious) agency (is activated) which consists of a perfectly stable state of conscious absorption in the power of omniscience.

* * *

The meaning is as follows. The functional energies (*kalā*) of the categories that range from Māyā to Earth are the material cause of the elemental body (*bhūtaśarīra*). Once they are generated (*niṣpādya*) as the aesthetic delight (*rasa*) of consciousness by connecting them together in the unifying perception of their oneness with one's own nature, the phenomenal body (*bhāvaśarīra*) which is the locus of sound and the other objects of the senses (also) manifests (*udeti*) as the aesthetic delight of uninterrupted (*ghana*) consciousness and bliss. In this way (the yogi) gains the energy (*vīrya*) generated by penetrating (*samāveśa*) into the plane of universal agency, etc., and so realises everywhere the supreme sovereign freedom (of consciousness) which is (the universal) cognizing and acting subjectivity that, full and perfect (*paripūrṇa*), (perceives and does all things).

Exposition

Again Kṣemarāja understands this aphorism differently, although in a way compatible with Bhāskara's interpretation. According to him it means: *By reflecting on one's own perception of things, that which was lost again emerges.* As Kṣemarāja reverses the order of the previous two aphorisms he understands this one as showing the way in which the yogi can regain the yogic consciousness of the Fourth State should he loose it when he enters one of the other states. Thus, according to Kṣemarāja, this aphorism basically teaches how the yogi is to experience his true nature not only in the Fourth State but also in the others where, through lack of awareness, the lower-order subject has taken over the functions of the higher. To do this the yogi need not attempt to check the flow of perceptions or thoughts. Instead, he should seek the knower and agent of the manifest aspect of the categories of existence apparent to him. By cultivating the awareness that 'I am all this', the yogi again catches hold of the bliss of the Fourth State in the moment of self-realisation and recognises that whatever he may see, hear, think about or apprehend is nothing but an aspect of his own universal nature. His mind becomes steady and he enjoys rest within himself. Kṣemaraja quotes the *Svacchandatantra* as saying:

> Even the mind of yogis is forceably made unsteady (by the desire for worldly pleasure).(But) the mind which is (pure) Being, the ultimate object of realisation (*jñeya*), stable and complete in all respects never wavers whatever be the state of its possessor. Reflect on the reality (all) seek to know (*jñeya*) wherever the mind happens to move for as all things are Śiva, once it moves where can it go?[55]

* * *

How is (the yogi) who is constantly dedicated (to this practise)? (The Lord) said:

śivatulyo jāyate
He becomes like śiva. 3/26 3.25

Amongst (all) the causes that concur (to give rise to phenomenal existence) Śiva stands supreme. His nature is consciousness and form boundless Light (*nirupādhijyotis*). Thus because (Śiva is such and) the adept constantly applies himself (to the practise of Yoga), he is like Him (in all respects) even while he acts (in this world) and is liberated in this very life by the vitality (*vīrya*) of that higher knowledge we spoke about before.

* * *

(The yogi) who is constantly dedicated (to this practise) has attained, through his intense pursuit of Śiva's true nature, (Śiva's own) level of existence and so savours the bliss of liberation in this very life even while the energies which function through the body (*dehakalā*) continue (to operate) and so is like Śiva. Eventually, when the worldly experience which has falled to his lot and that which he must still enjoy is exhausted, he is liberated after the death of the body (*videhamukti*) and then attains a state of identity (*tādātmya*, with Śiva).

Exposition

Kṣemarāja explains that once the yogi has succeeded in experiencing the Fourth State (*turīya*) which is self-realisation in all states, he rises to the level Beyond the Fourth (*turīyātīta*) in which he identifies with Śiva. This aphorism points out that he is not as yet absolutely identical with Śiva. Although the yogi is liberated in this life (*jīvanmukta*), it is not until the last traces of *Karma*, which still hold him down to the level of embodied existence, have worked themselves out and he quits the body that he becomes Śiva in every respect.

* * *

Now to what is one who practises in this way constantly dedicated? In reply, the Blessed One spoke the following aphorism which describes (this yogi's) vow:

śarīravṛttirvratam
The activity of the body is the vow. 3/27 3.26

(This yogi) performs the Great Vow of abiding in his own unfettered nature. (His) five insignias (*mudrā*) are the body, that is, the skeleton, the skull, the anklets, the backbone, which represents the stick, and the bones which are those of the hands, feet and neck. The ashes (he smears on his body) is the supreme radiance (of consciousness) and the three qualities (*guṇa*), the sacred thread. His banner is the Great Path[56] and ornaments, the senses. His sport is to play among the objects of the senses and he delights constantly in the cremation ground of the Heart (of consciousness) illumined in his body, speech and mind. Whatever he does is the eternal festival of the Lord of the Heroes.

* * *

He who is well practised in the way described attains success in the Great Vow, the Vow of the Pāśupatas.[57] The accessories he should use are not those visible to all. These include, the skeleton, skull, stick, five insignias, ash, sacred thread, banner, ornaments, dwelling and sportive behaviour. (The ascetic) who sports visible signs and so makes a show of himself as a follower of Dharma (*dharmadhvajin*) is sullied by impurity.

Exposition

Although the liberated yogi must continue to reside in his body until the remnants of the fruits of his past actions are exhausted, he accepts his lot joyfully. He lives without care for what he will eat or where he will find shelter, accepting whatever comes to him without concern for his personal well being. To the outer observer he appears to behave and talk like any other man. Concealing his true spiritual stature from the prying gaze of the public, the elevating powers of consciousness converge upon him. Untouched by good or evil, the reflective awareness he has of his own nature coincides with that of Śiva Himself. Thus, one with consciousness, he rests on the supreme plane (*anuttara*) where the brilliant radiance of his own nature is his constant worship.[58] This same self-awareness enlivens his body, mind and breath; it rises in an uninterrupted flow to the highest reaches of consciousness, like a flame from a fire, to dissolve in the infinite.[59] Thus his every action, however ordinary it may seem to others, is a ritual gesture (*mudrā*) which forms a part of his uninterrupted worship of his own nature manifest within him and everywhere around him. Thus, as all he does and his very body are the signs (*mudrā*) of his ascetic attainments, Bhāskara shows how these correspond to the outer signs that Pāśupata and other such yogi's wear. Indeed, without the former the latter are useless, merely outer shows that, far from being a token of spiritual development, restrict consciousness further.

* * *

Now how does one who performs this vow recite Mantra ?

kathā japaḥ

Common talk is (his) recitation of Mantra. 3/28 3.27

Once the awakened (*prabuddha*) yogi's level of consciousness has risen to that of (the universal) agent, all that he says is (his) recitation of Mantra. Observing his vow and reciting Mantra (in this way), he is the best of men (*puruṣottama*). His common talk is the flow (*sañcāra*) of his utterances (each) supported by the vitality (of consciousness) and is the recitation of Mantra which should thus be known to be of four kinds; namely, the empowered (*śākta*) recitation, the recitation of the Gander (*haṃsa*), the recitation of the individual soul (*paudgala*) and the recitation without parts (*niṣkala*). The recitation without parts is the (reflective awareness of) the components of OṂ (*praṇava*) while the recitation of the Gander (*haṃsa*) is (the awareness) of the energy of the divine resonance of consciousness (*nāda*). The recitation of the individual soul is (the abiding awareness) of the movement of the breath as it flows (ebbing and flowing) constantly 21,600 times (a day).

* * *

The Lord of the Heroes Who observes the Great Vow and has reached the level of consciousness to contemplate the Supreme Egoity (*parāhaṃbhāva*, of universal consciousness), recites Mantra constantly and without interruption. By means of the very essence of the reflective awareness (he has) of the deity of his own nature he recites the four types of Mantra; namely, that without parts, the Gander, that of the individual soul and the empowered.

Exposition

Established in the pure Mantric energy of the universal ego, the continuous flow of the yogi's awareness is the constant emergence and subsidence of Mantra. Empowered by the omniscient awareness of the pure cognition of universal consciousness, the yogi repeatedly rises to the highest state and redescends to that of everyday life. This vibration is the resonance (*nāda*)[60] or enounciation of energy (*śāktoccāra*) within consciousness. It is one level at which the yogi speaks and, in so doing, recites Mantra. Again, at another level, constantly mindful as he is of the sound of the movement of his breath, the yogi recites *Ajapa Gāyatrī Mantra,* i.e., *Haṃsa,* which is repeated automatically within his body 21,000 times a day. Finally, every word he utters, mindful of the 'soundless sound' of awareness from which it springs and to which it returns, is also his Mantra. Thus at every level of his being the yogi participates in the sacred and makes it manifest through his every perception, thought, word and deed.

* * *

What is the gift by which the wise (yogi) who is thus perfected, devoted to the observance of (this) vow and the recitation of Mantra may be known? (In reply) Śaṅkara said:

dānam ātmajñānam
Self-knowledge is the boon. 3/29

As we have already explained and will do so again later, the best and highest knowledge is insight into one's own nature (*ātmasvarūpa*). Its correct revelation (to others) is the greatest boon those awakened by the power of grace (can bestow) here in this world. Their gift (*dāna*) completely severs (*kṣapaṇa*) the bonds of the fettered and so is called "initiation" (*dīkṣā*) which bestows (*dāna,* self-realisation) and destroys (*kṣapaṇa,* all bondage).

* * *

The boon of those who have been blessed with an intense descent of the power of grace, observe the vow and recite Mantra in the way described, is the self-knowledge described previously which ought to be revealed, in the manner explained above and to be further explained, to the fettered. This is because those who are the objects of grace are fit for the initiation (that bestows) the boon of self-realisation and destroys all the fetters that restrict consciousness (*āṇava*).

Exposition

Graced with an intense descent of power (*tīvraśaktipāta*), the yogi is granted an insight into his true nature. To receive this boon is to be given the fullness and wholeness of one's own nature, to free it from all duality, to purify it of illusion and protect it from the forces which obscure the awareness it has of itself. Moreover, the yogi bestows the same gift he received through enlightenment to his disciples. Once the yogi enjoys the freedom and wisdom of the highest level of consciousness there is nothing left for him to do except elevate others. As Abhinava says:

> People, occupied as they are with their own affairs, normally do nothing for others. The activity of those in whom every stain of phenomenal existence has been destroyed and are identified with Bhairava, full of Him, is intended only for the benefit of the world.[61]

* * *

The all-pervasive Lord Who creates, preserves, destroys, protects and graces is nothing but the Self because Śiva is its true nature. (*Śiva*), Who bears the crescent moon, uttered (the following) aphorism which, (can be read) in sections and as a whole, in order to describe what it is:

yovipastho jñāhetuśca
Knowledge and the cause reside in the cosmic nature and the source (of the universe). 3/30 3.29

The Lord is the highest reality for He is the source (*yoni*) of the universe. He is both knowledge and action because He reduces (all that) should be abandoned to a worthless nothing (*tucchīkaraṇa*). Thus the yogi who, endowed with knowledge, abides in the cosmic nature is, as we have already explained, the most excellent cause of both liberation and worldly enjoyment (*bhoga*). The Lord of yogis who is thus perfectly (*samyak*) absorbed in the active agency (of consciousness, *kartṛṃśa*) and so has realised his stable state of

being (*sthiti*) resides in the cosmic nature and is the supreme cause of the (development of that) knowledge (in others).

The group of mothers (which operates in the limited consciousness of) the fettered governs them. The Self resides pulsing radiantly in the midst (of these obscuring forces) and so is the Lord of the Wheel (of Energies). Thus (these powers) are the functional potencies (*vṛtti*) of the Bhairava of Consciousness (*cidbhairava*) and are said to be the rays (of His divine light) which worship (Him) perpetually by (offering Him) the pleasures (*bhoga*) of sound and the other objects of the senses. The all-pervasive Lord of one's own consciousness is the means (*hetu*) by which (one achieves) knowledge of the group of Mothers.

* * *

Paraśiva is the universal cause of all things. His nature is knowledge and action and He reduces (all that) should be abandoned to a worthless nothing (*tucchīkaraṇa*). The yogi who, through His grace, abides in the abode from which all things emanate becomes, by virtue of the perfect omniscience and other (divine attributes he finds there), a veritable vessel of liberation and bliss.

(Again, another interpretation is the following): the lord of yogis whose consciousness has risen to the level of that of the (universal) agent attains thereby his stable state of being and so can, by the power of his insight, awaken those fit to receive instruction.

Yet another (way of understanding this aphorism is this): The Self shines radiantly as the Lord of the Wheel (of energies) in the midst of *Māheśvarī* and the other (powers which constitute) the group of Mothers that support (the limited consciousness of the) individual fettered perceiving subject. (These powers) are the functional potencies of consciousness which, sustained by *Mātṛkāśakti*, are the rays (of the light of the Self) that, drawing the essential being of the objects of the senses (towards the universal consciousness of the Self), worship it thus perpetually. Therefore, because these energies reside within (the Self) and can have no independent existence of their own apart from it, they sustain it in order to make themselves manifest. In short, (the Self) is the outpouring of divine power (*śāktollāsa*).

Exposition

Kṣemarāja offers two explanations of this aphorism. According to one interpretation, the meaning would be: *the Lord of yogis who is established in the abode of the consciousness which is his own essential nature by the power of (his) reflective awareness should be known to be the (universal) knower and agent (of all things).*[62] The second interpretation is the one Kṣemarāja prefers and largely coincides with the one Bhāskara offers. From this point of view, the aphorism means: *He who is established in the Wheel of Energies is the source of knowledge.*[63] The Wheel of Energies is in this case, as Bhāskara also says, the group of Mothers, *Māheśvarī*, etc., who preside over the various classes of phonemes. The enlightened yogi sets aside all the limited knowledge and action they engender to become the Lord of the Wheel, thus taking possession of himself as the universal agent in the centre of the circle from which the universe is emanated. As the Master and agent of the activity of the Wheel of Energies he has the power to enlighten others and bestow on them the supreme bliss and freedom of liberation.

* * *

(Śiva then) explained that His form as the energy (of consciousness) is the universe:

svaśaktipracayo'sya viśvam
The universe is the aggregate of his powers. 3/31 3.30

In this way the powers of (Śiva) the power-holder are those of consciousness and the rest. The pulsations (*spanda*) of their ever-renewed outpouring are said to be their aggregates. Know these to be the universe, for the all-pervasive Lord manifests as power in the form of the universe and in so doing manifests (only) Himself at all times.

* * *

The universe is Śiva in the form of His absolute energy and, because the yogi is similar to Śiva (in all respects), the power of his consciousness is fully expanded (in the same way) as the vibrant radiance of the power of action made up of the pulsation of its wonderfully diverse and constantly renewed outpouring. The entire range of objectivity, whether external like the colour blue, or internal, like the feeling of pleasure, participates, in the course of its perception, in the repose the light (of consciousness enjoys in its own nature). In so doing (each object) attains its own specific phenomenal form (*svavyavasthāpana*), for otherwise it would appear to be unreasonable to establish the nature (of anything) just as it is in itself (*svasiddhi*). Therefore, it is one's own consciousness alone that manifests itself in this way and that as the wonderful diversity of all things, like one who is free to desire whatever he likes. Thus, because the power (of consciousness) and its possessor are one, it is Śiva Himself Who manifests in this way.

Exposition

As nothing can exist apart from our perception of it, and consciousness, conceived as a state of pure cognitive awareness, is the necessary ground of all perception, the yogi who identifies with consciousness is the creator of all things. The constantly renewed outpouring of the powers of consciousness stimulated by the expansion of the yogi's universal power of action blossoms forth into a new universe at each instant. Thus, like Śiva, the yogi expresses the unmanifest universe without either aspect contradicting or impinging on the fullness of the other.

* * *

Now, (Śiva) the Destroyer of the Three Cities, uttered the following aphorism as he explained that the Self which is the author of creation is similarly also the agent of persistence and destruction:

sthitilayau
(Such is also the case with) persistence
and absorption. 3/32 3.31

The same conscious nature freely brings about the persistence and absorption (of all things) as it wishes by means of these same aggregates of energy which are the outpouring of (its) functional potencies (*vṛtti*).

* * *

The conscious nature thus sustains and destroys the universe (it has) generated through (its) power of action by the power of its will. What is meant by persistence (*sthiti*) is the external manifestation of the entire universe of phenomena established in its own sustaining ground for the specific time alloted for its existence according to its level (on the scale of the categories of existence ranging from the lowest) up to that of Śakti and the corresponding subjects which govern it. One's own plane of being dissolves away by the withdrawal back (into consciousness) of the one above it, so similarly, indeed all the more so, the (entire objective) universe which is below one's own (subjective consciousness) is (also dissolved away). In this way, absorption is repose in the (pure) conscious subject. Both manifesting in this way, they are nothing but the aggregate of one's own powers. Every single thing, its unfolding and withdrawal, is the power of consciousness, for were it otherwise (its) manifestation would not be reasonably possible.

Exposition

The yogi's powers not only stimulate creation but also maintain the universe and re-absorb it back into undifferentiated consciousness. Nothing is created that does not come to an end, nor is destruction ever ultimate or absolute—one follows the other consistently and without break. The cycle of arousal and subsidence of individual perceptions, states of consciousness, physical activity and emotions in the microcosm as well as the incessant changes in the entire universe are held together in the rhythm and harmony of the yogi's universal consciousness.

* * *

In the following aphorism, (Śiva) the Saviour (Hara) and ocean of scripture described one's own basic abiding state (*nijasthiti*), that is, the Self as it is during the phases of creation, persistence and destruction:

tatpravṛttāvapyanirāsaḥ saṃvettṛbhāvāt
Even when these are operant, (the subject) is not lost because (he is) the perceiving subjectivity. 3/33 3.32

The ubiquitous Lord of Consciousness does not forsake his own basic abiding state of being (*svasthiti*) even when those of creation and the rest are operant because He is always the perceiving subject. (Thus), it is the perceiving subjectivity that is described here as being 'not lost' and never ceases. States (of consciousness) can cease in this way but never the subject who experiences them (*avasthātṛ*)[64] because it is his very nature to thread through all (these states) as described (in the *Stanzas on Vibration*).[65]

* * *

The conscious nature persists unchanged even while creation and the other (phases of manifestation) take place. (It abides constantly) as the perceiving subjectivity, that is, the (pure) reflective awareness and awe-inspiring wonder of the Fourth (transcendental state beyond creation, persistence and destruction) and never falls from this condition.

The word *these* in the aphorism stands for the five operations (of creation, persistence, destruction, obscuration and grace). The conscious nature is the author of the five operations. Manifesting its sovereign power to perform each one, it engenders the realisation of its own state as the witnessing subject that, ever present (*sadodita*), (perceives these operations) and inspires with wonder at the beginning and end of these transitory phenomena. In this way the states of the imperishable subject who experiences them are of many kinds, repeatedly arise, are destroyed and undergo transformations, but it is not destroyed. Otherwise these phases (of creation and) destruction, etc., would be impossible, for there would be none to witness them.

Exposition

At one with the reflective awareness of the bliss of the Fourth State, the yogi is identified with the pure perceiving subjectivity that makes every state of consciousness apparent. As the subject of all these states (*avasthātṛ*), he is not bound by them, nor does any change in them occasion a change in himself. But while Bhāskara links this aphorism with the fourth verse of the *Stanzas* where this is explained, Kṣemarāja looks to verses 14–16 where the distinction is drawn between the outer transitory world of phenomena (*kārya*) and the inner subject who is the universal agent (*kartṛ*) that produces it. The agent, like the perceiver, must abide without change for him to produce his product. Destruction and change belong to the sphere of ignorance. It is that ignorance which arises and falls away, not one's own true nature that, by its very nature, is imperishable.

* * *

(The Lord) said the following to describe the nature of pleasure and pain:

sukhāsukhayorbahirmananam
(The yogi's) feeling of pleasure and pain
is external. 3/34 3.33

The feeling (*manana*) that one has within oneself of outer pleasure comes from savouring the (outer) profane objects of the senses, (while the feeling of) inner pleasure comes from getting what one wants.

Pain is of three, five or of endless forms due to (its countless) varieties. Spiritual (mental and physical) are the three types of pain. (The five types are called) "dullness" (*tamas*), "delusion" (*moha*), "great delusion" (*mahāmoha*), "darkness" (*tāmisra*) and "blinding darkness" (*andhatāmisra*). These and the other (three types) constitute the eight natural tendencies (*aṣṭaprakṛti*).

***Dullness* is pride of self; *delusion* is false identification with the body; *great delusion* is identification with one's son or other external things; *darkness* is hate for all who do harm (to oneself) or one's family, etc., while *binding darkness,* the fifth, is the fear of death. Again (these types) are divided into other countless varieties.**

(The yogi's) contemplative absorption in the acting subject is firm and constant and so the feeling of the states of pleasure and pain, etc., is one with consciousness (and so), for whatever reason it may arise, does not obscure it.

* * *

Pleasure is defined as the blissful state (*ānandavṛtti*) the perceiving subject experiences by obtaining some worldly object he finds extremely desireable. Pain (on the contrary) is the miserable state (*anānandavṛtti*) that arises if one fails to get it or, (worse), if the opposite happens (and one looses something one likes). (Pain) is of many kinds according to whether it is spiritual (mental or physical). But neither of these two can obscure (the liberated yogi's) true nature (*svarūpa*) because he maintains a constant and steady awareness (*vimarśa*, of it) so that when they arise he does not feel that they have anything to do with him (*anāhaṃmamatā*) but experiences them as he does (the colour) blue or any other (external sensation) and not as does the fettered, whose subjective awareness (*ahantā*) is affected by it.

Exposition

Kṣemarāja pertinently points out that although the awakened yogi experiences the whole universe as the expansion of his power, this does not imply that he must also experience the ups and downs of pleasure and pain.[66] This is because his vision of his own nature is not restricted to a physical body or to any other individual locus of consciousness subject to these alternations through its relation with other objects set in opposition to it as the limited subject. Once the yogi has discovered his true identity, the subtle body (*puryaṣṭaka*) is no longer the exclusive domain of his ego-sense. The pleasant or painful sensations, thoughts and emotions to which it is subject are now no longer experienced internally as happening to the yogi himself. Pain and pleasure are recognised to reside in the outer sphere of objectivity as states of mind and body not of the Self. Only the lower-order subject is caught in their opposition, while the higher-order subject, freed of all false identifications, delights in the innate bliss of his own nature for, as the *Stanzas on Vibration* declare, ultimate reality is free of both pleasure and pain as well as subject and object.[67]

* * *

(The lord then explained how the Self is if this external feeling (of pleasure and pain) does not penetrate inwardly and it is liberated from it:

tadvimuktastu kevalī

The one who is free of that is a liberated soul. 3/35 3.34

The lord is free of pleasure and pain as He is of all insentience.[68] Thus He is isolated (*kevala* in the oneness of consciousness) and established in Himself because He pervades all (things and every state of consciousness).[69]

* * *

If the feeling of pleasure and the rest does not penetrate inwardly, the yogi, unaffected neither by them nor by the delusion to which they give rise, does not loose the power (*vibhava*) inherent in his own nature. Thus, by reposing in the supreme subject who in independent (*kevala*) consciousness alone, he experiences the fruit of Yoga.

Exposition

When the opposites are out of balance man fails to achieve perfect harmony and the result is continuous agitation. But if they come together and become one, man is freed from duality and achieves 'isolation' from them. It is isolation with regard to things: abandonment by consciousness of that which is not integral with its own nature in order that it may return into itself and plunge into its centre. In so doing, consciousness withdraws from its objectively manifest state to that of subjectivity and the yogi recognises that nothing exists outside his own nature and is thus isolated in the supreme reality and liberated.

* * *

Does delusion obscure (one's own nature) or not ? (The Lord) said:

mohapratisaṃhatastu karmātmā
A compact mass of delusion, the soul is
subject to karma. 3/36 3.35

Stupidity (*maurkhya*), inertia (*anudyoga*), ignorance (*avidyā*), insentience (*jāḍya*), obscuration (*avṛti*), lack of discernment (*aviveka*) and loss of consciousness (*mūrchā*): these and other such expressions are synonymous with the delusion that extends its sway when one identifies with the body and the rest (of the psycho-physical organism). Pervaded by it completely, the Self (becomes) a mass (of delusion) and is then said to be the fettered soul object to *karma* (*karmātman*) that undergoes repeated rebirth. Then (in this condition) duality manifests, the mark of which is ignorance of unity.

* * *

If (the individual soul) is completely pervaded by the delusion and ignorance which gives rise to (his false) identification with the body, he becomes involved in the good, bad and mixed actions he does with the body and its limbs. Thus, disregarding his own true nature which is one with the Sky of Consciousness, he seeks the fruit of his many and diverse actions and so, full of desire, he is subject to repeated rebirth in many forms as man (or beast).

Exposition

Kṣemarāja quotes the *Kālikākrama* as saying:

> If (the yogi) is under the sway of discursive thought and enveloped in ignorance, he cannot generate (fully and) and at once (the principles of existence) from Śiva onwards (and so realise them to be one with consciousness). Thus, due to that (ignorance) he perceives various states of being, both good and bad, and from the bad ones he experiences great suffering.[70]

* * *

As long as delusion persists, the Self assumes the form of subject and object. By resting on the plane (of consciousness of the universal) agent and so (practising) the Yoga of its removal, the individual soul (*ātman*) is ever awake and Śiva's nature is its stable state of being. Now what happens when duality ceases? Śaṅkara said:

bhedatiraskāre sargāntarakarmatvam
When diversity has been eliminated (the yogi's) action is to give rise to another creation. 3/37

As explained by the mothers of the universe in their aphorisms,[71] there is no multiplicity at all here (when the yogi) realises that the Self is all things. If the abiding state of being of the awakened persists without changing, whether they act in this world or, (absorbed in contemplation) desist from all action, that is the imperishable, unborn unity (*sāmya*) of the world of sensory perception (*viṣaya*).

When diversity has been eliminated in this way, the Self (is realised) to have a single (all-encompassing) form. Thus, the other creation, never manifest before, different from (this) creation, is the action of the conscious nature which possesses the power to do (*kartṛtā*) whatever it wishes.

* * *

(The yogi) whose heart is full of the power of Śiva's grace practises Śiva's Yoga through which he divests himself of the bondage of *karma* and so is awakened and no longer considers that anything exists separately, independently of Paramaśiva. Thus he frees himself of the perception of duality (experienced by the) subjects (that belong to the lower orders of consciousness) such as the fully enveloped subject (*sakala*) who identifies himself completely with the body, etc., or the subject who experiences deep sleep (*pralayakalā*), etc. In this way (the yogi) realises his own true nature (*svasvarūpa*) and so attains a stable state of being and the (inner) strength of the highest order of empowerment (*paraśāktabala*). Thus, once he has attained the great power that belongs to Mantra, Lord of Mantra and other subjects (of the higher orders of consciousness) he can bring about new creations consisting of ever-renewed manifestations ordered diversely as he wishes.

Exposition

Objectivity and subjectivity abide at one without contradiction in the wholeness of the universal Self. The yogi comes to realise this as he gives up attachment to the body and the awareness of his pure conscious nature gradually takes over from the limited states of embodied subjectivity. In this way he quits the lower order of creation, consisting of the categories below Māyā, and rises through the higher order of creation from the category of Pure Knowledge to Śiva, generating it as he does so. Each stage in this ascent is marked by a transition from one order of experiencing subjectivity to the other. In this way a more universally conscious subject takes over from one less so below it that thus becomes an object for the former and, with it, the entire extent of objectivity that it encompasses. In this way, the world of experience based on diversity and division is brought to an end and a new world of experience based on unity is created. When this process is complete, the yogi becomes the agent of every action in the universe.

* * *

Then (Śiva), the Lord of the gods, explained what brings about (this) new creation:

karaṇaśaktiḥ svato'nubhavāt
The power of the senses (is proved) by
one's own experience. 3/38 3.37

The senses have the power to bring about (this) new creation, as one's own experience proves, because they are supported by the uncreated power (of consciousness). This is so because the power of the senses comes from the force of absorption in the Self (*ātmāveśa*).[72] Thus, the Supreme Lord resolves (to bring about) whatever phenomenon (*kārya*) (the yogi) desires (whose consciousness) is fixed on the authentic foundation (of his being).

Although all this has been said before, it is repeated here again in another way to make (this point) clear because the yogic powers (the yogi acquires) are of many kinds.

* * *

Even a tiny louse possesses a degree of the power common (to every living being) through which this wonderfully diverse universe is created. Indeed, we know from our own experience that we can create the gardens, forests, mountains, lakes, cities and other common things (of daily life) while we dream or let our thoughts wander freely. Similarly, the yogi who, by his intense and profound application, rises to a (higher) level of existence where he can take support from the uncreated vitality (of consciousness) is able thereby to generate whatever he wishes in the way he likes by the creative power (*karaṇaśakti*, of consciousness).

Even though we have already referred to this means of realisation based on the power (inherent in consciousness) to give rise to this wonderfully diverse universe, we have occasion to mention it again now in order to explain that there are many other kinds of yogic powers (the yogi acquires).

Exposition

We know from our own experience that we have the power to create mental images at will as well as the power to perceive them. Although the objects thus created and known are not apparent to others, we are assured by this fact of the power of consciousness to know and act.[73] For the average man, contact with the innate power of the Self (*ātmabala*) is attenuated by his lack of self-awareness, the yogi on the other hand, by virtue of his profound absorption and intense will, can tap this power to the full and, by his mere intention alone, creates objects which are equally apparent to himself and to others.

* * *

The Lord of the Worlds then reverently explained that once the Fourth State (of consciousness), which is the direct experience of one's own nature (*svānubhava*), manifests everywhere in (all the phases of the cycle of manifestation) from creation onwards, the (individual) soul attains its own stable state of being (*ātmasaṃsthiti*):

tripadādyanuprāṇanam
That which is preceded by the three states
vitalizes them. 3/39 3.38

That which is preceded by the three states is the Fourth (state of pure consciousness) which is preceded by the states of waking (dreaming and deep sleep) and is said to be the

fullness (of consciousness that permeates all three) simultaneously. (All) existing things are rightly vitalized by it in the sense that it infuses its own inherent power (into them).

* * *

Consciousness manifests itself and is clearly revealed, like a flash of lightening free of all obscuring coverings, in the course of daily life by (the power of the yogi's) introverted awareness when he savours (the aesthetic delight) of good music or other pleasing objects. This happens if (the yogi) manages, by applying the aforementioned means, to perceive the Fourth State that, (as dense) uninterrupted consciousness and bliss, is Śiva Himself Who, full and perfect, determines the nature of all things and vitalizes the three states of waking (dreaming and deep sleep).

Exposition

According to Kṣemarāja, this aphorism teaches that the Fourth State of consciousness (*turīya*) is not only to be infused in the three states of waking, etc.,[74] but is also discovered in all the three moments of the emergence, persistence and susbsidence of any perception in any of these states. For although the power of Māyā, which gives rise to multiplicity and the split between subject and object, operates throughout this cycle, everybody experiences the fleeting emergence of the Fourth State of consciousness, as sudden and powerful as a lightening flash, whenever one delights in any sensation. The pleasure one feels during sexual intercourse, seeing a close friend after many years, eating a good meal or listening to fine music is in fact the bliss of one's own nature, it does not come from outside.[75]

The sensations which pour into consciousness, either through the outer senses or the mind, as memories or imagined forms, are influxes of the power of awareness which arouse consciousness and heighten its inner vitality. The aesthetic delight we enjoy seeing a beautiful object or hearing sweet music is, from this point of view, not an intrinsic quality of the object but the result of the aesthetic sensitivity of the subject. It is the ability to experience the wonder (*camatkāra*) aroused by the subtle vibration (*spanda*) of the bliss of self-awareness in the Fourth State. Abhinava writes:

> For if a colour passing through the eyes is a source of pleasure, this is due to the separation of the great emission, which consists of the arousal of vitality (*vīryakṣobha*).

A little further ahead he goes on to say:

> The wonder (we feel) is limited to the degree in which this vitality does not feed (consciousness). For the complete absence of wonder is, in effect, an absence of life. Conversely, aesthetic receptivity—being endowed with a heart—is to be immersed in an intense state of wonder consisting of the arousal of vitality. Only he whose heart is fed by this infinite and nourishing vitality, only he who is dedicated to the constant practise (of taking delight in this form of) pleasure, only he and none other is pre-eminently endowed with the ability to feel wonder.[76]

The yogi is taught in this aphorism that, in order to heighten the awareness of his own nature, which the power of Māyā has obscured, he must try and fix his attention on the instant in which he feels this wonder welling up inside him in moments of intense joy, confusion, anger or fear. By attending to the sudden emergence of the vibration (*spanda*) of the transcendental Fourth State of consciousness at these times and establishing himself in a state of introverted absorption, as verse 22 of the *Stanzas* teaches, he should, as Kṣemarāja puts it, "vitalize the living Self by that very life itself."[77]

* * *

The compassionate Lord Śiva explained in the following aphorism how one should do (this):

cittasthitivaccharīrakaraṇabāhyeṣu
The same stability of mind (should permeate) the body, senses and external world. 3/40 3.39

The mind, the nature of which we have already discussed above, is stable when it does not wander, that is, if it does not deviate from its own essential nature (as pure consciousness). This same stability (*sthiti*) (operates) in the body duly fashioned (by consciousness) and in the internal and external senses as the vital force (*prāṇana* that vitalizes them). Similarly, one has the same perception (of the abiding state of consciousness) in whatever external things (the mind fixes its) attention (*prakalpana*) in this way.

* * *

When the principle of consciousness directs its attention to the object of perception it restricts itself and so becomes the mind (but even then we know that it never really changes) because, when one practises the means to realisation, it reverts to its (original) inherent nature, which is pure uninterrupted consciousness and bliss. (In the same way), the body and the rest (of the psycho-physical organism) created by it (never) deviates from its own true nature (as pure consciousness). (Similarly), all phenomenal creation (*bhāvajāta*) in the state prior (to its manifestation) is one with the juice (of the aesthetic delight, *rasa*) of consciousness (but when consciousness) directs its attention outside itself, it becomes gross as it were and manifests itself (externally in the form of phenomenal creation), as happens in a dream or while phantasizing. In reality, however, it is the same perception it has of its own nature (*svarūpaprathā*) that condenses, internally and externally, (to assume the form) of every individual existing thing and thus becomes manifest to then dissolve away again (and revert to its original form) as the juice (of the aesthetic delight) of consciousness.

Exposition

As usual with the Yoga taught here, the retraction of awareness inwards and the resultant experience of the Fourth State achieved through introverted contemplation (*nimīlana*) is perfected only when it issues out, through an expansion (*unmeṣa*) of consciousness, into the outside world. The psychic energy the yogi sought at its source within his own nature must flow out, as he maintains his inner awareness, to fill the world of his outer experience and the channels through which he apprehends it. The yogi thus comes to experience his body, senses and physical environment as pervaded by the bliss of the power of his own freedom and achieves mastery over all the states of consciousness and forms of awareness.

* * *

(Śiva) the Lord of the Daughter of the Mountains then explained how the world of phenomena that resides thus within (consciousness) flows out from it:

abhilāṣād bahirgatiḥ saṃvāhyasya
Due to (one's) craving, that which is transported moves outside. 3/41 3.40

The desire (*icchā*) that develops in the Self due to the abundance of its inherent power, to complete (outwardly) the absorption (it experiences in its own inner) activity is the craving (to which this aphorism refers). Due to this (desire) the senses and other (components of the psycho-physical body) that are transported (by it) 'move outside' in the sense that they perform their specific functions impelled by the energy of (the inner conscious) nature (residing in the body, which is) the object of its impulse (and the outer support of the senses).

Again, 'that which is transported' is both the fettered soul's object of desire and that craving itself which, once creation has taken place, is directed to all the objects of the senses and so is said to be the outward movement of the soul fettered by *karma* (*karmātman*) that is transported (by it). (The fettered soul) transported (by its desire) abandons its own essential nature. This is its movement directed to the outer objects of the senses. And so, if (the soul) is always transported (here and there) by the objects of the

senses, etc., the delusion (*moha*) which is foolish craving, goes on developing (within him).

* * *

The craving (to which this aphorism refers) is the desire the soul (*ātman*) has to infuse the power of consciousness into the senses of knowledge and action when the vitality inherent in its own nature abounds to excess and so wishes to see, hear or execute any other of the functions (*kriyā*, of the senses) on this, lower level (of consciousness). This (craving) impels the senses that are (thus) transported (by it) and so begin to operate in the domains of sound and touch and their other objects.

Again, 'that which is transported' is the fettered soul (*paśu*) who is bound by *karma* (*karmātman*) and so is transported from womb to womb (and reborn repeatedly) along with the veils that obscure its consciousness (*kañcuka*) and the other (principles of individualized existence) that are presided over by the powers known as *Khecarī, Gocarī, Dikcarī* and *Bhūcarī*. The fettered soul is affected by the craving which is the Impurity of Individuality (*āṇavamala*, that contracts its consciousness) and is the root cause of all the fetters (that bind it) and so it foresakes the pure experience of its own true nature (*svasvarūpānubhava*) and moves outside in the pursuit of pleasure, (directing its attention) to the objects of the senses. (Thus) the Wheel of *Bhūcarī* energies (which presides over the sphere of objectivity) transports the fettered, engaging them in the works of delusion (*mohakārya*) at increasingly grosser levels of existence.

Exposition

This aphorism warns the yogi to reflect constantly on the inner Fourth State of consciousness during the outflow of awareness. The spontaneous tendency of the Self to view outer objectivity creates the world of perceptions. The yogi carried along by this desire issues forth from the transcendental consciousness of his own nature into the immanent state of cosmic consciousness without being bound. However, when this creative will is conditioned by ignorance due to which the individual wrongly considers himself to be incomplete and turns away from his own nature, stimulated by the desire for an outer object to fill the gap he feels in himself, the outpouring of his awareness becomes binding. The individual soul, identified with the body, is thus carried from life to life by the limited powers of consciousness manifest as the forces which condition the soul's consciousness, mind, senses, sensations and physical world. These are the spheres governed by the energies to which Bhāskara's anonymous commentator refers.

* * *

(The Self) is known as the individual soul bound by *karma* when the impure desire (for the objects of the senses) prevails (within him). (Śiva) the Great Lord said the following to explain what happens to the Self when that (desire) ceases:

tadārūḍhapramitestatkṣayājjīvasaṃkṣayaḥ
Then (when the yogi) is established in pure awareness
(his craving) is destroyed and so the individual
soul ceases to exist. 3/42 3.41

The state which heralds the arising of desire is said to be the domain of the perceiving subject and the awakened yogi who knows ultimate reality then resides within it. When he penetrates into the domain of the perceiver, (stimulated and sustained) by the vitality that comes from the exertion of the power inherent in his own nature he, the subject whose consciousness is firm, is then said to be awake.

The pure awareness of the subject is his knowledge of his own pure consciousness nature. Then, (when the yogi) is established in that pure awareness, his craving is destroyed and, as a result, the individual soul bound by *karma* also ceases to exist.

* * *

This impure craving thus (persists) together with the conditioned ego (of the fettered soul) due to his deluded experience. However, it happens at times (that despite this craving the yogi) is graced by virtue of his many good deeds and, intent on discerning (the true meaning of) the Śaiva scripture, (his) consciousness develops and rises to the level of the (pure) perceiving subject. (Thus he) savours his own inherently blissful nature which illumines itself with the rays of its consciousness both inwardly and extenally from the level of the principles which obscure consciousness (*kañcuka*) down to that of the subtle elements of sensation and is made manifest by the powers known as *Khecarī* (*Gocarī, Dikcarī* and *Bhūcarī*) because now the consequences of their activity is the very opposite of that (experienced by) the fettered. Thus, the very moment (the yogi) abandons the craving of the fettered, (the activity of) the subtle body (*puryaṣṭka*) which is transported (from life to life) is stilled.

Exposition

The yogi whose inner nature unfolds through the power of the grace of universal consciousness to ultimately fill the entire field of awareness, absorbs into itself the limited subjectivity associated with the subtle body (*puryaṣṭaka*) of sensations and mind. Now firmly established in the flow of cognizing subjectivity present at the initial moment of the emergence of desire, the yogi is freed of the flux of differentiated perceptions and plunges through the centre between inner and outer, being and non-being, to merge in the bliss of the Fourth State. Enlightened by the unfolding vision of the eternal Now, past and future fall away and the awakened yogi, solely intent on devouring time (*kālagrāsaikatatpara*),[78] is liberated from the flow of the sensory activity which dragged him away from the peace and tranquillity of resting in his own nature.

* * *

The individual soul is bound and so is said to be fettered (*paśu*) and subject to transmigration (*saṃsārin*). (The

Lord then) explained how the Self is when the mass of fetters (that bind it) are destroyed:

bhūtakañcukī tadāvimukto bhūyaḥ patisamaḥ paraḥ
(The soul) clad in the cloak of elements is not free but, like the Lord, becomes supreme once more. 3/43 3.42

The cloak is made of the five gross elements, which are the fetters (that bind the soul), and one should know it to be the obscuring covering (that veils his consciousness). Then, (the fettered soul), clad in the cloak of the elements, is not free but bound, (even so), by fixing (his attention), in the manner described, on the plane of the omniscient (Lord) Who does all things, he becomes supreme once again like the Lord by experiencing his own nature truly and directly. There can be no doubt about this!

* * *

Even when it appears that (the yogi) is not free because of his persisting relationship with the material body, he emerges from his fettered state when the impurity of desire is destroyed in this way and, through the development of the plane of universal agency and cognitive subjctivity, he experiences the Śivahood of his own nature which is the uninterrupted (*ghana*) bliss of absolute consciousness. However, the embodied condition is not superceded and so (the yogi is merely) similar to Śiva and not Śiva Himself for His state (can) only be attained after death.

Exposition

Free of craving for outer things, the well awakened lays aside, as belonging to the objective sphere, the thoughts and sensations which had formerly usurped the office of the perceiving subjectivity. The destruction of the lower-order subject, bound by the diversity and change of the world of transmigration, marks the emergence of the higher-order subject which subsumes diversity and change into the unchanging unity of its experience of wholeness. The elements which constitute the body do not cease to exist even after liberation, but they are then merely an outer shell, no longer felt to be 'I'. Quoting from various sources, Kṣemarāja stresses in his commentary that the realisation of one's own true disembodied identity takes place in an instant. The enlightened teacher need only say a word, or just a glance may suffice if the right moment has come for the disciple to understand his true nature and be freed of his false identification with the body.

* * *

The link (which connects the soul), clad in the cloak of the gross elements, (with the body) is the vital breath (*prāṇa*). But how is it that (this link persists even when the soul is liberated)? The Lord Whose Insignia is the Bull, uttered the following aphorism (by way of explanation):

naisargikaḥ prānasaṁbandhaḥ
The link with the vital breath is natural. 3/44 3.43

The link between the vital breath and the physical body comes about quite naturally because the vital breath is life itself.

* * *

Once consciousness has risen (to the highest level) in the way explained above and the false identification with the subtle body (*puryaṣṭaka*) ceases, the physical body linked with it that envelops (consciousness) should also fall away (but this does not happen) and so we accept that the link between the subtle body and the vital breath that sustains (the physical body) is naturally established.

In order to make the wonderful diversity of the universe manifest, consciousness initially manifests limitation (*saṃkoca*) and then (descends) to the level of the subject that serves as the vital force (*prāṇana*, that gives life to the body and senses) and so manifests itself as the universe, which is the object (the subject perceives). It then spontaneously forgets its own infinite power (*vibhava*) and accumulates meritorious and sinful *karma* by the good and bad thought constructs to which it gives rise while its condition is that of (the subject) who gives life (to the psycho-physical organism). (Thus) it wanders from life to life (reincarnating) as man, beast or god according (to its *karma*). This continues until it is blessed with the power of grace (that the Lord freely bestows upon it), independently (of its merits), and so craves to ascend by degrees along the ladder of the Śaiva teaching (*śaivajñāna*) to the upper abode of the absolute. But even when all (the soul's) *karma* has been burnt away by the fire of knowledge, it goes on experiencing (the consequences) of the *karma* that has already begun to take effect (*prarabdhakarma*) and so the physical body (*bhūtakañcuka*) and the life breath linked with it persist just as the potter's wheel continues to spin (for a while) even when the stick (that impels it) is removed from it.

Exposition

By now the reader will have become familiar with the Kashmiri Śaiva view of reality or, more specifically of consciousness, as an undivided continuum or medium of free becoming. All nature forms an unbroken chain whose links rest on the immutable law of the progress of a universal power constituting the unity of all things. The emergence of a modality of experience that the Indian tradition as a whole characterizes as a constraining wandering from life to life, state to state (*saṃsāra*) is, from this standpoint, understood to be the result of a spontaneous disruption from within of the stable tranquillity (*praśama*) of this flow. Turbulence (*kṣobha*) disturbs its unity, splitting it up into discrete elements, thus marking a transition from continuum to process, from the paradox of the changeless becoming of Being to the intermittent appearing and disappearing of phenomena. The movement (*spanda*) of consciousness, undefinably neither successive nor nonsequential,[79] becomes manifest as unending cycles of creations and destructions stretching from infinitely long spans of time to infinitesimally short.

Thus the manifestation of the finite is a process of emergence of the temporal order from the eternity of consciousness.[80] The transformation of the unmanifest state into that of manifestation is a shift from atemporal Being-Becoming (*Śiva-Śakti*) to a state of movement (*kriyā*) from the past into the future. In this way the inner activity of consciousness becomes the outer activity of objectively projected phenomena:

> Time measures in minutes, etc., action (*kartṛtva*).[81] Thus that which time measures is (not pure action but) the limited activity of phenomena (*kāryāvacchedi*).[82]

The power of time (*kālaśakti*) gives rise to past, present and future on the plane of Māyā,[83] it is thus one with consciousness's creative power of action (*kriyāśakti*).[84] Through it consciousness projects the diversity of experience onto the screen of its own nature.[85] It is through the power of time that the power-holder, while beyond the realms of the temporal, diversifies the universe.[86] It divides up our action,[87] diversifying the unity of the All through a compounding process of differentiation (*kalanā*) and thus manifests individual being out of universal being. Creating the diversity (*vaicitrya*) of manifestation, Śiva simultaneously gives rise to time.[88] Ultimately, time and diversity are one, hence all that is objectively manifest is conditioned by time.

Kālī, also called *Kālasaṃkarṣiṇī* ("The Attractress of Time"), is the hypostasis of the creative autonomy (*svātantrya*) of consciousness identified with the power of time. Her name, derived from the root *kal*, is interpreted in five ways, indicative of the five cosmic functions of the power of time, as follows:

1) *Kal* in the sense of casting forth (*kṣepe*): the emergence of time marks an arousal from the state of absorption in the unity of the Self giving rise to the differentiation of reality and the projection of the multiplicity of objectivity.

2) *Kal* in the senses of knowing (*jñe*): time accompanies all object-centred knowledge in the absence of an awareness that the universe of experience is a differentiated aspect of the Self.

3) *Kal* in the sense of enumeration (*saṃkhyāne*): time is the measure

of thought. To fall from the atemporal unity of the All is to become a prey to differentiated mental representations (*vikalpa*) issuing from the perception of relative distinctions.

4) *Kal* in the sense of movement (*gate*): through insight into the true nature of time we can move forward to catch hold of our own nature made externally manifest as the cosmic reflection in the mirror of undifferentiated consciousness.

5) *Kal* in the sense on resonance (*nāda*): time is a mode in which the light of consciousness, reflecting on its own nature, is made manifest.[89] Thus, it is also the resonance (*nāda*) of the reflective awareness of one's own nature as the essence of all things when their outer form is transcended.[90]

We can distinguish in this account of the five functions of the power of time, two distinct levels. The first three functions entagle the subject in time as a process, i.e., events, occurences, happenings felt to be the outcome of a continuous series of operations that have no agent as their author. The last two functions form part of a praxis in which the subject recognises himself to be the autonomous agent of these events now apparent to him as deeds. At the lower level, time functions in relation to conditioned consciousness; at the higher, it is freely created by unconditioned consciousness:

> "Always," "occasionally," "now," "'then," etc., is the play of the notions of time made manifest by the freedom of consciousness, nor is the Supreme Lord touched by the phases of time.[91]

At this level, time is the medium through which all things are manifest and is the inner nature of all the categories of existence. It is the very essence of Śiva's consciousness identified with Īśvara, the category of experience (*tattva*) in which Śiva reflects on the oneness of the All, the objective elements of which—although in a state of emergence or production—are still united with the subject.[92] At the lower level of Māyā where the subject is limited by his perception of external objects as separate from himself and by his subsequent identification with them, time serves to condition the subject further. Abhinava explains:

> Time (*kāla*) is that which is initially responsible for the successive changes in the limited subject in which it manifests itself. It subsequently arouses a corresponding idea in relation to the object as well, for example (in notions such as): 'I who was thin am now fat and will be fatter still'. Thus the subjective limitation imposed by time is responsible for the idea of the successive change in the body assumed to be identical with the Self. This arouses a similar idea in relation to the limited subject's object of knowledge.[93]

Abhinava does not mean to say that time is a self-existent reality. For although time is described as an attribute (*viśeṣaṇa*) of object-centred awareness,[93] the reality of the truly existent (*vastutattva*) as the All, containing in its fullness both subject and object, is undivided by time (*akālakalita*). Time is not an external measure of activity, but is this activity itself. For while action consists of an association of previous and subsequent elements (*pūrvāparabhūta*) ordered into a continuous succession of events, time is the differentiated perception of that which went before in relation to that which follows after (*purvāparavikalpana*).[95] Days, hours or minutes are merely subdivisions of the movement of the earth in relation to the heavenly bodies. There is no independent time apart from our conception of it.[96] It is a format through which we order our experience but is nowhere to be found either in the sphere of objectivity or within the pure consciousness of the unconditioned subject.[97] The distinction between psychological and objective time is false, the awareness of time passing is always a mental construct (*kalpanā*). Abhinava points out:

> The power of time consists of the multiplicity of action and hence is based on the will (*icchā*), externally it has no fixed form. For when one dreams that one is in a dream, simply dreams or is in deep sleep, or abandons oneself to one's imagination, or is in a state of contemplative absorption in which one discerns the sequence of creation and destruction of all things in an instant, however short it may be, can appear to be a very long (time).[98]

Time is the result of our memory (*smaraṇa*) of the past and anticipation (*utprekṣaṇa*) of the future. When that which IS is realised to be just as it IS (*vastutattva*) past and future fade away together with all the other projections superimposed upon it. Free of past and future, the present also disappears, and the relativity of time is annulled in the absoluteness of complete (*saṃpūrṇa*) and undivided (*abhinna*) awareness (*bodha*). Abhinavagupta writes:

> The subject who recalls or phantasizes, etc., remains always the same and is ever present: past and future do not exist. For it is said, "it is not conditioned by the two times." This subject always remains the same as it is, it does not differ from what it was before, nor does it tolerate the sort of limitations that find expression in statements such as "he knows this again and does this," etc. This subject, it is said, shines once and for all. This is why one says that the present is such in relation to the past, etc., and that when they do not exist nor does that; thus the true reality is not measured by time.[99]

Time is thus nothing but an unfolding (*sphāramātra*) of consciousness,[100] into the field of the finite, i.e., the realm of objectivity (*meyatva*). For this to happen, the unconditioned subjectivity of pure consciousness must first limit itself to the status of an individual subject to allow for the existence of similarly limited objects,[101] which is the necessary condition attending the emergence of time. The present in relation to the past and future is the result of the perception and activity of an individual locus of awareness. Thus, at the individual level, the inherent rhythm of consciousness expresses itself as the passing of time in accord with the emergence and subsidence of each act of perception.

Moreover, another aspect of the spontaneous movement of consciousness is the manifest rise and fall of the breath. Exhaled and inhaled breaths are the gross manifestations of the current of conscious energy moving to and fro between subject and object. The act of perception follows the course of the breath,[102] which moves in association with the conjunction and separation of the senses with their objects.[103] Again, the breathing cycle (*prāṇacakra*) is also the cycle of time (*kālacakra*). Consequently, the three breaths, namely, inhaled, exhaled and the one that rises in the centre between them, correspond to past, present and future.[104] Thus time, perception and breath are linked together in the universal vibration of consciousness:

> This entire expanse of time rests thus on the vital breath, this on movement and this on the void which rests in consciousness. Thus all the universe rests within (consciousness). As the arising and falling away of all things is based on consciousness in its true nature, and these movements right up to the (supreme) power are expressions of its vibration (*tatspanda*), it is manifest in countless ways.[105]

The initial condition for the emergence of the breath, time and differentiated perception (*vikalpa*) is the same, namely, the spilt between subject and object. Consciousness, through its inherent power, denies the plenitude of its unity and so gives rise to 'I' and 'This'—subjectivity and objectivity—which exclude each other reciprocally in a state of negation conceived as an emptiness (*śūnya*). The subsequent stages represent phases in the development of a link connecting these two poles. The first movement towards reuniting them is an intent on the part of the subject to appropriate the object. Out of this urge arises the flux of vitality (*prāṇana*) which give life to the body (microcosm) and universe (macrocosm) and is said to be the intial transformation of consciousness. Abhinava explains:

> Time, consisting of succession and non-succession, rests entirely within consciousness. For, according to the scriptures, Kālī (the Goddess of Time) is the supreme power of the Lord, Who, making manifest and affirming externally as an objective reality the succession and non-succession She bears within Herself, appears as the life force (*prāṇavṛtti, prāṇana*). This unique and pure consciousness, the supreme reality of the light (of consciousness), is manifest as a Sky void of all things. That alone is said to be the voidness of consciousness. It is the supreme state for those yogis who reflect (upon the world) as 'not this, not this' (*neti, neti*).[106] This etheric subject, overflowing and falling onto the knowable separated from it, desiring to make it its own is called the "vital breath" (*prāṇa*), "vibration" (*spanda*) or "wave" (*ūrmi*).[107]

The vital breath, *prāṇa* (or more precisely, *prāṇana*, i.e., *prāṇa* in its generic aspect) is understood in its most general sense as the vital energy or élan (*vīrya*) of consciousness and the principle of life in living beings. Thus, it is figuratively described as preventing the 'stiffness' (*stabdatā*) of *rigor mortis*. At the cosmic level it is the vibration (*spanda*) or effulgence (*sphurattā*) of consciousness that makes manifest the universe. As such, *prāṇa* is the primal causal movement or fundamental urge in the ground reality manifest as the manifold of a possible universe. As the Sun (*bhāskara*) of Life,[108] it illumines the entire universe and supplies the energy for the eternal rhythm of cosmic creation and destruction:

> He, the Great Lord and ocean of eternal consciousness, the essential nature of all things (*ātman*), makes manifest and withdraws creation and destruction in consonance with the arising and subsidence of the power of the vital breath (*pavanaśakti*).[109]

At the microcosmic level the breathing cycle passes through three principle phases, namely, exhalation, retention and inhalation. These correspond to the creation, persistence and withdrawal of the universe of perceptions. In fact, all the cycles of universal creation and destruction are contained in the arising and subsidence of the vital breath circulating throughout the body.[110] Yoga, in this context, is the practise of following the movement of the breath and recognising it to be the flux of the Cosmic Path of universal manifestation. When the yogi exhales, he turns outward to attend to objectivity, and subjectivity contracts. Once the breath has returned and rests internally, all differentiation vanishes. This incessant expansion and contraction is a natural, spontaneous process. To know it is to find release:

> He who constantly exerts himself and realises the true nature of the pure conscious Self to be the power of the vital breath that transcends time and is associated with the cycles of creation, persistence and destruction, achieves liberation (*bhairavībhāva*).[111]

Thus, this aphorism declares that although the Awakened yogi is detached from his body and so, in a sense, is dead to the world of embodied existence, he lives a higher mode of life, realising that the divine vitality that gives Being to all things is inseparable from his true nature.

* * *

(The breath) consisting of the Resonance (*nāda,* of consciousness) and the Point (*bindu,* of divine light) courses along three paths. (The Lord then explained) whether it is necessary to conquer it or not in order to realise one's own nature (*svasiddhi*):

nāsikāntarmadhyasaṃyamāt kimatra
savyāpsavyasauṣumneṣu
(The movement of the vital breath is stilled) by concentrating on the centre within the nose. Of what use (then) are the left and right channels or Suṣumnā? 3/45 3.44

The nose (in this context) means the inner Twelve-finger Space (where the breaths come to rest). Those who fix their attention there merge (into universal consciousness) and so, conquering (the breath), their own fundamental and abiding state of being (*svātmasthiti*) becomes clearly apparent. The centre is here the Heart (of consciousness). When the vital breath is set aside there (within it), all mental activity is absorbed (into consciousness) and so (the yogi experiences) the Supreme Arising of the Self. Once it has been conquered in this way what use then are the left and right channels or *Suṣumnā* along which the breath (normally) flows? For (the yogi who conquers the breath) it possesses the power of life itself and bestows every perfection. Śiva declares the same in the venerable *Svacchandatantra* (where we read):

> The vital breath is life itself (*prāṇamaya*) which engenders exhalation (*visargāpūrṇa*) and inhalation (*prāṇa*).[112]

Consequently, (Śiva goes on to) talk of the conquest of the breath and the vital channels (*nāḍī*) by virtue of which the soul is free, pure and one with Śiva.

* * *

(Bhāskara explains in his commentary) how (the yogi) can attend to the Absolute Word (*Śabdabrahman*) which is the Unstruck Sound (*anāhata*) of the vital force (*prāṇa*) in order to achieve liberation so that he can exercise the many yogic powers (*siddhi*) his true nature possesses (to the full).

The psychic channels (*nāḍī*) are conquered (and the yogi gains mastery over them) when the vital breath which includes (both the inhaled breath technically called) the "Point" (of divine light) and (the exhaled breath called) the "Resonance" (of consciousness) which moves along the three channels, *Iḍā*, (*Piṅgalā* and *Suṣumnā*), merges (into consciousness). This happens in the case of yogis who concentrate steadfastly on (the centre) within the nose, that is, on the Twelve-finger Space and the other centres where the sun of the vital breath sets (and the movement of the breath ceases) by virtue of the excellence of their practise.

When the movement of the breath ceases, the activity of the mind comes to rest in the Unstruck Sound of the absolute (*anāhatabrahman*) and (the yogi's) perception (*pratyaya* of the absolute) forms a single clearly evident flux (of awareness) by virtue of which (the yogi's consciousness) becomes one with it (*tanmaya*) and so all division between between the meditator (and his object of meditation) falls away and Śiva, Who is one's own supreme nature, manifests. Once the goal has been attained in this way (all) practise belonging to the lower levels, such as the recitation of Mantra as taught in the Individual Means,[113] ceases for the higher level (of practise) does not depend on the other levels that precede it.

Exposition

According to Kṣemarāja the word *nāsikā*, which normally means "nose," here denotes the power of the vital breath (*prāṇa-śakti*) because it "moves on a crooked or curved path" (*nāsate*). Again, the centre within the vital breath, as Kṣemarāja says, is "consciousness, the centre of which is the sustaining ground (*pradhāna* of existence) because it is the inner being of all things."[114]

The process of differentiation continues after the vital breath has emerged from the emptiness of universal consciousness. In its descent from the higher regions, it successively gives life to the mental faculties, then to the body where it opens up channels for itself through which it courses in the form of *Nāda*, the vitalizing resonance of awareness.[115] Abhinava writes:

> The currents of the vital breath are expressions of the vibration (*spanda*) of consciousness; the extreme limit of grossness that they assume is called the "cavity" (*suṣi*) which forms a channel (*nāḍī*) that connects the body together. It is said in the *Svacchandatantra*: "Just as a leaf is pervaded by its filaments, so the body is pervaded by the channels, both principle and secondary."[116]

In the *Heart of Recognition* (*Pratyabhijñāhṛdaya*), Kṣemarāja writes:

> The Centre is the Goddess of Consciousness alone for it is the inner being of all things as nothing would have a nature of its own were it not fixed on the screen of that (consciousness). However, even though it is such, it conceals its real nature at the level of Māyā and, in accord with the dictum *initially consciousness is transformed into the vital breath*, it assumes the form of the power of the vital breath (*prāṇaśakti*). It then gradually descends through the planes of the intellect and body, etc., and reposes there following the course of countless vital channels (*nāḍī*). The principle form it assumes is that of the Central Channel (*madhyanāḍī*, i.e., *suṣumnā*) whose substratum is Brahman, the power of the vital breath. It travels from the Cavity of Brahmā (*brahmārandhra*) (at the top of the head) to the genital region (*adhovaktra*) like the central rib of a leaf.[117]

The primary psychic channels are ten in number and radiate in a circle (*cakra*) from the navel.[118] From there they travel to every part of the body branching out into 72,000 secondary channels,[119] which then go on to form further subdivisions, thus permeating the body and ensuring the free circulation of the vital breath to every part of the psycho-physical organism.[120] Of the ten primary channels, three are the most important for the practise of Yoga. Again, of these, the most important is *Suṣumnā*, which issues from the circle of energies around the Cavity of Branmā at the top of the head and runs down the body to the genitals.[121] It is through this channel that the pervasive vitality of consciousness travels down through the body, and through that it again rises up, as *Prāṇā Kuṇḍalinī*, to reunite with its infinite nature and so connect the microcosm with the macrocosm. Described as the "Channel of Consciousness" (*cinnāḍī*) or as the "filament of pure awareness" (*jñānasūtra*),[122] it is conceived to be a line without thickness, which thus transcends the limitations of space and is symbolic of the infinite. When the vital breath travels through it at a level with consciousness, the yogi experiences it as the Sky of Consciousness (*cidvyoman*) into which his awareness expands.[123] To the left and right of *Suṣumnā* run *Iḍā* and *Piṅgalā*, the channels for the descending and ascending breath and the manifestation, at the individual (*āṇava*) level, of all polarities, which they symbolize as the Sun and Moon. They emerge and subside into the vacuum of *Suṣumnā*, which is the pure energy (*Śakti*) of the Goddess of the Centre (*Madhyā Devī*) in which the opposites fuse. By fixing his attention on the void between the breaths, the yogi experiences the expansion of consciousness in the centre (*madhyavikāsa*). The process of descent is then reversed as bodily consciousness merges into thought, thought into mind and mind into the Heart of consciousness beyond mind (*unmanā*):

> If (the yogi) desires to discern the eternal and undifferentiated outpouring of his own Heart, he must penetrate into the point in the centre where the Sun and Moon set.[124]

The 'crooked' (*kauṭilya*) or irregular movement of the breath is thus spontaneously stilled. The yogi breathes freely with mindfulness and thus experiences an inner peace of mind (*cittaviśrānti*).[125] Penetrating deeper into the primal source of energy (*kalā*) permeating the breath, *Kuṇḍalinī* rises and the two breaths are sucked into *Suṣumnā*. When this process is complete and the yogi emerges from his absorption (*samādhi*), he is effortlessly carried by the grace of the Goddess of the Centre to the highest level of consciousness through the movement of the breath, now recognised to be one with the flow of time and space. The three moments of the dialectic of consciousness ranging through thesis, antithesis and synthesis symbolized by the triad of channels is overcome and assimilated into a unity. The yogi becomes one with the supreme power of consciousness which instigates the flux of the breath and, with it, the flow of time from the centre within the nose:

> The Attractress of Time residing in the space at the base of the nose constantly instigates the two breaths, attracting to the heart the three forms of time. By inhalations she lends access (to pure consciousness), by suspending the breath She maintains (that state of awareness) and, by exhalations, She absorbes (diversity). (Thus), in an instant, (She) is born of the exhalation of the breath and absorbs all time. She, the power of the will is called the "supreme energy" which awakens the three (times) and, worthy of worship, attracts all the vital breath (*prabhajñana*) which is (the basis) of the flux of time.[126]

* * *

Now (to conclude), the all-pervasive Lord explained the ultimate purport (*siddhānta*) of the means to realisation He has taught and ranged together in (all) these sections (of the *Aphorisms*):

bhūyaḥ syāt pratimīlanam
May (the soul) merge (in the Lord) once again. 3/46 3.45

All this universe is, in the way we have explained before, the development (*vijṛmbha*) of the will of the ubiquitous Lord from which the individual soul is separated by the vitality of the power of Māyā. (The Lord) awakes the soul (from the slumber of ignorance) once again by imparting the means described herein so that, by destroying the impurity (which sullies consciousness), it may merge in the Lord (again) and, becoming one with Him within Him, be Śiva Who is full, perfect and uninterrupted bliss. This is basically what this excellent commentary on the *Aphorisms of Śiva* has described correctly and succinctly in 390 verses.

* * *

(This aphorism) explains briefly the essence of all the Śaiva teachings imparted (herein). (The word) *again* (implies the following process): Paramaśiva is the absolute, the nature of which is pure consciousness. When He chooses out of His own free will to utilise His divine power (*vīrya*), He instigates the development (of the principles) Śiva, Śakti (*Sadāśiva, Īśvara* and *Śuddhavidyā*) that emerge (out of Him) as the subtle beginnings (*pallava,* of cosmic manifestation) and once He has done so He enters the Pure Path (constituted by these principles). (He resides) on this Path without falling from His true nature which is uninterrupted consciousness. On the lower Path, however, He takes upon Himself the condition of a worldly soul (*māyāpramātṛ*) for He wishes to exhibit the game (He plays) of forgetting His own nature and so acts out the cosmic drama. He attains His own abiding state (*svasthiti*) (once again) when, through a supreme act of grace, it becomes clearly apparent (to the soul) that the glory of its power to know and do all things has not been lost and so the state of the individual perceiver is submerged (into universal consciousness) by following the path indicated by the Śaiva teachings. (Thus), when the impurity (which sullies consciousness) has been destroyed, (Śiva) engenders the emergence of His supreme Śiva-nature which is the absolute consisting of perfect, uninterrupted consciousness and bliss and having done so (the soul) realises its own fundamental state.

Exposition

Kṣemarāja explains what *merger* means in this aphorism in the following way:

> The universe arises out of one's own nature which is pure consciousness and, once freed of the latent traces of multiplicity, merges again into pure consciousness. Thus, through the repeated unfolding of his own essential, pure conscious

nature (and repeated merger), the yogi is centred on the practise of the highest form of Yoga.[127]

Kṣemarāja goes on to explain that this "happens again," in the sense that "the Śiva-nature the yogi possesses is not something new but is in fact his own essential nature. It is only due to the negative influence of his own thought constructs, generated by the power of Māyā, that he is unable to reflect on it even though it is clearly manifest. Thus, it is by explaining the means to realisation discussed herein that this (supreme truth) is made fully evident (to everyone)."[128]

On this note the *Aphorisms of Śiva* end.

APPENDIX: THE STANZAS ON VIBRATION

The Spandakārikā

1. We praise that Śaṅkara who is the source of the power of the Wheel of Energies by whose expansion (*unmeṣa*) and contraction (*nimeṣa*) the universe is absorbed and comes into being.
2. That in which all this creation is established and from whence it arises is nowhere obstructed because it is unconditioned by (its very) nature.
3. Even when division prevails due to the waking and other states, it extends through that which is undivided (*tadabhinna*) because the perceiving subjectivity forever remains true to its own nature.
4. No notions such as "I am happy," "I am miserable" or "I am attached" (exist independently). They all clearly reside elsewhere, namely, (in that) which threads through (all) the states of pleasure and the rest.
5. That exists in the ultimate sense where there is neither pleasure nor pain, subject nor object, nor an absence of consciousness.

6.–7. That principle should be examined with effort and reverence because this, its uncreated freedom, prevails everywhere. By virtue of it, the senses, along with the inner circle, (although) unconscious, behave as if conscious in themselves and move towards (their object), rest (there) and withdraw (from them).

8. Indeed the individual soul (*puruṣa*) does not activate the impulse of the will (which directs the body's activity) by himself alone, but through his contact with (his) own (inner) strength (*bala*), made in such a way that he identifies with it, (thus acquiring its power).

9. An individual who, (though) desirous of doing various things, (but) incapable of doing them due to his innate impurity (experiences) the supreme state (*parampadam*) when the disruption (*kṣobha*, of his false ego) ceases.

10. Then (the soul realises) that his (true) uncreated quality (*dharma*) is (universal) agency and perceiving subjectivity, and so he knows and does whatever (he) desires.

11. How can one who, as if astonished, beholds his own nature as that which sustains (all things) be subject to this accursed round of transmigration?

12. Nothingness can never be an object of contemplation because consciousness is absent there. (It is a mistake to believe that one has perceived nothingness) because when reflection (subsequently) intervenes, one is certain that it was.

13. Therefore consider that to be an artificial state similar to deep sleep. That principle is forever perceived and not remembered in this way.

14. Moreover two states called "the agent" and "product of action" abide here. The product of action is subject to decay, whereas agency is imperishable.

15. Only the effort directed toward the product of action disappears here (in states of intense introverted contemplation). When that ceases, the unenlightened believes that his own existence ceases (with it).

16. That inner being is the abode of omniscience and every other divine attribute. It can never cease to exist because nothing else can be perceived (outside it).

17. The fully awakened (yogi's) perception of that (reality) is constant (and abides) unaltered in all three states, whereas others (perceive) that only at the end of the first (*tadādyānte*).

18. The omnipresent Lord appears in two states in union with (His) supreme power whose form is knowledge and its object. Elsewhere, apart from these (two states, He manifests) as pure consciousness.

19. The streams of the pulsation (*spanda*) of the qualities, along with the other (principles), are grounded in the universal vibration (of consciousness) and so attain to being. Therefore they can never obstruct the enlightened.

20. Yet for those whose intuition slumbers, (these vibrations of consciousness) are intent on disrupting their own abiding state of being (*svasthiti*), casting them down onto the terrible path of transmigration, which is so hard to cross.

21. Therefore he who strives constantly to discern the *spanda* principle rapidly attains his own (true) state of being even while in the waking state.

22. *Spanda* is stable in the state one enters when extremely angry, intensely excited, running or wondering what to do.

23.–24. Once entered, that state which (the yogi) takes as his support and firmly resolves that "I will surely do whatever He says"; both the sun and moon set, following the ascending way, into the channel of *suṣumna*, once abandoned the sphere of the universe.

25. Then in that great sky, when the sun and moon dissolve away, the dull minded (yogi is cast down) into a state like that of deep sleep. The awakened, however, remains lucid.

26. Seizing that strength (*bala*), mantras, endowed with the power of omniscience, perform their functions, as do the senses of the embodied.

27. It is there alone that they, quiescent and stainless, dissolve away, along with the adept's mind, and so partake of Śiva's nature.

28.–29. Everything arises (out of) the individual soul and so he is all things because he perceives his identity with the awareness (he has) of them. Therefore there is no state in the thoughts of words or (their) meanings that is not Śiva. It is the Enjoyer alone who always and everywhere abides as the object of enjoyment.

30. Or, constantly attentive and perceiving the entire universe as play, he who has this awareness (*saṃvitti*) is undoubtedly liberated in this very life.

31. This indeed is the arising of that object of meditation in the mind of the meditator, namely, the adept's realisation of his identity with it by the force of (his) intent.

32. This alone is the attainment of the nectar of immortality, this indeed is to catch hold of oneself, this is the initiation of *nirvāṇa* which bestows Śiva's true nature (*sadbhāva*).

33.–34. Requested by the will, the benefactor makes the sun and moon rise and bestows on the embodied, while they wake, the objects that are in (their) heart—so also in the dream state (Śiva), residing in the centre, manifests without exception, always and most vividly, the things (His devotee) desires because he never desists from (his) prayerful request.

35. Otherwise, (as happens normally), the generation (of images) would be continuous and independent throughout the waking and dreaming states in accord with their character, as happens to the worldly.

36.–37. Just as an object which is not seen clearly at first, even when the mind attends to it carefully, later becomes fully evident when observed with the effort exerted through one's own (inherent) strength (*svabala*), similarly, when (the yogi) lays hold of that same power, in the same way, then whatever (he perceives manifest to him) quickly in accord with its true nature (*paramārthena*), whatever be its form, locus, time or state.

38. Laying hold of that (strength) even a weak man achieves his goal and so in the same way a starving man can still his hunger.

39. When the body is sustained by this, one knows everything that happens within it. Similarly, (this same omniscience) will prevail everywhere (when the yogi) finds his support in his own nature.

40. Lassitude ravages the body and this arises from ignorance, but if it is eliminated by an expansion of consciousness (*unmeṣa*) how can (ignorance), deprived of its cause, continue to exist?

41. The expansion of consciousness that takes place when one is engaged in a single thought should be known as the source form whence another arises. One should experience that for oneself.

42. Shortly after, from that (expansion) arises the point (*bindu*), from that sound (*nāda*), from that form (*rūpa*) and from that taste (*rasa*) which disturb the embodied soul.

43. When (the yogi's consciousness) pervades all things by (his) desire to perceive, then why speak much? He will experience it for himself.

44. At all times (the yogi) should remain well awake. Having with (his) perception observed the field (of awareness), he should deposit all in one place, and so be untroubled by any alien (reality).

45. He who is deprived of his power by the forces of obscuration (*kalā*), and a victim of the powers arising from the mass of sounds (*śabdarāśī*) is called the fettered soul.

46. Operating in the field of the subtle elements, the arising of mental representation marks the disappearance

of the flavour of the supreme nectar of immortality; due to this (man) forfeits his freedom.

47. Moreover, his powers (of speech) are always ready to obscure his nature, as no mental representation can arise unpenetrated by speech.

48.* This, Śiva's power of action, residing in the fettered soul, binds it, (but) when (its true nature) is understood and it is set on its own path, (this power) bestowes the fruits of yoga (*siddhi*).

49.–50. (The soul) is bound by the City of Eight (*puryaṣṭaka*) that resides in the mind, intellect and ego and consists of the arising of the (five) subtle elements (of sensory perception). He helplessly suffers worldly experience (*bhoga*) which consists of the arising of mental representation born of that (City of Eight) and so its existence subjects him to transmigration. Thus we will explain how to end this transmigratory existence.

51. But when he is firmly established in one place which is then generated and withdrawn (by him at will), his state becomes that of the (universal) subject. Thus he becomes the Lord of the Wheel.

52. I revere the wonderful speech of the Master whose words and their meaning are marvellous; it is the boat which carries one across the fathomless ocean of doubt!

---

*According of Bhagavadutpala this stanza should be read to mean: This, Śiva's power of action, is completely under his control (*paśuvartinī*). (Although) it binds (the fettered soul), when (its true nature) is understood and it is set on its own path, it bestows the fruits of yoga (*siddhi*).

LIST OF ABBREVIATIONS

Ī.P.	Īśvarapratyabhijñā
Ī.P.v.	Īśvarapratyabhijñāvimarśinī
Ī.P.V.V.	Īśvarapratyabhijñāvivṛtivimarśinī
C.G.C.	Cidgaganacandrikā
Chān.Up.	Chāndogya Upaniṣad
T.Sā.	Tantrasāra
T.Ā.	Tantrāloka
N.T.	Netratantra
P.T.V.	Parātrīśikāvivaraṇa
P.T.L.V.	Parātrīśikālaghuvṛtti
Pr.Hṛ.	Pratyabhijñāhṛdaya
Bṛh.Up.	Bṛhadaraṇyaka Upaniṣad
M.N.	Mahānārayaṇīya Upaniṣad
M.M.	Mahārthamañjarī
M.V.	Mālinīvijayottaratantra
M.V.V.	Mālinīvijayavārtika
Y.Hṛ.	Yoginīhṛdayatantra
V.B.	Vijñānabhairava
Ś.Dṛ.	Śivadṛṣṭi
Ś.Sū.	Śivasūtra
Ś.Sū.vā.	Śivasūtravārtika
Ś.Sū.vi.	Śivasūtravimarśinī
Ś.St.	Śivastotra
Sp.Kā.	Spandakārikā
Sp.Nir.	Spandanirṇaya
Sp.Pra.	Spandapradīpikā
Sv.T.	Svacchandabhairavatantra

NOTES

Introduction

1. See bibliography.

2. *The Doctrine of Vibration* by Mark S. G. Dyczkowski. State University of New York Press, Albany, 1988.

3. In his commentary on aphorism 1/20, Bhāskara writes:

śaktimān nirupādānaḥ saccidrūpaḥ prakāśakaḥ
antaḥsthitānām bhāvānām icchayaiva bahiryataḥ.

This means: "Consciousness and Being is the nature of the possessor of power for without any material cause He illumines externally by (His own) will alone the phenomena that reside within (Him)." Compare Ī.P., 1/5/7, which reads:

cidātmaiva hi devo' ntaḥsthitam icchāvaśād bahiḥ
yogīva nirupādānam arthajātaṃ prakāśayet.

This means: "The Lord Whose essential nature is consciousness, externally manifests, like a yogi, all the objects that are within (Him), according to (His free) will, without (requiring) any material cause."

4. Abhinavagupta quotes from two works which he attributes to the "son of Divākara," whom we know was Bhāskara, as he expressly tells us so himself (see below p. 11). These works are the *Collyrium of Discrimination* (*Vivekājñana*) and the *Hymn to Power* (*Kakṣyāstotra*). For details of these works and where they are quoted, the reader is referred to my forthcoming *Stanzas on Vibration.* There I devote an appendix to an analysis of the texts and authors quoted in the commentaries on the *Stanzas on Vibration* among which is the *Hymn to Power*.

5. See my introduction to the *Stanzas on Vibration*.

6. Accordingly, I have appended a translation of the *Stanzas on*

Vibration at the end of this book to which the reader will be referred throughout this work in the relevant places.

7. I prove that it was Utpaladeva who first formulated this profound metaphysical insight in my paper "Self Awareness, Own Being and Egoity," Varanasi, 1990.

8. T.Ā., 2/39.

The First Light

1. The anonymous author of the Sanskrit notes to Bhāskara's commentary is alluding here to the etymology of the word *deva*, meaning god or lord. This word is derived from the root *div* to which grammarians assign as many as six meanings, namely: play (*krīḍā*), desire to overcome (*vijigīṣā*), behave variously (*vyavahāra*), manifest or illumine (*dyuti*) praise (*stuti*) and movement (*gati*). Abhinavagupta explains what these mean in this context:

i) Play (*krīḍā*): Free of any desire to gain or avoid anything, God (*deva*) plays the game of pouring Himself out into cosmic manifestation, inspired by His own uninterrupted (*ghana*) bliss.
ii) Desire to overcome (*vijigīṣā*): His intention is to be superior to all and such is His freedom.
iii) Behave variously (*vyavahāra*): Although His varied acting always takes place within His own undivided nature, He makes Himself manifest in the form of the discourse (*saṅkalpa*) of thought.
iv) Manifestation or illumination (*dyuti*): He manifests all things and it is because of this that He shines.
v) Praise (*stuti*): He is praised because all things incline towards Him in all their varied functions from the moment they acquire their individual existence.
vi) Movement (*gati*): His movement is consciousness; it consists of the totality of all activity and its qualities are knowledge and action.

Abhinava's source here is the *Śivatanuśāstra* which he quotes in T.Ā., 1/100b–103.

2. The movement of the moon is thought to continuously regenerate the universe. The moon is the visible form of the divine source of the life-giving ambrosia (*soma, amṛta*) which, as it gradually wains, empties out of it to feed the entire universe of objectivity, including the gods and manes, as well as the sun and the other cosmic bodies along with man's body, senses and mind. During the bright fortnight, as the moon waxes, it gradually reabsorbs into itself from its hidden source what it had lost in the dark

fortnight. In this way, the moon, which consists of fifteen digits, (*kalā*) increases and decreases continuously. This cyclic process of nourishment and self-regeneration is grounded in an unchanging, underlying reality that persists as the permanent element that guarantees the continuity and regularity of this process. This element is conceived to be the sixteenth digit of the moon, known as *amākalā*. Although invisible, it is the source of all the other digits and hence the one which ultimately nourishes the whole universe (*viśvatarpiṇī*), and so is identified with the divine energy of the emission (*visarga*) of consciousness that incessently renews all things. See T.Ā., 6/92b–97.

3. See below p. 11.

4. See below p. 11. The anonymous author of the Sanskrit notes reads: *sā cāstyahantedantādi* (in place of *sadāstyahantedantādi*).

5. See below p. 12.

6. Cf. *vṛtti* on Sp.Kā., 1.

7. This line is drawn from Kallaṭa's *Tattvavicāra*.

8. Concerning these energies see my *Doctrine…*, pp. 129–131.

9. Cf. Pr.Hṛ., pp. 40–47, where Kṣemarāja declares that the conclusions various philosophical systems reach concerning ultimate reality are all roles that the universal Self assumes and that they vary according to the degree in which it discloses its true nature. Similarly, Abhinavagupta maintains on the authority of the *Svacchandatantra* that other schools of thought such as the Sāṁkhya or Veda all originate from Śiva and so should be respected. But even so, these traditions are mere fragments of a much vaster tradition and so mislead these who follow them (T.Ā., 35/36–40a). It is for this reason that other schools teach only partial aspects of reality and so lead to only partial attainments and cannot rise to the level of insight of the higher, more complete tradition or, if they do, they immediately fall to lower views thus clearly demonstrating that they are under the sway of Māyā (ibid., 37/3–8).

10. Cf. Sp.Kā., 2. For references to the *Stanzas on Vibration* see the appendix where they are translated. The words *caitanyamātmano rūpam* (the nature of the Self is consciousness) are taken, according to Abhinavagupta, from Kallaṭa's commentary on the *Aphorisms*. Ī.P.V.V., II p. 183.

11. Abhinava writes: "(The word) consciousness is an abstract noun that expresses the concept of freedom, that is, (absolute) Being beyond all specification. This is what (Lord Śiva) has said in the ancient *Aphorism*" (*caitanyam iti bhāvantaḥ śabdaḥ svātantryamātrakam anākṣiptaviśeṣam sad aha sūtre purātane*). T.Ā., 1/28.

12. Sp.Kā., 47.

13. There are three basic impurities that seemingly sully consciousness. The first, called the Impurity of Individuality (*āṇavamala*), apparently contracts consciousness from its infinite plenitude down to an atomic point (*aṇu*) which thus assumes the form of the individual soul. The second impurity is that of Māyā (*māyīyamala*). It entangles consciousness, thus contracted, in the net of duality. The third is the Impurity of Karma which subjects individualized consciousness to suffer the consequences of its actions. Utpaladeva defines these impurities as follows:

> The Impurity of Individuality (*āṇavamala*) operates when one looses consciousness of one's own true nature (*svasvarūpa*) and is of two kinds, namely, the loss of consciousness of one's freedom and the loss of freedom of one's consciousness. The (impurity) called Māyā is the perception of the object as separate (from the subject). It engenders (repeated) birth and worldly experience (*bhoga*). The Impurity of Karma affects the acting subject ignorant (of his true nature). All three are due to the power of Māyā. (Ī.P., 3/2/4–5.)

14. Ś.Sū.vi., p. 18.

15. Cf. Sp.Kā., 9.

16. Cf. Sp.Kā. 45, 47. On the development of speech and its binding effects on individual consciousness, see my *Doctrine...*, pp. 195–200.

17. The five obscuring coverings are: 1) Time (*kāla*), 2) Attachment (*rāga*), 3) Power of merely limited action (*kalā*), 4) Power of merely limited knowledge (*vidyā*) and 5) Constraint to fixed laws (*niyati*), particularly those of *Karma*. See my *Doctrine...*, p. 131. Abhinavagupta deals with these obscuring coverings and their development in detail in T.Ā., 9/174 ff. See also below p. 97.

18. Sp.Nir., p. 68.

19. Each of the fifty letters of the Sanskrit alphabet symbolize a phase in the flux of energy that generates and withdraws the cosmic and transcendental order as it assumes or abandons aspects of its nature, each of which are energies in their own right. 'A', the first letter of the Sanskrit alphabet, stands for *Anuttara*, the absolute. Its four principle powers are depicted as forming part of the letter 'A' thus:

20. See my *Doctrine...*, pp. 129–130.

21. Abhinavagupta explains the nature of these three energies as follows: "*Vāmā* is the mistress of those immersed in transmigratory existence and bestows the power of the Lord (*prabhuśakti*). *Jyeṣṭhā* (presides) over those who are well awakened and *Raudrī* over those who seek worldly pleasure. *Vāmā* (is so called) because She vomits phenomenal existence (*saṃsāravamana*). *Jyeṣṭhā* because She is of Śiva's nature and *Raudrī* because She dissolves away all evils and fixes every action." T.Ā., 6/56–57.

22. Kṣemarāja writes: "The arising of mental representation (*pratyaya*) consists of the flow of cognitive consciousness which is both discursive (*vikalpaka*) and non-discursive (*avikalpaka*). That cannot take place unpenetrated by speech, that is, without being coloured by the subtle (inner) speech of the sort "I know this" and without being associated with gross (outer speech). In this way, even the intentions of animals are made clear without linguistic conventions. Within oneself is an inner understanding that is communicted by a (silent) gesture of the head and this is the reflective awareness of (the inner) speech (of understanding). Were this not so, a child could not grasp the initial (indication of) the convention (which links a particular word to its specific meaning) because he would be devoid of the inner awareness which distinguishes (between one thing and another). Thought constructs (*vikalpa*) are, as everyone's personal experience proves, pervaded by gross speech." (Sp.Nir., p. 71.)

23. *ajñātā mātā mātṛkā viśvajananī*. Ś.Sū.vi., p. 25.

24. T.Ā., 15/130b–131a.

25. N.T., 21/38.

26. See below under aphorism 2/7.

27. Ś.Sū.vi., p. 89.

28. See below, pp. 130–133.

29. See my *Doctrine...*, p. 7, for this and other Tantric etymologies of the name *Bhairava*. Also T.Ā., 1/96–100a.

30. Ś.Su.vi., p. 30.

31. *aunmānasaṃ dhāma*. Ś.Sū.vā., app. p. 100.

32. These words are taken from a famous quote drawn from the *Sarvamaṅgala* (alias *Pārameśvarī*) Tantra.

33. This is one Tantric etymology of the word *cakra*. Abhinava adds others: "The term *cakra* is said to be derived from the roots *kas*, because it expands, *cak*, because it is satisfied, *kṛt*, because it cuts and *kṛ*, because it acts. Thus *cakra* is that which unfolds, is satisfied, severs and acts." T.Ā., 29/106b–107a.

34. Ś.Sū.vi., p. 33.

35. Abhinava writes: "All this universe is a reflection in this way in the Lord Who is the pure Sky of Bhairava's consciousness, (produced there) unaided by anything else. The perfect independence of the Lord is His cosmic nature. This, they say, is Supreme Intuition, the Goddess Absolute." (T.Ā., 3/65–66.)

36. For the practise of *Bhairavamudrā*, see my *Doctrine...*, pp. 158–162.

37. Ś.Sū.vi., app. p. 10, fn. 95, of the K.S.T.S. edition.

38. Cf. Sp.Kā., 3.

39. Cf. ibid., 3–4.

40. See my *Doctrine...*, pp. 84, 213–216.

41. T.Ā., 6/83 and commentary.

42. "The waking state prevails when creatures (*bhūta*) such as (the persons called) Caitra and Maitra, the principles from Earth onwards, words, which are the instruments of denotation, the tetrad consisting of the subject, object, means of knowledge and knowledge (itself, in short, all) this universe (manifests objectively) as that which is supported (by consciousness, *adhiṣṭheya*)." (Ibid., 10/232–233.)

43. Ī.P., 3/2/17; Ś.Sū.vi., p. 41; M.M., p. 156.

44. T.Ā., 10/242.

45. Ś.Sū.vi., p. 43; Sp.Nir., p. 13; Sp.Kā. vi., p. 20.

46. T.Ā., 10/244

47. Read *dṛṣṭṛsvabhāvasya* for *dṛṣṭisvabhāvasya*.

48. T.Ā., 10/253–254.

49. Ibid., 10/247–250.

50. Ī.P., 3/2/16.

51. Ś.Sū.vi., p. 41.

52. Sp.Nir., p. 13.

53. T.Ā., 10/255.

54. Each state is thus related to the others, giving three states for each basic one. These nine states are described below in the exposition to this aphorism.

55. 'Lord' (*pati*) is defined in the appendix of the printed edition of Bhāskara's commentary (p. 104) as "the subject of the Pure Path which consists of Mantra, etc. He is the liberted soul whose own true nature is unobscured by (his) powers." Bhāskara is here trying to point out that the nature of these three states is not absolute but relative to the subject who experiences them. They are one thing for the illumined soul and quite the contrary for the fettered; they operate in opposite ways.

56. Cf. Sp.Kā., 18 and also 35.

57. T.Ā., 10/258

58. Ī.P., 3/2/13–15 and commentary.

59. T.Ā., 10/257.

60. Ī.P. 3/2/15.

61. M.V.V., 1/975.

62. T.Ā., 10/258.

63. Ibid., 10/261.

64. Ś.Sū.vi., p. 43.

65. T.Ā., 10/262.

66. Cf. Sp.Kā., 19.

67. M.M., p. 172; Ś.Su.vi., p. 48.

68. Ś.Sū.vi., p. 48.

69. Cf. Sp.Kā., 11.

70. Cf. ibid., 42.

71. Ś.Sū.vi., p. 54.

72. M.N., section 22.

73. Sv.T., vol. I, p. 5.

74. Ś.St., 1/9.

75. Cf. Sp.Kā., 28–29.

76. Ś.Sū.vi., p. 57.

77. Cf. Sp.Kā., 25.

78. Cf. Kallaṭa's commentary on Sp.Kā., 34.

79. Chān.Up., 8/1/1–3.

80. Bṛh.Up., 3/9/19–25, 5/3/1–2.

81. Ibid., 4/1/7.

82. Chān.Up., 8/1/1–2.

83. *Kathā Upaniṣad*, 4/12–13.

84. The reader is referred to Paul Müller-Ortega's excellent study on the symbolism of the Heart: *The Triadic Heart of Śiva*, Albany: State University of New York Press, 1989. See also a no less interesting thesis on the same subject by Javier Ortez: *A Hermeneutics of Symbolic ("Spatial") terms (Śūnya, Ākāśa, Kha, Vyoman) and the Relationship with the "Centre" ("Heart," Hṛdaya) in the Śivaism of Kashmir*, Varanasi: Banaras Hindu University, 1989.

85. *hṛdayaṃ bodhaparyayaḥ*, T.Ā., comm. on 4/183.

86. P.T.V., p. 61.

87. Ś.Sū.vi., p. 59.

88. T.Ā., 4/181b–182a; T.Sā., p. 27 fn. 12.

89. C.G.C., 1/5.

90. M.M., pp. 127–128; Ś.Sū.vā. by Varadarāja, 1/77.

91. P.T.L.V., p. 18.

92. Ī.P.V.V., 11, pp. 205–206.

93. *ahaṃparāmarśātmā paraṃ hṛdayaṃ viśrāntidhāmatayāvasthitam.* T.Ā., comm. 5/61.

94. T.Ā., 5/20. *anantaṃ paramaṃ jyotiḥ sarvaprāṇihṛdi sthitam.* Quoted from the *Navaśatīśāstra* in Y.Hṛ., p. 63.

95. P.T.L.V., pp. 9–10.

96. Ibid., p. 1 (intro. v. 3).

97. Ibid., p. 10.

98. M.M., p. 25.

99. P.T.L.V., p. 10; cf. M.M., v. 14.

100. Sp.Kā., 53. This verse is found only in Kṣemarāja's recension of the *Stanzas on Vibration*. It says: "May this wealth of knowledge always lead, as it did Vasugupta, to the welfare of all who, once they have obtained (this) the Unattainable, have stored it in the cave of their hearts."

101. M.M., p. 25.

102. P.T.L.V., p. 19.

103. M.M., v. 52.

104. Ś.Sū.vi., p. 59.

105. Cf. Sp.Kā, 33–34.

106. Ś.Sū.vi., p. 62.

107. Ibid., p. 64.

108. Cf. Sp.Kā., 18.

109. M.M., v. 60.

110. See my *Doctrine...*, p. 178.

111. Ś.Sū.vi., p. 38.

112. Sp.Kā., 48.

113. Cf. Ī.P., 1/5/7.

114. Cf. Sp.Kā., *vṛtti* 1.

115. *Śivasūtra con il commento di Kṣemarāja* by Raffaele Torella, Roma: Ubaldini Editore, 1979, p. 60.

116. The Pure Knowledge of a higher enlightened consciousness is a recurring topic in Bhāskara's commentary. See, for example, under aphorisms 2/3, 2/4, 3/3, 3/7 and 3/19. For 'impure knowledge' see under 2/10 and 3/19.

117. These eight yogic powers form a standard group cited together in many treatises on Yoga and are drawn from the *Yogasūtra*. Kashmiri Śaivites explain these powers as aspects of the divine power the yogi acquires through the expansion of consciousness thus:

1) The power of atomicity (*animā*) is the power to be aware of one's presence within all things.
2) The power of lightness (*laghimā*) is the power to free oneself of the grossness of diversity.
3) The power of greatness (*mahimā*) is the power to experience the all-pervasion of consciousness.
4) The power to make oneself heavy at will (*garimā*) [which has been omitted in this text] corresponds to the power to evolve gross forms out of one's own consciousness.
5) The power of attainment (*prāpti*) is the capacity to rest within one's own nature.
6) The power of forebearance (*prākāmya*) is the power to grasp cosmic diversity.

7) The power of control (*vaśitā*) is the power to do whatever one wishes.
8) The power of lordship (*īśitva*) is the yogi's unbroken (*akhaṇḍita*) freedom. P.T.V., p. 37 fn. 74; cf. M.M., pp. 126–127.

118. Sv.T., 4/396–397.

119. M.V.V., 1/245–246, 2/100–102.

120. *Mālinī* is the name given to the alphabet when the order of the letters has been disarranged in such a way that the 'seed' letters (i.e., the vowels representing aspects of Śiva's transcendental consciousness) and the 'womb' letters (i.e., the consonants which represent aspects of Śakti's immanent consciousness) are thoroughly mixed together. It is symbolic of the union of Śiva and Śakti through which the universe of diversity is destroyed and the pure consciousness of Paramaśiva is awakened in the yogi. *Mālinī* represents the awakened power of *Kuṇḍalinī* that rises inwardly making a sound like that of a black bee: "*Mālinī* is supported (*mālitā*) by the Rudras and bears supernatural powers and liberation; the fruits it bestows are like a garland of flowers (*mālā*) and as such is worthy of adoration; the sound it creates, like a bee, is that of reabsorption." (T.Ā., 15/131b–132b.)

121. T.Ā., 3/229b.

122. Ibid., 4/181b–183.

123. Pr.Hṛ., p. 57 and P.T.V., p. 55.

124. Pr.Hṛ., p. 93.

125. *uccāra* means "pronounciation," "articulation" or "utterance." It denotes the act of uttering a Mantra (*mantroccāra*). It literally means "an upward movement." Moveover, the term *uccāra* conveys different meanings according to the yogi's level of practise. At the individual (*āṇava*) level, it is the recitation of Mantra in harmony with the movement of the breath. At its height, it is the upward moving current of vitality through *suṣumnā*. At the empowered (*śākta*) level, it is the persistent force of awareness that impels individual consciousness and merges it with universal consciousness. At the Śiva (*śāmbhava*) level, it is the exertion that impels the cycles of creation and destruction.

126. Sp.Pra., p. 109.

127. See below, p. 199 fn 10.

The Second Light

1. Pr.Hṛ., sū. 5 and commentary.

2. Ś.Sū.vi., p. 23.

3. *Mano bindu* is the light of consciousness. It is said to be like a brilliant star that shines in the calix of the lotus of the Heart of consciousness and is equally Śiva, Śakti and the individual soul (*nara*) (T.Ā., 3/111–113a). It is also, more concretely, the final nasal sound that is written at the end of the seed-syllables that are recited alone as Mantras in themselves or as part of Mantras. To make his recitation effective, the adept should recite this final nasal sound with the full force of his awareness. Compare this passage from the *Muṇḍaka Upaniṣad* about the recitation of OṂ which also ends with the nasal sound, *bindu*:

> Taking as a bow the great weapon of the Upanishad, one should put upon it an arrow sharpened by meditation. Stretching it with a thought directed to the essence of that, penetrate that Imperishable as the mark, my friend. The mystic syllable OṂ (*praṇava*) is the bow. The arrow is the soul (*ātman*). Brahman is said to be the mark (*lakṣya*). By the undistracted man is It to be penetrated. One should come to be in It, as the arrow (in the mark). *Muṇḍaka Upaniṣad*, 2/2/3–4 (Hume's translation).

4. Ś.Sū.vi., p. 89.

5. ...*parameśī bodhākhyā śaktirviśvaṃ garbhīkṛtya parā kuṇḍalikā satī*... Sv.T., vol. II, p. 261.

6. See above, p. 00 fn. 00.

7. Ś.Sū.vi., p. 90.

8. T. Ā, comm. 3/67.

9. T. Ā, 6/217.

10. Also called "Half of Ka" (*kakārārdha*) (see above p. 00), it is referred to as *hakārārdhārdha*, i.e., "half of half of Ha." Half of Ha is *visarga*, which is the last letter in the vowel series of the Sanskrit alphabet, written as two dots, one above the other. Thus, half of that again is the single dot or point that represents *bindu*, which is the seed born of the union of the female (*kuṇḍa*) and male (*golaka*) elements. It is the bliss (*ānandātman*) of the supreme emission (*paravisarga*) of cosmic consciousness in the field of universal awareness. Referred to as the seventeeenth *kalā*, it is the life-giving nectar of 'I' consciousness which vitalizes and transcends the sixteen aspects (*kalā*) of object-centred awareness that constitute individual embodied consciousness, namely, the five gross elements, the ten sense

organs and mind (*manas*), for it is said that "an immortal part (*amṛtakalā*) is present in man who is made of sixteen parts." Quoted in comm. T. A., 3/137b–140a.

11. *Kuṇḍalinī* is called *Haṃsa* because of its intimate association with vitality and breathing. As the supreme form of speech and the source of all lower orders of speech, *Kuṇḍalinī* is also the supreme form of the breath (*prāṇanarūpā*), the vehicle through which speech is generated. At the lower level of articulate speech, the breath rises and descends in the usual way making the sound 'Ha-Sa' as it does so (comm. Sv.T., 4/257). This unstruck sound (*anāhata*) is the lowest order of Divine Sound, *Nāda*. The middle level (*parāpara*) of *Nāda* is *Haṁsa*, as the sound of the breath rising in *suṣumnā* (corresponding to *Prāṇa Kuṇḍalinī*), while the supreme form (*para*) of *Nāda* is the pure reflective awareness of consciousness (*vimarśa*) (corresponding to *Parā Kuṇḍalinī*). See comm. T. A., 3/67.

12. Sv.T., comm. 4/257.

13. 'A' is the first letter of the alphabet and represents *anuttara*, the absolute, as the primordial unity from which all the other letters are emitted. See above, p. 00 fn.00.

14. The spiritual energy of *Kuṇḍalinī* can be experienced at any time by anybody, irrespective of caste, colour or creed. Yogic discipline or any other practise is only secondarily instrumental in awakening this power. It is Śiva's grace alone that can arouse it and this He bestows when and where he wishes.

15. Abhinava writes: "That undivided light (which shines) when the power of action emerges in the abode of the Moon (object), Sun (means of knowledge) and Fire (subject) is our supreme *Bindu*. The Lord has said in the *Tattvarakṣāvidhāna*: "*Bindu*, residing in the centre of the circle of the lotus of the Heart, is known by progressive merger of the individual soul (*nara*) into Śakti (and that) into Śiva. It is the immaculate saviour (*tāraka*)" (T.Ā., 3/111–113a). *Śakti Kuṇḍalinī* rests here, unconcerned with outer manifestation, in Her own nature alone (T.Ā., comm., 3/137b–140b), full of the potential energy of the power of action. At the universal level, *Śakti Kuṇḍalinī* rests initially in the root centre at the base of the spine (*mulādhāra*).

16. The Moon, Fire and Sun represent, as usual, the object, subject and means of knowledge, while the stars symbolize differentiated perceptions (*vikalpa*). All is absorbed in the pervasion (or 'poison', *viṣa*) of the reflective awareness of 'I' consciousness in the deep sleep (*suṣupti*) state of *Śakti Kuṇḍalinī*.

17. The vitality (*vīrya*) of Śiva's seed (*bindu*) is activated by one-pointed and repeatedly refreshed awareness of the movement of the breath. The resonance (*nāda*) of the reflective awareness permeating the

breath as the supreme life-force (*parā jīvakalā*) thus aids in the churning and arousal of the spiritual power of *Kuṇḍalinī*.

18. The four aspects (*kalā*) of *Bindu* are subject, object and means of knowledge together with the 'Inexplicable' (*anākhyā*), which is the transcendental consciousness of the pure awareness (*pramitibhāva*) that contains the other three as a single undivided whole.

19. The yogi experiences *Jyeṣṭhāṣakti* in a state of introverted contemplative absorption (*nimīlanasamādhi*) when subject and object fuse with the rise of *Kuṇḍalinī*. He must however inevitably emerge from this state of contemplation. This emergence (*vyutthāna*) is due to the power of *Raudrī*, which distracts him from the absorption of contemplation and causes the power of his awareness to flow out through the three channels of will, knowledge and action into the domains of individual subjectivity, the senses and objectivity, respectively.

20. *Ambikā* is the energy which allows the yogi to re-enter into his own introverted absorption and then emerge from it again repeatedly in an arch-like movement, as is that of the breath, to ultimately achieve a state of pervasive awareness equally present inwardly and externally.

21. These three energies correspond to those of the absolute (*anuttara*), the will (*icchā*) and the expansion (*unmeṣa*) of the power of knowledge from which all the other phonemic energies emerge (see T.Ā., 3/220b–221a). The first of these energies operates in the superior yogi whose mind has dissolved away (*cittapralaya*) in the unity of cosmic and transcendental consciousness. The second operates in the yogi when his mind is awakened (*cittasaṃbodha*) and he seeks to enjoy the pleasures of the world with his senses illumined by the power of awareness. The last power operates in the inferior yogi who limits himself to enjoying the stillness of resting his mind (*cittaviśrānti*) in introverted contemplation.

22. *Sadyojata*, *Vāmadeva*, *Īśāna*, *Tatpuruṣa* and *Aghora* are the names of Śiva's five faces. To each face corresponds a Mantra. The reader is referred to Sv.T. 1/45, 4/103, 158, 173, 189, 195. See also Gnoli's Italian translation of Abhinavagupta's *Tantrāloka* (pp. 716–717, fn. 8).

23. Ś.Sū.vi., p. 97.

24. T.Ā., 32/1–2.

25. Ibid., 32/9b–10a.

26. Ibid., 32/3.

27. Pr.Hṛ., p. 88.

28. Y.Hṛ., p. 71.

29. Cf. *Kulacuḍāmaṇi*, quoted in Ś.Sū.vi., p. 99.

30. Ś.Sū.vi., p. 99.

31. Ibid.

32. T.Ā., 32/64.

33. Ibid., 32/65.

34. Ibid., 4/200.

35. M.V.V., p. 16–17.

36. This is the most popular and well-known etymology of the word *guru*. There are others as, for instance, the following found in the *Gurugītā*, v. 46: *gukāraṃ ca guṇātītaṃ rukāraṃ rūpavarjitam / guṇātītasvarūpaṃ ca yo dadyāt sa guruḥ smṛtaḥ* (*Gu* stands for "beyond the qualities" and *ru* for "devoid of form." He who bestows that nature which transcends the qualities is said to be a *guru*).

37. Ś.Sū.vi., p. 102.

38. M.V., 2/10.

39. T.Ā., 13/329.

40. Ibid., 13/309–310.

41. Ibid., 13/335–336.

42. Ibid., 15/38b–39a.

43. Y.Hṛ., pp. 174–175; T.Ā., 4/77, 13/158.

44. T.Ā., 4/59.

45. Y.Hṛ., p. 185.

46. T.Ā., 13/298.

47. M.M., p. 4.

48. Ibid., p. 6.

49. *Śāmbhavīśakti*, also called *Jyeṣṭhā* or *Rudraśakti* (T.Ā., 13/202–203, 13/249b), is a middlingly intense (*tīvramadhya*) and weakly intense (*tīvramanda*) descent of power (*śaktipāta*) which leads the disciple to the true Master and along the Śaiva path. It annuls the power of *Vāmāśakti* which leads the disciple away from the path.

50. P.T.V., pp. 14–15.

51. Sv.T. quoted in V.B., p. 7. See also my *Doctrine…*, pp. 167–168.

52. T.Ā., 1/275.

53. M.V.V., 1/918b–921a.

54. See my *Doctrine...*, p. 178.

55. For details of the process of emanation and how the letters relate to the categories and energies, the reader is referred to chapter 3 of Abhinava's *Tantrāloka* and his commentary on the *Parātrīśikā* (pp. 165–200). Kṣemarāja himself says that his own account, which essentially constitutes his commentary on this aphorism, is a summary of Abhinava's exposition as found in these works (Ś.Sū.vi. on sū. 2/7). For an excellent study based on these sources, see A. Padoux, *Recherches sur la symbolique et 1'énergie de la parole dans certains textes tantrique*, Paris, 1963.

56. See my *Doctrine...*, pp. 185–188, 198–199.

57. The *Siddhāmṛta*, quoted in Ś.Sū.vi., p. 105; this same passage is quoted in T.Ā., 3/220b–225 as part of the *Siddhayogeśvarīmatatantra*.

58. Cf. Sp.Kā., 48, to which Kṣemarāja refers in this context.

59. Ś.Sū.vi., p. 119.

60. V.B., v. 149, quoted ibid.

61. Ś.Sū.vi., p. 121.

62. Ibid.

The Third Light

1. T.Ā., comm. 13/191.

2. Cf. Sp.Kā., 49–50, to which Kṣemarāja refers in his commentary.

3. In the place of *parimitapramātṛbhāvābhimānānām grāhitānām*, read *parimitapramātṛbhāvābhimānagrāhitānām*.

4. See my *Doctrine...*, p. 166.

5. See ibid., chap. 7, on the categories of practise (*upāya*).

6. Ibid., pp. 210–211.

7. V.B., v. 56.

8. T.Ā., 11/50.

9. Ī.P., 2/1/5.

10. Ibid., 2/1/3.

11. T.Ā., 6/21b–22a and comm.

12. The word *adhvan* is here supposed to derive from the root *ad*, to eat. T.Ā., 6/28b–30.

13. The five Cosmic Forces (*kalā*) are the binding energies that operate within consciousness to hold its outer manifest form together into one coherent whole. They are visualized as five concentric circles containing the various categories of existence, as follows:

i) *Nivṛttikalā*—the Earth Principle (*pṛthvītattva*) alone falls into the sphere of this energy.
ii) *Pratiṣṭhākalā*—includes the categories from Water to Nature (*prakṛti*).
iii) *Vidyākalā*—this is the energy working through the five obscuring coverings (*kañcuka*) and Māyā.
iv) *Śāntakalā*—includes the categories from Pure Knowledge (*śuddhavidyā*) to *Sadāśiva*.
v) *Śāntātītakalā*—this is the sphere of Śiva and Śakti.

14. M.V.V., 1/1014–1017.

15. T.Ā., comm. 6/30.

16. Ibid., 8/4.

17. Ibid., 11/92.

18. Ibid., 11/107–108.

19. *Doctrine...*, pp. 210–211.

20. Cf. Sp.Kā., 8.

21. Sv.T., 7/297

22. Ś.Sū.vi., p. 147.

23. Sv.T., 4/393–397.

24. Ś.Sū.vi., p. 152.

25. *harṣānusārī spandaḥ krīḍā*, Ś.Dṛ., p. 29.

26. M.M., v. 19.

27. T.Ā., 4/10.

28. Ś.Dṛ., 1/35–36.

29. Ibid., 1/37b–38a.

30. M.M., p. 51.

31. Ibid., p. 55.

32. Ibid., p. 49.

33. Cf. Sp.Kā., 8.

34. Cf. ibid., 39.

35. T.Ā., 3/141b.

36. Ibid., comm. 4/132.

37. Ibid., 3/128b–129a.

38. Ibid., comm. 13/206b–207a.

39. M.V.V., 1/678–680.

40. Cf. Sp.Kā., 36–37.

41. Ś.Sū.vi., p. 162.

42. The "movement of the fish," according to the glossary appended to the edition of Bhāskara's commentary, refers to the "lower power" (*adhaḥśakti*), i.e., *Kuṇḍalinī* at rest in the body.

43. See above, aphorism 1/23.

44. N.T., 8/41–45.

45. Cf. Ī.P., 1/5/15.

46. Cf. Sp.Kā., 45.

47. Cf. ibid., 47.

48. Read *cittena* for *citte.*

49. See my *Doctrine...*, pp. 158–162.

50. Cf. *vṛtti* on Sp.Kā., 6–7.

51. V.B., v. 138.

52. Quoted in Ś.Sū.vi., p. 177.

53. Cf. Sp.Kā., 26.

54. Ś.Sū.vi., p. 180.

55. Sv.T., 4/311–314.

56. The Great Path (*mahāpatha*) is the last journey made, to the place of its execution, by those who have vowed to commit ritual suicide. They must travel towards the northeast, which is Śiva's quarter, in a straight line without altering their course, whatever the obstacle, and eat only air and water until their body drops "like a dry leaf." See *Mānavadharmaśāstra,* 6/1/32.

57. For the *Pāśupatas* and their Great Vow (*mahāvrata*) see my *Canon of the Śaivāgama and the Kubjikā Tantras of the Western Kaula Tradition*, Albany: State University of New York Press, 1987, pp. 19–26.

58. *Sphuraṇarūpā pūjā*. P.T.L.V., p. 23. Cf. V.B., v. 147: "The offering of flowers and the rest does not constitute worship: (true) worship is that which fixes the mind firmly and, with reverence, dissolves it away in the Supreme Sky of consciousness free of all thought constructs."

59. Sv.T., 4/398.

60. V.B., v. 145.

61. T Ā., 2/39.

62. Ś.Sū.vi., p. 194.

63. Ibid.

64. Cf. Sp.Kā., 16.

65. Ibid., 4.

66. Ś.Sū.vi., p. 205.

67. Sp.Kā., 5.

68. Cf. ibid.

69. Cf. ibid., 4.

70. Ś.Sū.vi., p. 206.

71. That is, Ś.Sū., 1/4, 2/7 and 3/20.

72. Cf. Sp.Kā., 6–8 and 26.

73. Ī.P., 1/6/11. Cf. also T.Ā., 11/101.

74. Ś.Sū., 3/21.

75. V.B., v. 69–73.

76. P.T.V., pp. 47–49.

77. Ś.Sū.vi., p. 212.

78. Ibid., p. 220.

79. T.Ā., 4/179b–180a.

80. M.V.V., 1/816a.

81. Drawn from M.V., 1/29.

82. T.Ā., 9/201b–202a.

83. Cf. ibid., 13/206.

84. Ibid., 6/39.

85. Sv.T., vol. VI, pp. 167–168.

86. M.M., p. 131.

87. M.V.V., 1/876.

88. Ibid., 1/99b–100.

89. T.Ā., 13/204.

90. Ibid., 3/252b–253a, 4/173b–175.

91. M.V.V., 1/663–664a. Cf. ibid., 1/815.

92. T.Ā., 6/38–40b.

93. Ī.P.v. II, p. 208.

94. M.V.V., 1/56.

95. Ibid.

96. Ibid., 1/664.

97. Ibid., 1/678–685.

98. T.Ā., 6/182b–184; also, P.T.V., p. 246.

99. P.T.V., p. 246; cf. M.V.V., 1/815.

100. T.Ā., comm. 13/206b–207a.

101. Ī.P. v. II, p. 206.

102. Cf. T.Ā., 10/187b–227a.

103. T.Ā., 7/26–30.

104. Ibid., 15/336.

105. T.Ā., 7/62b–64a.

106. According to the teachings of the Upaniṣads (e.g., Bṛh.Up., 3/9/26, 4/2/4, 4/5/15), the Self can only be described in negative terms, i.e., as that which it is not.

107. T.Ā., 6/7–11.

108. Ibid., 15/52.

109. T.Sā., p. 62.

110. T.Ā., 7/70b.

111. T.Sā., p. 61.

112. Sv.T., 7/25; also quoted in Ś.Sū.vi., p. 224.

113. There are three categories of practise, the supreme (*para*), which is called the "Divine Means" (*Śāmbhavopāya*), the middling (*parāpara*), called the "Empowered Means" (*śāktopāya*), and the lowest (*apara*), called the "Individual Means" (*āṇavopāya*). For a brief account of these categories see my *Doctrine*..., chapter VII.

114. Ś.Sū.vi., p. 228.

115. T.Ā., comm. 8/283.

116. T.Ā., 7/66–67. See Sv.T., 7/7b–11a.

117. Pr.Hṛ., comm. sū. 17.

118. Sv.T., 7/8, 7/16, 7/301.

119. Ibid., 7/9; cf. Bṛh.Up., 2/1/19.

120. T.Sā., p. 57.

121. T.Ā., comm. 7/66–68.

122. M.M., p. 60.

123. V.B., v. 35.

124. M.M., v. 56.

125. V.B., v. 27.

126. T.Ā., 15/336–338.

127. Ś.Sū.vi., p. 230.

128. Ibid.

BIBLIOGRAPHY

Īśvarapratyabhijñākārikā by Utpaladeva with *vimarśinī* by Abhinavagupta. Vol. 1, K.S.T.S., no. 22, 1918. Edited by M. R. Śāstrī. Vol. 2, K.S.T.S. no. 33, 1921. edited by M. S. Kaul.

Īśvarapratyabhijñākārikā by Utpaladeva. English translation of the *vimarśinī* by K. C. Pandey. In *Bhāskarī*, vol. 3. Sarasvati Bhavan Texts, no. 84, Benares, 1954.

Īśvarapratyabhijñākārikā with *vivṛtivimarśinī* by Abhinavagupta (3 vols.). K.S.T.S., no. 60, 1938, 62, 1941 and 66, 1943, respectively. All edited by M. S. Kaul.

Cidgaganacandrikā. Edited by Swāmī Trivikrama Tīrtha. Tantrik Texts 20. Calcutta: Āgamānusaṃdhāna Samiti, 1936.

Tantrasāra by Abhinavagupta. K.S.T.S., no. 17, 1918. Edited by M. S. Kaul.

Tantrāloka by Abhinavagupta (12 vol) with *viveka* by Jayaratha. Part 1 edited by M. R. Śāstrī. Parts 2–12 edited by M. S. Kaul, K.S.T.S., no. 23, 1918; 28, 1921; 30, 1921; 36, 1922; 35, 1922; 29, 1921; 41, 1924; 47, 1926; 59, 1938; 52, 1933; 57, 1936 and 57, 1938.

Netratantra with *uddyota* by Kṣemarāja. Vol. 1, K.S.T.S., no. 46, 1926; vol. 2, no. 61, 1939. Both edited by M. S. Kaul.

Paramārthasāra by Abhinavagupta with *vivṛti* by Yogarāja. K.S.T.S., no. 7, 1916. Edited by J. C. Chatterjee.

Parātrīśikālaghuvṛtti by Abhinavagupta. K.S.T.S., no. 67, 1947. Edited by J. Zadoo.

Parātrīśikāvivaraṇa by Abhinavagupta. K.S.T.S., no. 18, 1918. Edited by M. S. Kaul.

Pratyabhijñāhṛdaya by Kṣemarāja. English translation: *The Secret of Recognition*, with notes from Baer's German translation. Adyar: Adyar Library, 1938.

Māharthamañjarī and *parimala* by Maheśvarānanda. Edited by Vrajavallabha Dviveda. Yogatantragranthamālā, no. 5. Benares, 1972.

Mālinīvijayavārtika by Abhinavagupta. K.S.T.S., no. 31. Edited by M. S. Kaul. Srinagar, 1921.

Mālinīvijayottaratantra. K.S.T.S., no 37, 1922, Srinagar. Edited by M. S. Kaul.

Yoginīhṛdaya with commentaries *dīpikā* by Amṛtānanda and *setubandha* by Bhāskara Rāya. Sarasvatībhavanagranthamālā no. 7, 2nd ed. Edited by G. Kaviraj. Benares, 1963.

Vijñānabhairava with commentaries by Kṣemarāja (incomplete) and Śivopādhyāya. K.S.T.S., no 8, 1918. Edited by M. R. Śāstrī.

Śivadṛṣṭi by Somānanda with *vṛtti* (incomplete) by Utpaladeva. K.S.T.S., 54, 1934. Edited by M. S. Kaul.

Śivasūtravimarśinī by Kṣemarāja.

English translation: *Śiva Sūtra: The Yoga of Supreme Identity* by Jaideva Singh. Delhi: Motilal Banarsidass, 1979.

Italian translation: *Śivasūtra con il Commento di Kṣemarāja* by Raffaele Torella. Rome: Ubaldini Editore, 1979.

French translation: *Étude sur le Śaivisme du Cachemire, École Spanda, Śivasūtra et Vimarśinī de Kṣemarāja* by Lilian Silburn. Paris: E. de Boccard, 1980.

Śivastotrāvalī by Utpaladeva with commentary by Kṣemarāja. Edited with notes in Hindi by Swami Laksmanjoo. Benares: Chaukhamba, 1964.

Siddhitrayī by Utpaladeva. This consists of three works: *Ajaḍapramātṛsiddhi, Īśvarasiddhi* and *Saṃbandhasiddhi*. K.S.T.S., no. 34, 1921. Edited by M. S. Kaul.

Spandakārikā with *vṛtti* by Kallaṭabhaṭṭa. K.S.T.S., no. 5, 1916. Edited by J. C. Chatterjee.

Spandakārikāvivṛti by Rājānaka Rāma. K.S.T.S., no. 6, 1916. Edited by J. C. Chatterjee.

Spandanirṇaya by Kṣemarāja. K.S.T.S., no. 43, 1925. Edited with English translation by M. S. Kaul

Spandapradīpikā by Bhagavadutpala. Published in the *Tantrasaṃgraha*, vol. 1. Yogatantragranthamālā no. 3, pp. 83–128. Edited by G. Kavirāja. Benares, 1970.

Svacchandabhairavatantra with *uddyota* by Kṣemarāja. 7 vols. K.S.T.S., 21, 1921; 38, 1923; 44, 1925; 48, 1927; 51, 1930; 53, 1933; 56, 1955. All edited by M. S. Kaul.

The Thirteen Principle Upanishads by R. E. Hume, Oxford University Press, reprint U.S.A. 1975.

INDEX

Avarṇa (absolute), 71
Avasthātṛ, 150
See also Subjectivity
Avasthiti, 131–132
See also Contemplation
Āveśa, 22, 77, 135
See also Absorption
Āveśa (penetrating), 69
See also Consciousness, pure
Avidyā (ignorance), 153
Avilkalpaka (non-discursive), 193
Avilupta (ever-persisting), 113
Avisista (common), 89
Aviveka, 153
See also Discernment, lack of
Avṛtākṛti, 10
See also Self, obscured
Avṛti, 153
See also Obscuration
Avyakta, 13
Awakening
conquest of delusion and, 108–111, 142
in the deep sleep state, 33, 43
in the dream state, 33
of Kuṇḍalinī, 72, 85
Master's Grace and, 23, 82–85
mātṛkā and, 82–85
universal consciousness and, 19, 42, 46, 100–104, 201
Awareness
deep sleep state and, 30–32
duality and, 16, 29, 70, 127–128, 137–139, 150–152, 161–163, 164–166
Fourth State of, 27, 27–28, 31, 46, 78, 103–104, 130–132, 157–159
and the heart, 44–46
language and, 20–21, 70, 128–130, 134–135, 193
mantra and, 62–63, 66–67, 69–75, 76–79, 93–95, 142–144
mātṛkā and, 21, 61–63, 70–74, 82–85, 128–130
mudrā and, 78–79
power of, 18, 19, 23, 24, 44, 47, 57, 63, 71, 116–117, 146–147, 163–164, 169, 175, 177, 184, 200
right discernment and, 48, 69, 94, 134–135
steadfastness of, 25, 30, 59–60, 68–69, 101–104, 111–112, 122–123, 130–132, 135–137, 139–140, 151–152, 159–161
time and, 169–173
See also Consciousness; Heart
Awe, 37
See also Wonder, state of
Ayukta, 94
See also Yoga

Bahirmukha, 25
See also Senses
Bāhyākāratā, 132
See also Reality
Bala (uncreated force), 59, 60, 62, 76, 94, 126, 135–137, 182, 183
elements and, 105
obscuration and, 96
Being, unidivided, 27, 113–115, 117
mantra and, 69–75, 142–144
Śakti and, 48
Being-Becoming, 168
See also Śakti; Śiva, Lord
Bhagavadutpala, 63
Bhairava, xiii, 8
Churning-, 36
and the heart, 44–45
and inner circle of deities, 40
Kuṇḍalinī and, 72–74
power of, 21, 24, 79, 129–130, 194
as upsurge, 22–23, 25, 84
See also Effort
Bhairavamudrā, 25, 132–133
See also Practice, yogic
Bhairavībhāva, 173–174
See also Liberation
Bharaṇa (fill), 22
See also Consciousness, undifferentiated

Knowledge *(continued)*
power of, 78, 111–112, 144–145, 201
Pure-, of the Self, xiv, xvi, 6, 14, 19, 21, 22, 23, 44, 48, 49, 54, 56–57, 62, 70, 73–74, 74, 76–79, 89–91, 98, 111, 113–115, 128, 143–144, 166, 179, 186, 196, 197, 204
rebirth and, xvi, 86–87, 127–128, 163–164, 165–166
union and, 14, 16, 18, 23, 26, 27, 41, 45, 46
Wheel of Energies and, 24
See also Jñāna; Mātṛkā
Krama (movement of consciousness), 25, 26
objectivity and, 101
Krama tradition, 4, 25
See also Tantra
Krīḍā (play), 190
Kriyāśakti, 78, 162, 168
mantra and, 85
See also Action; Śakti
Kriyāvaicitrya, 101
See also Action(s); Diversity
Kṣapaṇa (severs), 143
Kṣatrīya, 42
and study of the Vedas, 43
See also Caste system
Kṣemarāja, ix, 1
commentary by, ix, 1, 2, 4, 6, 18, 21, 23, 25, 26, 45, 47, 49, 61, 67, 68–69, 73–74, 76, 90, 191, 193, 196
on conquering delusion, 109–111, 128, 133, 154
on Fourth State, 140, 158–159
and Impurity, 17–18, 20
Krama tradition and, 5, 25
on mantra, 21, 60–63, 67, 68–69, 75–76
and nature of consciousness, 14, 45, 49, 50, 53, 58, 60–63, 70–75, 80, 90–91, 101, 121–122, 126, 179–180
on obscuring energies, 18, 36, 47, 134–135, 146
on right discernment, 49, 88, 131–132, 133
subjectivity consciousness and, 16, 50, 56, 84–85, 86–87, 138–139, 193
on upsurge of Bhairava, 23, 25
and Virgin Will, 39
and vital breath, 106, 124–125, 136–137, 175–178
See also Vimarśini
Kṣepe (casting forth), 168
Kṣobha (turbulence), 167, 182
Kula (wholeness), 79
See also Oneness
Kumārī, 38–39
See also Virgin
Kumar (to play), 39
Kuṇḍa (female), 199
Kuṇḍalinī
awakening of, 72, 85, 198
mantra and, 60, 62, 71–74
mudrā and, 78
state of, 18, 200
vital breath and, 59–60, 177
See also Shakti; Śiva, Lord
Kutsa (abhorrent), 39

Laghimā (lightness), 57, 197–198
Lakṣya (mark), 199
Language, xii
awareness and, 20, 70, 82–85, 134–135, 192
gutteral consonants of bondage, xvi, 128–130
knowledge and, 24, 71–74, 82–83
mantra and, 60, 69–70, 93–95, 129
See also Mātṛkā; Speech
Lassitude, 185
Laukika, 13, 17
See also Materialists; Self
Layabhāvanā, 101
See also Contemplation, of dissolution

Silence
deep sleep state and, 31–32
Śiva, Lord, x, 9–10
attributes of (divine), 14, 16–19, 40–41, 48, 49, 61, 71–74, 79–80, 94, 125, 144–145, 170, 186, 200, 201
compassion of, 12
and consciousness, xi, xiv, 10, 11, 12, 16, 45, 47, 54, 56–57, 59–60, 65–67, 71–74, 98, 125–126, 135–137, 146–147, 149–150, 178, 186
contraction of, 12, 13, 19, 24, 26, 41, 45, 54, 61, 66, 99–104, 115–116, 132, 149–150, 161–163, 181
expansion of, 12, 13, 22, 23, 24, 41, 45, 46, 49–50, 52, 59–60, 63, 69, 98–99, 104–106, 132, 149–150, 151–152, 161
grace of, 79–82
Kashmiri Śaivism and, 3
and mātṛkā, 21, 71, 82–85
–nature, 10–12, 14, 20, 21, 24, 40–41, 45, 47, 56, 63, 71, 78, 79–82, 83, 98, 104–106, 110, 113–115, 125–126, 130–132, 139–140, 144–145, 147, 154–156, 165, 180, 184, 200
obeisance to, 10
obscuration and, 10–11, 12, 17–19, 54–55, 96–97, 106–108, 116–117, 128–130, 150–152, 153–154, 161–163, 167
realizing, xiv, xvi, 8, 10–11, 13, 25, 56, 63, 78–79, 100–104, 125–126, 134–135, 139–140, 178
and Śakti, 48, 51–52, 60–61, 71–74, 79–82, 85, 103–104, 168, 179, 198
Tantras and, 5, 71–74, 80–82
Śivabindu, 72
Śivacaitanya (Śiva-consciousness), 47
See also Śiva, Lord
Śiva-consciousness. *See* Śivacaitanya; Śiva, Lord,–nature
Śivānanda, 4–5
Śiva rock, xii
Śivarūpatā (Śiva's Being), 134–135
Śiva Sūtras, ix
and arising of innate knowledge, xiv–xv
and light of consciousness, xiii–xiv
mythic origin of, x
and vibration of power, xv–xvii
Śivatā, 66, 130–132
See also Śiva, Lord,–nature
Śivatanuśāstra, 190
Śivatattva, 100
Śivavyāpti, 110
See also Śiva, Lord,–nature
Śivo'ham [mantra], x
Sky of Consciousness, xiv, 76, 77, 172–173, 183, 194, 206
elements and, 104–106
mudrā of, 78–79
vital breath and, 177–178
Sleep state, xvii, x–xi, 182, 200
awakening within, 33, 43
and consciousness, 27, 30–32, 42, 46, 131–132
dream state during, 34
of Kuṇḍalinī, 73
Māyā and, xiii, 30, 32
and samādhi, 35, 43
tamas guṇa and, 36
vitality of, 157–159, 184
Smaraṇa, 170–171
See also Memory
Snowy Mountains, 9
Soma, 42, 190
See also Nectar
Somānanda, 2, 114
Soul, xvi, 13
dream state and, 29–30
fettered, individual, 13, 18, 20, 28, 31, 35, 51, 54–55, 80, 94, 97–99, 128–130, 142, 143–144,

Soul *(continued)*
153–154, 161–163, 164, 167, 182, 186
guṇa and, 35–36, 96
karma and, xvi, 86–87, 153–154, 167
liberated, xvi, xvii, 86–87, 143–144, 152–153, 163–164, 166, 195
Śiva-nature of, 10–11, 20, 21, 24, 46, 71–74, 78–79, 86–87, 89–91, 115–116, 125–126, 130–132, 135–137, 139–140, 154–156, 178
Supreme-, 24, 111
Sound
articulate, 70–74, 128–130, 134–135
of awareness, 44, 60, 128–130, 199
Kuṇḍalinī and, 71–74
manifest universe and, 21, 53, 69–70, 185, 200
mantra and, 63, 67, 70, 82–85
unstruck-, 21, 62, 71, 83, 84, 175, 200
See also Mantra; Mātṛkā
Space
path of, 102
twelve-finger, 124, 175
Spandakarikās, 2, 45, 181–186
See also Stanzas on Vibration
Spanda (pulse of consciousness), 61–62, 146–147, 167, 183
emission and, 120–122
mātṛkā and, 83–84
mind and, 67, 159
vital breath and, 176
See also Śakti
Spandasūtra, 11
See also Aphorisms on Vibration
Sparśa (tactile sensation), 83
Speech
articulation of, 70–74, 93, 128–130, 134–135, 198, 200
knowledge and, 15, 24, 60, 128–130, 193
Kuṇḍalinī and, 71–74
mantra and, 60–63, 70–75
obscuration and, 20, 113–115, 128–130, 186
Spharamatra (unfolding), 171–173
Sphuraṇa (effulgent flow), 45, 50
mantra and, 69–75
See also Act, the Pure; Awareness
Sphurati, 28
See also Cognition
Sphurattā, 10, 118, 173
See also Light; Radiance
Śrīkaṇṭhabhaṭṭa, 11
Śrītantrasadbhāva, 21, 71, 73–74
See also Tantra
Sṛṣṭi (emission), 39, 59, 121–122
mudrā and, 78
See also Rebirth
Stabdatā (stiffness), 173
Stability, 104, 159–161
Stanzas on Recognition, 2
Stanzas on Vibration, 1, 2, 149–150, 152
Bhāskara's commentary and, 46
excerpt, 181–186
and Fourth State, 28
on mantra, 76
and pure I AM concept, 4, 6, 56, 61–62, 90
and union of elements, 56
See also Spandakarikās
Sthiti, (stable state), 19, 42, 144–145, 159–161
mudrā and, 78
See also Persistence
Stupidity, 153–154
See also Ignorance
Stuti (praise), 190
Subjectivity, xvi, 12, 172, 181, 193, 201
bondage and, 15–16, 86, 96–97, 128–130
deep sleep state and, 34
and discernment of consciousness, 14, 32, 33, 39, 128–130,

effort in, 23, 25, 51, 52–53, 56, 58, 59, 67–69, 93, 94, 103, 105, 123–125, 154–155
of the heart, 42–46
and lake of consciousness, xvi, 59–60
meaning of, 7–8
and penetration of mind, xvi, 26, 30, 42, 74–76, 106, 132–133, 135–137, 159–161, 177
and pleasure or pain, xvi, 97–99, 150–152
powers of consciousness and, 18–19, 25, 26, 36, 37, 42, 46, 48, 52, 56, 58, 59–60, 71–74, 78, 80–82, 89–91, 130–132, 154–155, 159–161, 186
and Pure Knowledge, xiv, 22, 23, 27, 56–58, 76–79, 100–104, 106, 139–140, 161, 179
and state of wonder, 37–38, 82, 129, 159
visions and, xiv, 22, 37, 42, 56, 76, 83, 89–91
vital breath and, xvii, 21, 30, 42, 46, 59–60, 93, 105–106, 135–137, 171–173, 174–178
See also Practice(s), yogic; Siddha
Yoganibhālana (practice of union), 121–122
Yogasūtra, 197
Yoginīs, 52
Yoginīvaktra, 52
Yoni (sources), 16, 128
Yonivarga (group of sources), 18
See also Power, four sources of
Yoni (womb), 84
See also Universe, womb of
Yukta, 94
See also Yoga